Cameras into
the Wild

Cameras into
the Wild

*A History of Early Wildlife
and Expedition Filmmaking,
1895–1928*

PALLE B. PETTERSON

McFarland & Company, Inc., Publishers
Jefferson, North Carolina, and London

LIBRARY OF CONGRESS CATALOGUING-IN-PUBLICATION DATA

Petterson, Palle B., 1967–
Cameras into the wild : a history of early wildlife and expedition
filmmaking, 1895–1928 / Palle B. Petterson.
p.   cm.
Includes bibliographical references and index.

ISBN 978-0-7864-6166-0
softcover : 50# alkaline paper ∞

1. Wildlife cinematography — History.   2. Wildlife films — History
and criticism.   3. Nature films — History and criticism.   I. Title.
TR893.5.P48   2011   777'.832 — dc23   2011020108

BRITISH LIBRARY CATALOGUING DATA ARE AVAILABLE

Cover image: Percy Smith filming in a pond, 1910 (Science Museum/SSPL)

Manufactured in the United States of America

*McFarland & Company, Inc., Publishers
Box 611, Jefferson, North Carolina 28640
www.mcfarlandpub.com*

For my father
Poul Bøgelund Thomsen
(1933–1996)

TABLE OF CONTENTS

Sufficient tribute can never be paid to these pioneering cameramen; it is one thing to carry into the jungle a lightweight camera equipped with zoom lens—a courageous enough action in itself—but to lug a machine that, with its tripod, weighed anything from seventy-five to one hundred pounds, and to crank the handle evenly while positioned only yards from the fiercest creatures on earth—this took more than enthusiasm. "I find that turning the crank will not answer the purpose when the camera man is looking into the eyes of a rapidly advancing lion," Carl Akeley remarked, mildly. "It is not in human nerves to stand the strain without excitement." However, not even he could provide as reliable an alternative, despite experiments with compressed air and spring-operated motors.

Whatever history we can see in photographic form, we owe to courageous and skillful cameramen. Our own lives are richer for the risks they took, and for their sheer hard labor. The most astonishing scenes ever put on the screen were captured by cameramen working for newsreels and documentaries.—Kevin Brownlow, *The War, the West and the Wilderness* (1978)

He had killed many elephants, and his long experience had given him a great deal of that knowledge about elephants which would enable him to kill them without himself being killed. On the other hand, Cunningham hunted elephants for ivory, and when a man approaches a herd looking for ivory, he is not likely to see much excepting tusks. It is natural, therefore, that from the ivory hunters we learn comparatively little of the more intimate things that we should like to know about the everyday life of the elephant. The world has no record of the knowledge of wildlife that their experience should have given the ivory hunters.

It is for this reason that the camera hunters appeal to me as being so much more useful than the gun hunters. They have their pictures to show—still pictures and moving pictures—and when their game is over the animals are still alive to play another day. Moreover, according to any true conception of sport—the use of skill, daring, and endurance in overcoming difficulties—camera hunting takes twice the man that gun hunting takes. It is fortunate for the animals that camera hunting is becoming popular.—Carl E. Akeley, *In Brightest Africa* (1927)

PREFACE

I first got the idea for *Cameras into the Wild* in September 1997. In the beginning it was meant to be a thesis in film history at the University of Copenhagen. At this time my plan was to focus on the history of nature and wildlife filmmaking. But I abandoned this due to the lack of literature on the subject. It was difficult to find anything at all on early wildlife and expedition filmmaking. No literature had at that time focused on nature and wildlife films from a historical viewpoint. As the years passed I realized I was not alone in encountering this problem. Authors Kevin Macdonald and Mark Cousins, for their *Imagining Reality*, decided to abandon the subject of non-fiction filmmaking because there hadn't been enough written about it. This included nature and wildlife films. In their foreword, Macdonald and Cousin write:

> Among the topics that we would like to have included were: Chinese documentary, ethnographic filmmaking, nature documentaries and the effects of the digital revolution [x].

Well, I ultimately decided to persevere; and in my hunt for literature on nature filmmaking, several people at the Danish Film Institute Library helped me in my research. Together we found a few articles and books that briefly mentioned nature documentaries, or wrote about companies producing wildlife films. On the Internet it was the same story. I found homepages for a few nature film producing companies, some of which wrote about their company's background. But it was all too little, and I decided instead to write about the competition between the ITV and BBC nature film units. I didn't give up though; the history of nature and wildlife filmmaking needed to be written. So in 1998 I contacted the Danish Royal Library, where Michael Gregaard offered to help with my research. And what a help he was. He would spend several hours trying to find something in particular, accessing databases around the world. His help was invaluable. His unquestioning support and recognition of the importance of my work became fuel for my efforts.

During the years since, I have visited several libraries in the USA and Europe, and have searched an uncounted number of international databases, cardex and book indexes. As years passed, I amassed more than 150 books and articles on the subject of expedition films, wildlife films, nature films and travelogues. Most of these could not be found in Denmark. Some were sent to me from abroad, others I went to read at different libraries, and still others I had to secure through photocopying. I obtained material from Switzerland, Austria, Germany, Holland, Sweden, Norway, Denmark, Italy, France, Great Britain, Canada, the USA, India, Australia and Canada. And nearly all my sources were written during the period about which I am concerned — 1895 to 1928.

Searching for and finding the films themselves is a story of its own, but here I would just like to thank the following institutions: Det Danske Filmarkiv (Copenhagen), British Film Institute's Archive (London), Library of Congress (Washington, D.C.), the American Museum of Natural History (New York), Det Svenska Filminstitut's Archive (Stockholm), and, finally, Svensk Ljud och Bild (Lund). Their importance cannot be overstated, because they are the ones who saved these films for the future. Without them everything would be lost by now. Their preservation standards are unparalleled, and they have been so very helpful to my work.

A very special thanks goes out to the people at the Danish Film Institute Library, who were both enthusiastic and motivating whenever I came to them with my odd questions. A special thank to Lars Ølgaard and Casper Tybjerg, who kept me on the right track. Ølgaard was always happy to find books in storage that had never been used before, and his cheering comments made me smile.

A special thank-you to the providers of many photographs: Karen Akerson, Martin and Osa Johnson's Safari Museum in Kansas, Milestone Films and the Danish Film Institute's Stills Archive.

As years passed, I collected more and more new books and articles that touched on the subject. They became the inspiration for several written works while I studied film and media, and in this way my long research period didn't seem wasted. Concentrating on the audio-visual areas I cared most about, I once had to change teachers, but this was better than changing the subject. So for the past 13 years I have remained connected to my favorite subject — all the way to this book. I have been writing a Ph.D. dissertation about the way film can show people's changing thoughts about nature. All along I have refined and kept contact with the work I present here, which I hope someone else will find interesting and inspiring. A big thanks to my translating collaborators Maria Christensen and David Bouch.

INTRODUCTION

Most books on documentaries and other non-fiction films ignore the historical development of nature, wildlife and wilderness films, and I have always wondered why. On those rare occasions when these films *have* been discussed, it has been in a rather superficial manner. The fact that so little has been written about the topic has made me eager to delve into this unexplored area. You might say that the feeling of entering unknown territory has been the prime mover in my endeavors.

Cameras into the Wild seeks to answer the following questions: 1. Which non-fiction films dealt with nature and wild animals? 2. Who made these films, and in what way did they influence the development of nature, wildlife and wilderness films? 3. How and why did contemporary film technology, projection facilities and narrative techniques influence the development of films about nature and animals?

Since nature, wildlife and wilderness films are able to bring into focus environmental problems (indeed, they have already done so), wildlife and wilderness films deserve to become a political, popular and scientific field of interest. In addition, nature films have proved extraordinarily viable. They have kept up with developments within the film media in general, and have maintained their popularity in the present digital age.

Which types of films does the term "wildlife and wilderness film" include? The shortest answer to this question is: any film that portrays nature/wilderness and animals/wildlife. This includes many subgenres, such as expedition, travel, natural history, hunting, adventure and, of course, wildlife films. Together I label these films as either wildlife and wilderness films, or simply as nature films.

This book will demonstrate that not only has the nature film genre been developing steadily for the past 100 years, it has also dealt with environmental protection for some 90 years. *Cameras into the Wild* will make it easier to place nature film-related issues in perspective for future scholars and others interested in this rather overlooked field. The concluding remarks will offer ideas for future research topics.

To enhance the reading experience, the following paragraphs will define the most important words, concepts and characteristics mentioned in the book — words and concepts that might otherwise strike the reader as ambiguous or imprecise.

Although the structure of this book may appear fairly complex, it has been carefully planned out. Before the text turns to the actual wildlife and wilderness films, the section titled "Getting Around the Subject" will go through the most important theories and methods upon which the book relies. It will also outline the historical development of the concept

Martin and Osa Johnson with Bell & Howell cameras in Africa (Martin and Osa Johnson Safari Museum).

of nature. Moreover, it will illustrate how I have dealt with issues such as silent films and written sources.

The historical sections have been subdivided into a number of sub-sections. Each historical section has the same structure. First, there is a description of the overall development of the period in regards to cameras, lenses, techniques and exhibition venues. These descriptive paragraphs will focus mainly on conditions that may have influenced the production of wildlife and wilderness films. Next comes a section on the historical development of nature-related films, its sub-genres and cinematographers. Some cinematographers are mentioned briefly, whereas the description of others occupies an entire section. This depends entirely on their importance to the nature-related film genres. The sections on cinematographers have a similar structure covering their road to wildlife and wilderness filmmaking, the beginning of their careers, their work and their films. So little information is available on certain cinematographers that it has been impossible to describe them in detail.

The first time the title of a film appears I will indicate the year of its first screening in parentheses. Whenever possible, the original title and year will be listed, but in some cases I have had to rely on the title and year cited by a secondary source.

When relevant, my discussion will include films that especially illustrate natural scenery and that have been shot during travels. I will divide travel films into travelogue, expedition films and adventure/globetrotter films. The term "travelogue" was coined by Burton Holmes in 1904. It was meant to capture his special mixture of lecture and screening, and he came up with the term by combining the words "travel" and "monologue." "Travelogue" will be defined as films shot during travels by boat and or train to civilized countries — in other words, travels that did not require a huge amount of preliminary research or that had no scientific goal. This distinguishes them from the "expedition films."

In this book, "expedition films" will be defined as journeys that were not undertaken for the sake of the camera. Expedition films had another purpose. This could be to conquer land, to mark nationality or find answers to scientific questions.

"Adventure/globetrotter films" include amateur expeditions where the journey is somewhat harder than the one undertaken for a travelogue. The adventure/globetrotter journey does not have a scientific goal — rather, it has a filmic, commercial goal. We might even say that it functioned as self-promotion.

Hunting films make up another genre of which a major part consists of nature scenery and wild animals. The main goal of the hunting film is to depict the tracking and capturing of wild animals. The purpose of the pictures is to depict the actual hunt, but the films also document the abilities and accomplishments of the hunter, and so may be said to have an additional function — namely, self-promotion.

I will define less important themes and film categories as I go along, but one term should be mentioned here: "knowledge imparting films" is used as a collective term for popular science, information and educational films.

GETTING AROUND THE SUBJECT

Literature About the Subject

Criticism of Source Material

In order to study the period 1895–1928, we must establish a number of facts concerning the period in question, but it is difficult when so few sources are available. The validity and authenticity of information increases when it comes from several factual and informed sources. For this reason I have tried to gain access to as many original sources as possible. Historical information and facts inherent in original sources have been collected and adapted as part of the book's foundation concerning the history of wildlife and wilderness film. Criticism of these sources relies partly on common sense and partly on additional source information.

Literature on Wildlife and Wilderness Film

No books have yet appeared that deal explicitly with the history of nature films. However, four works have been written that deal somewhat with the topic at hand. Each of them includes sections on historical matters; but in general, these sections are short and have no great bearing on the main focus of the individual books. A couple of theses touch upon the topic of natural history films, but their coverage of the history of the genre is fairly superficial.

In my opinion, Danish Tomas Fibiger Nørfelt's MA thesis, *Naturbilleder* (*Pictures of Nature*), from 1992, presents a distorted view of the matter, and the organization and focus of the historical sections appear almost accidental. Among other things, Nørfelt claims that the National Geographic Society (NGS) played a crucial role as communicator and sponsor of nature films. First of all, the Society was established in 1888 — not, as Nørfelt states, in 1885. Secondly, it was not until 1965 that NGS began producing nature films. They had sponsored nature films in the 1950s, but to claim that they played a crucial role is to distort matters.[1] Those NGS expeditions that had the greatest influence on the history of nature films were Jacques-Yves Cousteau's expeditions. Cousteau mixed scientific exposition, reporting and classic nature film in a new and exciting way, which helped create respect for, as well as interest in, the nature film genre. But to claim that NGS was the foundation of Cousteau's success is wrong. He started making his own films back in the 1940s.

Norwegian Kari Norstad has clearly used Nørfelt's *Naturbilleder* as a source for her short sections on "historical development" in her MA thesis *Natur i Naturprogrammer* (*Nature in Nature Programmes*) from 1995.

I feel that both Nørfelt and Norstad misapply the concept of the travelogue. They use the term about the film *90° South*, which is not a travelogue but an expedition film by Herbert Ponting. Perhaps the two students became confused by the term "travel film" as used by the film historian Richard M. Barsam. Barsam's term "travel film" is much broader, as it includes *90° South*, as well as *Nanook of the North*, *Moana*, *Grass* and *Chang*.[2]

Norstad and Nørfelt only use about two pages each to describe the period that will be the main focus of this book, and they reach pretty much the same conclusion. For instance, they both mention *Voyage au Congo* (1926) in relation to the history of nature films, despite the fact that it is clearly an ethnographical expedition film. I have seen *Voyage au Congo* at the British Film Institute in London, and only two minutes of the 113 minutes of this picture are relevant within the context of nature films. Emphasizing *Voyage au Congo* within the context of nature films is problematic, taking into account that many, more relevant, films are not mentioned in the two theses (such as the films of Oliver Pike and William Finley, which show nature and wildlife in the same period).

It must be remembered that the purpose of these theses was not to write about the historical development of the genre but to address nature programs made for television. Where Nørfelt deals with the genre of nature programs, Norstad seeks to outline the presentation of nature as it appears in television programs. Nonetheless, their work demonstrates that there is an obvious need for a book like *Cameras into the Wild*— an in-depth historical reading of wildlife and expedition films that will give the reader an overview, making it easier to judge what films have been important for the development of the genre.[3]

In recent years, two books on the topic of wildlife and wilderness films have been published. Derek Bousé's *Wildlife Films* (2000) may be said to be the first of its kind in that it focuses totally on nature film. Bousé's focus is animal films. The work contains a section on historical matters, but its presentation of the early history of nature filmmaking is sketchy to say the least — especially as it does not include William Finley, Herbert Ponting or Bengt Berg. As I will demonstrate, these men played a major historical role in the development of both wilderness and wildlife films. Moreover, I disagree with Bousé's priorities in the section on silent films. Of a total of 17 pages, 5 deal with the pre-film days, i.e., cave paintings, Muybridge and Marey, and 4 pages are used to describe Martin and Osa Johnson. Over 50 percent of the total number of pages deals with the historical development of nature filmmaking.[4]

I read Bousé's work late in my writing process, as I did not want it to influence my own approach to the topic. His book *Wildlife Films* concerns animals filmed in their natural environment. Bousé considers the ethical implications regarding the manipulation occurring during the shooting and editing phases. Moreover, he depicts how animal films, from a historical perspective, have chosen a narrative track in which everything from human civilization has been discarded. People, electricity pylons, houses, vehicles and roads go unmentioned, and the focus is on wild nature without any human "interference." This is what the wildlife film industry calls the "blue-chip wildlife film."[5]

The fourth work, Gregg Mitman's *Reel Nature* (1999), is an historical work about American films that deal with the American romantic notions of nature. Mitman focuses on the period between 1885 and 1990, mainly on hunting films and expedition films produced in America. In the book, Mitman suggests that nature films have gradually been seduced by the entertainment industry, and that this has given the genre a dubious authenticity.

Although these four works deal with topics related to nature filmmaking, they have not been relevant for my arguments and conclusions in *Cameras into the Wild*. None of the books mentioned above have included the issue of technical development, and they have only been of limited use in this regard.

Contemporary Sources

I consider the sources from the period 1895–1928 to be of considerable importance, as they give us a sense of contemporary conditions and problems; but as they are often quite subjective in their approach, we should consider them with reservations. Two fundamental problems are that the authors either do not justify their claims or that they themselves rely on unreliable/unqualified sources. Richard Griffith makes some comments regarding source criticism in his introduction to the 1970 edition of Benjamin B. Hampton's *History of the American Film Industry* (1931). Griffith compares the book to other, earlier books on the same topic and writes about Hampton that

that is the best history of the movie business to date there can be no doubt. Ramsaye is far less exact, Jacobs is far less complete, and neither conveys to the same extent the sense of being in the thick of events, and deeply affected by them, yet committed to a perspective based on the need to make an objective choice between competing business policies [Griffith 1931/1970, ix].

Griffith has previously criticized Terry Ramsaye's *A Million and One Night's* (1926). He finds fault with the author's journalistic background as well as his inhibited relationship with the film industry. "It is in sum, romantic journalism of a high order."[6] In my use of these sources, I have attempted to avoid quoting sources uncritically, and I have double-checked the information whenever possible.

I have read Ernest A. Dench's (1919) and Homer Croy's (1918) works concerning

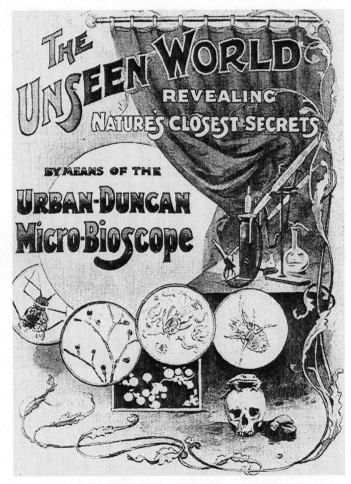

Catalogue front page from Charles Urban Co.

film production. Both are entertaining, but today they appear totally amateurish, and quite often there are no references regarding the locations, years, titles or people mentioned. Moreover, both works are totally uncritical and express an appalling naivety. Dench's *Making the Movies* is by far the worse of the two. Dench writes about intelligent ants that are unable to behave naturally once the camera is running, and grasshoppers endowed with such empathy that they die if you play beautiful or sad music to them.[7]

Old distribution catalogues often contain rather detailed depictions of film plots, but it is a good idea to consider these as "cinema trailers." They are "goodies" meant to tempt people to go to the cinema — or rather to make cinema owners buy the films. Thus, superlatives are used very frequently, and it is more than obvious that the films would never have been able to live up to such fantastic descriptions. Another problem concerning the film catalogues is that they do not mention the dates of the films included. Thus, it is only possible to give tentative dates for the year in which the films premiered.

An example of this is evident in the catalogues of Nordisk Films Kompagni. In 1911, Nordisk Film published *Norsk Natur, Bilbao, Spansk Natur,* and *Højskotland.* Unfortunately, I have not been able to obtain these films, and most likely they have been lost. The only thing that might give us an indication of what kind of films they were is the summaries in the catalogues, but these do not present us with a realistic idea of what the films might have contained. In order to illustrate my point, I have inserted an example of such a summary below:

> This time our cinematographer brings us a series of visuals from the memorable rocky Highlands of Sir Walter Scott — the country with its strange, callous and rough appearance, whose black, naked mountains seem to have been created for the lives of goblins and trolls. In the depths of the large dark forests the druids and nymphs dance and practice their magic — each brook has its own fairy, whose charming song sounds through the murmuring of the clear water. And the broad-shouldered sons of this magic country know these mountain folk and trolls. They remember and love the legends and fairy tales that flow mist-like round the old, strange and decaying palaces and castles. No one is more attached to the old dresses and customs. They wish to — and do — stand apart [Plot-description folder from The Danish Film Institute's library].

The description of *The Scottish Highlands* tells us nothing about the contents of the film. We must assume that the film showed images of mountains, forests, brooks, lochs, palaces, castles and Scots dressed up in national costumes. This remains plain guesswork, however, as the fairytale-like text gives us few hints. The above description is a good example of how non-fiction films were presented by Nordisk Film. Such descriptions were commercials, and had little to do with reality, which makes them useless for my present purposes.

Examples of Applied Literature

Charles Guggisberg's *Early Wildlife Photographers* (1977) deals mainly with still photography of birds and mammals, and does not discuss technological development, which appears to be a relatively undescribed topic in general. I have found information concerning film technology from various sources, but the main works are Brian Coe's *The History of Movie Photography* (1981), Brian Salt's *Film Style and Technology* (1983) and Raymond Fielding's *A Technological History of Motion Pictures and Television* (1967).

One major problem with Brian Salt's book is the lack of source references. Salt includes a list of literature but does not use any specific references in his actual text, and it is next to impossible to test the points he makes or trace the foundation of his knowledge about the technical development of the film media.

Pascal and Eleanor Imperato have written a well-researched biography about the lives of Martin and Osa Johnson, who produced wildlife and safari films in the silent era. The Imperatos spent three years researching and writing about the adventurous lives of the Johnsons. The purpose of the Imperatos was to puncture the many myths surrounding the famous couple — to get at the truth about them — a truth which is no less exciting than the Johnsons' spiced-up autobiographies and travel journals.

One problem with the Imperatos' book is their uncritical depiction of the content of the films they describe — they never reflect independently on the work of Martin Johnson. Nonetheless, the book is a fantastic source of knowledge about the lives of the Johnsons.

Despite the fact that contemporary reviewers were not impressed with the literary endeavors of the couple, the books by Osa and Martin Johnson describing their exotic travel experiences sold like hotcakes. Osa Johnson's book *I Married Adventure* was published 17 May 1940, and was an immediate success. The book was number one on the national bestseller list, and within a year 500,000 copies had been sold.[8] Although the books by the Johnsons leaned towards the fantastic side in their depiction of reality, they have provided me with useful and interesting information regarding the equipment and recording conditions of those days.

I have made extensive use of articles from newspapers and magazines, as well as books on non-fiction films and film in general. Through the reading of such material, I have found clues to new sources, which in turn (in some cases) have led me in the direction of new material. In this way, a list of over 100 indispensable works has been compiled — books, reference books, compiled lists of films, articles, etc.

The Locations of Neglected Films

The Mortality and Preservation of Film

The research for *Cameras into the Wild* has been complicated by the fact that the international film archives have great difficulty finding and preserving the works created in the silent film era, not to mention the fact that a great number of films have disappeared for good. Silent films were not considered to have any long-term economic value. Metaphorically, this situation might be compared to the development of a child. During the first couple of years, the child goes through a massive physical development, including motor function and language. The child quickly grows out of its old clothes and develops so fast in so many ways that one quickly loses sight of the attributes the child possessed in its infant stage. Once the child reaches a certain maturity, it will no longer grow out of its clothes so fast; rather, it will be the style and taste that changes. Moreover, the linguistic capacity and motor function will have reached a level from which all earlier stages will appear infantile. Still, the early childhood holds enormous significance for the later development of the child. It is through childhood experiences that we may interpret the actions of the adult man or woman. Similarly, all facets of early film history are of crucial significance, a fact which the world of film studies — and the industry itself — has been slow to recognize and integrate.

Film archive with nitrate films on the shelves (Karin Bonde Johansen).

Opposite: Corridor in a film archive with 16mm and 35mm films (Karin Bonde Johansen).

Thus, a film company like the Douglas Fairbanks Studio destroyed enormous amounts of film in order to get at the small amount of silver it contained, as it seemed more profitable than keeping the films in storage. The historical value of the films was not recognized at all.[9]

Moreover, the raw film stock of those days was hampered by technology. A film reel then consisted of three layers, including an outer layer that held a light-sensitive emulsion, and a middle layer that bound the emulsion layer to the base layer. In the period between 1888 and 1951, cellulose nitrate secured the flexibility, strength, surface texture and transparency of the base layer. Cellulose nitrate is a chemical substance extracted from animal tissue that is chemically related to gunpowder, making it an explosive element. Moreover, cellulose nitrate disintegrates as it oxidizes over time and emits gasses that can work independently and contribute to further disintegration of the film. Today, old films are copied onto acetate-based film or a digital storage device; but lack of funding often prevents an effective transmission procedure, which means that many films are ruined before they can be saved.

When it is decided what films deserve to be preserved, non-fiction films generally have a very low priority. Thus, technological and financial factors have contributed to today's situation in which very few non-fiction films of the silent era exist. A significant silent film historian, Kevin Brownlow, states, disheartened:

> The tradition that these films follow has been clouded by neglect. The men who made the early films of fact deserve to be remembered, and their work deserves to be exhumed. The evidence of the past is too precious to be destroyed [Brownlow 1978, 566].

Only a small percentage of films from the silent era exist — and very few of these are non-fiction. In 1985, Gomery and Allen estimated that about half of America's feature films have been destroyed.[10] In 1997, Casper Tybjerg suggested that about 80 percent of all Danish silent films have been lost, which corresponds with estimations on a more global level. Thus, in the year 2000, Paolo C. Usai states that film historians and archivists estimated that 80 percent of all silent films have been lost.[11]

Existing Films and My Reservations

I have done everything possible to see the wildlife and wilderness films available in Denmark, Sweden, America and England. I have naturally had to report only on the copies I saw — which often were merely one of several versions of the same film, and which may well have been of a different appearance or condition than what the film looked like when it first appeared.

On many occasions the producer of a given film had to send out different versions of the same film in order to comply with censor regulations, national tastes or the acceptable length for a particular cinema audience. These demands varied, depending on the target audience and its geographical location.

On other occasions, the same film material has been edited several times. This has occurred due to the fact that the development of the media gradually overtook the old version in terms of technique or stylistic ideas. Thus, it is difficult to know if the intertitles

Opposite, top: Dry, decomposed 35mm film (Karin Bonde Johansen). *Opposite, bottom:* Wet, decomposed 35mm film (Karin Bonde Johansen).

of a film belong to the original release or were inserted at a later time. An illustrative example of the difficulties facing the film historian in the matter of determining and analyzing film versions is Herbert G. Ponting's film material from Captain Falcon Scott's 1910–1912 Antarctic expedition. Over a period of some 20 years, Ponting's material was edited and revised into countless versions. Such a long period has naturally witnessed an incredible technological and narrative development. Thus, in the 1933 version of *90° South* the soundtrack changes the effect of the editing, and it differs significantly from earlier versions. For this reason, it is crucial to include all existing information concerning any given copy.

Another problem, which is especially relevant for the nature film genre, is the fact that films may be composed of material belonging to several independent productions, which is the case with the film *Partite di caccia grossa in Africa* (1926). This film depicts the expedition of an Italian explorer, Vittorio Zammarano-Tedescod, along the River Giuba in Somalia in 1925. The film includes hunting scenes depicting hippopotami, rhinoceroses, crocodiles, lions, leopards and elephants. Some of the material used in the film was not shot during the expedition that the film claims to portray, but can be identified as belonging to earlier films, such as *Hic sunt Leones* and *Il rifugio deel pleiadi* (1923?).[12] In this instance, it has been possible to trace the original sources of the material, but it is not always possible to judge whether a film has included material shot at a different time and place.

The Choice of Films

The Films

When choosing the films to be discussed in *Cameras into the Wild*, obviously the first criterion has been availability — the films must have been available for viewing. For those cases when this has not been possible, I have insisted on having a detailed written description of the plot. Another criterion stems from the fact that I wish to acknowledge the contemporary tendencies of the times. Therefore I have on occasion included films that may not have changed the course of film history, but that nonetheless indicate what went on in the minds of the cinemagoers. Film history is much more than just citing masterpieces or listing who achieved what first. If we examine the viewers, the films, and the industry's current production practice, we will find that all films have their place in history. We will discover that the direction of film history has not merely been determined by a small group of classics. Indeed, the aesthetic development has occurred through slow changes.

The Concept of Nature

In the following section I will describe my definition of nature — a definition that has determined what films should be included in the compiled list of films and, by implication, in *Cameras into the Wild*. The relationship between man and nature has changed considerably throughout man's existence on earth. These changes have led to new conceptions and reflections concerning the "nature" of nature and the meaning we ascribe to it.

Today, nature is so complex a notion that it includes everything from the mysteries of the universe, sexual urges and throat cancer to the mechanism of emotions, the attraction of the earth and natural gas. Nonetheless, research conducted in 1997 by Professor Svend Erik Larsen, the former manager of the basic research center Menneske og Natur (Man and

Nature) at the University of Southern Denmark, shows that what most people associate with the concept of nature is the word "landscape." Svend Erik Larsen has divided the defined notions of nature into a simple and concrete form, systematizing his notion of nature into points that situate the concepts of nature, culture and man in relation to each other.[13]

1. *Inside culture*: Nature as an available space in the form of a landscape that has been adjusted to the human need for knowledge and relaxation — zoological gardens, parks, village ponds.

2. *Outside culture*: Nature as a wilderness, existing outside human scale and control — catastrophes of nature, arctic landscapes, cancer tumors, and untamed nature in general.

3. *The borderline between nature and culture*: Larsen divides this borderline in three sub-sections. A. Nature as a resource — which also includes the body as a tool. B. Nature as garbage — a kind of nature that is unprofitable and which is difficult to control (Larsen here includes old, ill and tired people, and, by implication, corpses). C. Nature as non-inclusive or difficult to estimate — e.g. instincts, urges and other species-specific character-istics. The fear of death, hunger and the sexual urge are other examples.

4. *Cultural loans and leftovers in which nature is both inclusive and non-inclusive*: Nature comprising a sixth sense or a great indefinable power — this includes primitive cultures' understanding of nature, or that of healers, grass roots movements and other alternative viewpoints.

Larsen's description of the concept of nature has been very useful to me, and I have used it as the basis for my deliberations concerning the definition and discussion of nature in the context of the film media. What kind of films can be deemed "nature films" or wildlife and wilderness films? I immediately sensed that my discussion and definition of nature would have to differ significantly from Larsen's on one important aspect. Nature in the con-text of nature film should not include human behavior and physiology. For this reason, none of the films mentioned in this book deal with human nature — i.e. human illness, instincts, urges or behavior.

Here I will — for the sake of clarity — present how the concept of nature has been delimited when determining whether or not a given film was a "wildlife or wilderness film" to be discussed in *Cameras into the Wild*: The concept of nature in this project refers to nature as "natural scenery" with its wildlife — animals, plants, natural catastrophes and phe-nomena. The highest priority has been assigned to wild nature, untouched by human civ-ilization and culture. After this priority comes wild nature existing in rural and cultivated landscapes; while the lowest priority has been given to urban nature, including zoological gardens, parks and the animals and plants that live in such spaces. Man and his nature have been left out completely, and so has the problematical and complex concept of nature which is rooted in medical science and ethnography.

The Compiled List of Films

Over the last 10 years I have compiled a long list of non-fiction films that contain nature aspects. This list of films is founded on numerous written sources; but in the choice of films to be included I have decided that only films living up to my definition of nature films may be part of the list. For the period 1895–1928 I have registered 715 films. These films have been chronologically divided as follows:

There were 62 films produced in the period 1895–1902.

Year	Films	Number of series/ (films in each)
1895	2	0 (0)
1896	7	1 (5)
1897	14	2 (11)
1898	8	0 (0)
1899	7	0 (0)
1900	8	0 (0)
1901	2	0 (0)
1902	10	0 (0)

There were 74 films produced in the period 1903–1906.

Year	Films	Number of series/ (films in each)
1903	26	4 (12)
1904	6	0 (0)
1905	17	2 (14)
1906	21	0 (0)

There were 91 films produced in the period 1907–1910.

Year	Films	Number of series/ (films in each)
1907	14	0 (0)
1908	14	1 (1)
1909	26	0 (0)
1910	36	1 (2)

There were 242 films produced in the period 1911–1921.

Year	Films	Number of series/ (films in each)
1911	27	0 (0)
1912	32	1 (1)
1913	26	2 (3)
1914	30	1 (1)
1915	25	0 (0)
1916	10	0 (0)
1917	10	0 (0)
1918	12	2 (7)
1919	12	2 (3)
191?	5	3 (4)
1920	19	3 (7)
1921	34	3 (6)

There were 262 films produced in the period 1922–1928.

Year	Films	Number of series/ (films in each)
1922	63	3 (26)
1923	58	2 (23)
1924	24	1 (6)
1925	31	1 (2)
1926	34	2 (9)
1927	28	1 (11)

Year	Films	Number of series/ (films in each)
1928	20	0 (0)
192?	4	2 (6)

The same series may appear more than once and so "overlap."

Diagram Explaining the Selection of Film:

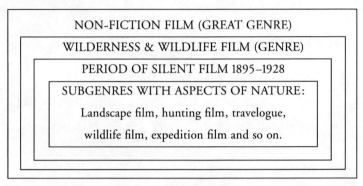

NON-FICTION FILM (GREAT GENRE)

WILDERNESS & WILDLIFE FILM (GENRE)

PERIOD OF SILENT FILM 1895–1928

SUBGENRES WITH ASPECTS OF NATURE:

Landscape film, hunting film, travelogue,

wildlife film, expedition film and so on.

Nature

How do people come to believe that it is interesting or important to see and learn from wildlife and wilderness films? First and foremost, the individual must no longer be dependent on nature, for until then he cannot liberate himself from it mentally. This is a necessary part of the creation of an aesthetic contemplation of nature, which makes it an important foundation for any literature and film about this particular topic.

Nature Emancipation and the Road to Romanticism

It is difficult to determine when the aesthetic conception of nature became dominant, but in some circles it probably appeared in the 16th century. At that time the word "landscape" took on a new meaning in both France and Italy. Prior to this, the word referred to a clearly demarcated region with its own law (for instance the Jutland Law). But during the 16th century the word attained its modern meaning — namely, natural scenery. At first this referred to landscape painting, but later it was used to denote the "actual" landscape — a new meaning, indicating that nature began to be perceived as scenery. In other words, nature came to have an aesthetic significance. At this time, however, such an understanding of nature was not widespread; it probably only existed among a minority until the middle of the 18th century, when the growing number of middle-class citizens began to prosper financially and achieved a sense of "physical surplus." This gave people new opportunities, and taking a walk in the park or in the countryside became popular among the well-to-do classes.

This new group of "surplus people" soon became attached to the notion of "tourist trips," which enhanced the conception of nature as beautiful. The tourist trip represented something new, for quite often the tourists went to places with raw and wild natural scenery. Earlier, the walk was limited to rural areas just outside the city gates, but now people began travelling to more untouched places, like the Alps. Not only were the Alps reachable but by 1789 their highest peak, Mont Blanc, had been climbed.

Mont Blanc.

With the ascent of Mont Blanc, the separation from nature seemed complete for humans. Yet until the 19th century, the journey abroad usually had one of the following purposes: Exploration, trade, government post, visits to health resorts, education or pilgrimages. Even a stay at a health resort or sanatorium in beautiful surroundings may not — at this point in time — be called a tourist trip. Such trips were considered a necessary evil and not at all a pleasurable experience. A real boom in the mixture of tourism and nature only occurred later. The 1860s and the 1870s saw an increase in the interest in nature tourism and circumnavigations of the globe. I believe that the literature of the times spurned the wanderlust. For instance, Jules Verne's *Around the World in Eighty Days* was published in 1873. Fictional accounts of life in, and journeys to, exotic countries were very popular at this point in time.

Nature Preservation and Education

The ordinary city population, workers and officials, only got the time, money and energy to enjoy nature sometime during the 20th century, when they had fixed work hours and, by implication, a certain amount of free time. They could spend this new free time in parks or at entertainment venues. One of the entertainments offered at these venues was the "magic lantern" show — a European invention which may be said to be the forerunner of the modern slide projector. The magic lantern, projecting hand-painted slides, was in use from the 1840s, around the time when the photographic slide was invented. The most popular topics in the magic lantern's heyday (1860–1885) were journeys to foreign cultures, as well as nature and places of outstanding beauty. For the first time in their lives, the people who attended these magic lantern lectures were able to see pictures of crocodiles, jungles or mountains.[14]

Man's understanding of nature had changed drastically by the end of the 19th century, so much, in fact, that certain parts of the population, as well as governments, could see the advantages of maintaining patches of untouched, wild nature. In America in 1872, Yellowstone National Park was established as the world's first wildlife sanctuary. Other countries joined in later, and in 1898 the Kruger National Park was opened in South Africa.[15] In England, nature protection was administered by the National Committee of Places of Historical Interest and Rural Beauty from 1895.

Until 1880, the biological mechanisms of nature were not part of the school curriculum, but a teacher in Boston, G. Stanley Hall, took an important step when he introduced a form of nature pedagogy. Nature became a popular source of learning and meant that curiosity about, and interest in, nature became widespread throughout society. Hall's nature pedagogy spread like rippling rings in water. Camps and field trips became popular, and school books about nature were published. The children were not merely to learn about nature in the class room, they had to get out into nature and be confronted with it physically.[16] At the same time, America's Ornithology Society was established (in 1883), and around the turn of the century different scouting organizations began. An interest in and understanding of nature was no longer a matter for the professionals, but was part of ordinary people's lives.[17]

Laterna Magica, or magic lantern (photograph by author).

There was an enormous increase in nature tourism during the first decades of the 20th century. This situation was caused mainly by a shortened working week, better public transport, and better economic conditions for the ordinary citizen. The national parks became popular tourist attractions for Americans, just as the Alps became a tourist attraction for Europeans. Around 1900, the German youth hostel association was established, which spread to the rest of Europe during the 1920s and 1930s. In America, the National Park Service was established in 1916. It was a common administrative body, chaired by Stephen Mather. He established beautiful stretches of road, walking paths and camping facilities within the national parks. He had a good reason for this — the number of cars in America tripled between 1916 and 1925, and thus reached 17.5 million. For the American middle classes, auto-camping became a favourite holiday form.

Four conditions were especially important in the popularization of nature interest and nature tourism[18]:

1. A growing middle class that had a decent income and free time away from work and other duties.
2. Better and faster modes of transportation, as well as an improved infrastructure. Roads were built that led directly to areas of natural beauty.
3. A regular tourist industry sprung up, handling and offering everything from accommodation and souvenirs to travel equipment.
4. Nature education became part of the school curriculum.

The changed understanding of nature that had gradually developed over time led to nature tourism, nature interest and the wish to maintain and protect nature in the wild. This was a good foundation for the appearance and development of nature films. The following review from 1910 of the film *The Egret Hunter* demonstrates how important nature had become for people's everyday lives around this time. Nature had become a source of joy and aesthetic pleasure — at least for some:

> Whatever might have been the purpose of this film, it should have the effect of influencing women to wear no more egrets on their hats. If it exerts an influence in that direction it will perform a useful service and possible will accomplish more than its makers really intended. Anything that tends to reduce the slaughter of birds of any sort performs a public service of importance [*The Moving Picture World*, May 21, 1910, 832].

The function of nature was no longer merely to serve man. Nature now denoted aesthetics, pleasure, experience, and challenges. Man had moved away from nature — so much so that he no longer looked at it from the inside, but rather stood apart and contemplated it from the outside. Man and nature had indeed become separated.

The Invention of Motion Pictures

The Beginning of Film

Many different inventors came up with inventions necessary for showing moving pictures, but some historians are keen to establish *one* originator of the media. Thus, Benjamin

Opposite: Nature tourism in 1916: Bright Angel Trail, Grand Canyon (photograph Kolb Brothers; provided by the estate of Janice P. Akerson, Alameda, California, United States).

Hampton states that Thomas Edison "was the 'father' of the movies because of his use of perforated film."[19] Giving an in-depth exposition of *who* had *what* influence on the development of the film camera falls outside the scope of this book. Nonetheless, I will shed a little light on those developments of the media that may be said to have had a special significance for wildlife and wilderness film.

Eadweard Muybridge (1830–1904) and the French physician Étienne-Jules Marey (1830–1904) were two enthusiastic photographers obsessed with movement; the two men analyzed movements in order to find their motor function. They took pictures of the way people and animals moved, as well as fast movements in general. They used very fast shutters, and in this way the picture could show the position of the body when at its fastest. Marey's photographic gun from 1882 was used to photograph such fast motion.

As early as 25 February 1888, Muybridge gave a lecture at Edison's laboratory in West Orange about his experiences with sequence photography. Two days later, Edison and Muybridge were to meet one another to discuss the possibility of connecting the Zoopraxiscope Projector with Edison's Phonograph. The inspiration for making motion pictures may well have commenced inside Edison's head at this meeting. At any rate, on 8 October of the same year he applied for a patent concerning his idea.

Edison's assistant and official photographer, William Kennedy Laurie Dickson, was responsible for the development of two apparatuses for recording and showing motion pictures. The projects had not progressed very far when Edison, in August 1889, attended an exhibition in Paris. There he, for the first time in his life, saw Marey's sequence film reel camera. In July 1891, Dickson visited the Eastman factories in Rochester, New York, and ordered 4 film reels, each 50 feet long; these were used for various experiments.

After three years of work, the cameras of Dickson and Edison were finished (in 1891) and presented to the public as the Kinetograph (camera) and Kinetoscope (projector). They contained 50 feet of film, which corresponds to about 20 seconds of screen time. These bits of film were shown on a commercial basis in the so-called "peepholes" from 1894. The content of these films was quite simple, but the novelty value attracted a lot of people. Real nature recordings were not part of the repertoire, yet there were short films showing a horse eating hay or a strong man flexing his arm muscles. Because the film was very insensitive to light, it was necessary to shoot the films in a Black Maria—a huge "tin can." Inside the tin can it was easy to control the shooting: the light was managed from the roof, and due to the pitch-black background, the pictures looked much clearer.

The Kinetoscope was presented in Paris and London in the summer of 1894, and Antoine, the owner of a

Étienne-Jules Marey.

factory producing photographic plates, attended one of these. He was immediately inspired by what he had seen, and due to the high prices set by Edison's agents, he asked his sons, Louis and Auguste, to begin working on a similar motion picture camera. In February 1895 they received a patent on their device, and on 22 March they presented their very first public showing on a screen. The two sons were, of course, none other than the Lumière brothers, and their apparatus was the *Cinématographe.* Their first commercial showing took place in the Salon India at the Grand Café in Paris on 28 December, 1895.*

Film Technology

Technical development is very important for any discussion of wildlife and wilderness films, for within this genre the quality of the raw film, the lenses, camera equipment (and its physical weight) and functionality all have a crucial significance. This is especially evident on those occasions when the cinematographer is working with shy animals or animals that live in isolated parts of the Earth.

"Trials of a Cameraman" is the title of an article written for the *Moving Picture World* in 1917 by the cinematographer William E. Fildew. In the article, Fildew argues that the skills of the cinematographer play a very important role in the production of any kind of film. Among other things, he describes his work in zoological gardens, which was clearly not his cup of tea, for he concludes, "I would rather photograph anything else than a wild beast" (July 21, 1917, 392). I mention Fildew's article for another reason, however; namely for his pointing at the importance of decent equipment, and for his remarks concerning the film's technical development:

> Years back when I worked at the old Biograph studios ... the quality of the film was an obstacle to be reckoned with. But now both film and emulsion have made rapid strides toward the ideal. Of course there have been improvements in the mechanical end, too — lenses, stops, apertures, revolving heads and tilting tables. Nearly all cameramen have made his own improvements [sic] in some detail or other, but the basic foundation of camera work still remains the lens and box [Fildew 1917, 391].

Fildew had no way of knowing that the road to the film-technical ideal would be long and winding. The wildlife and wilderness cinematographer was especially in need of technical improvements — improvements in the film's sensitivity to light and its grain quality, not to mention the cameras' and the lenses' improvements of prisms, mirror reflexes, shutter speed, etc.

In the period of 1895–1928, there came amazing developments in the equipment used in film production. The best inventions may be said to be the pioneer models presented to factory owners, and the most practical and innovative developments in many cases became standard parts of all models.

The next section describes the development of film emulsions and sound. Other relevant innovations within the history of film technology will appear in the following chapters under the headings depicting the technological development that characterized the period in question.

---

*It should be mentioned that the Skladanowsky brothers had their first showing in a vaudeville theatre in Berlin two months *before* the Lumiére brothers.

Film Emulsions

The earliest film emulsion, Ordinary, was sensitive to blue and violet colors, and slightly sensitive to the tint of green. Ordinary emulsion was not at all sensitive to yellow and red.

Around 1914, orthochromatic emulsion had become widespread; it was sensitive to tints of green and blue. Tints of yellow and red were hardly registered; indeed, these colors seemed almost pitch black on the developed film, whereas purple and blue were overexposed and appeared almost white. Since the film was not sensitive to the tints of red, it required clear daylight during outside shootings, and because the film was not sensitive to purple and blue, cloud formations or blue skies with clouds were flattened out into a clean white palette on the finished film. Nonetheless, orthochromatic film emulsion had a clear advantage over Ordinary, an advantage which bettered the results for, especially, the wildlife cinematographers: it was light sensitive to the whole palette of shades of green, which meant that it created a more beautiful image of the landscape than had been possible earlier in history.

Panchromatic film was developed by Eastman Kodak towards the end of 1912 for Gaumont Pictures, but it was not widely used until around 1925.[21] This was mainly due to the fact that until the '20s, panchromatic film had been too expensive. Moreover, the exposure was quickly consumed by the atmospheric air, which meant that the films had to be developed soon after shooting. The first panchromatic raw films were not very light sensitive either; the advantage of panchromatic film was that it was sensitive to all natural colors.

In 1925, Eastman Kodak launched a new panchromatic raw film that was cheaper and more atmospherically stable than the first one. This was the film with which Robert Flaherty created the beautiful *Moana — A Romance of the Golden Age* (1926). Robert Flaherty sensed — and made use of — the nuances within the many varieties of black and white, which gave the picture both depth and density. In other words, Flaherty made full use of the potential offered by panchromatic film.[22]

After the screening of *Moana*, the light sensitivity of panchromatic film was further improved, and it became increasingly popular. The improved light sensitivity was caused by a fast reacting film emulsion. This super-speed film had an ASA value of 40–50, and was launched almost simultaneously by all the major film producers — e.g., Eastman Kodak and Agfa. Thus, from 1927, panchromatic emulsion was by far the preferred emulsion.[23]

Silent Films with Sound

The cinemas of the silent film era were full of sounds — and not only in the form of talk, coughing, laughter, crinkling candy paper and the monotone noise from the projector. Indeed, only very seldom has the screening of films been completely silent. The film might have been accompanied by piano or orchestra music, sound effects, readings, lectures and commentaries made by professional actors behind the screen. Often, a "barker" presented the titles of the films, commented on them and read aloud the intertitles. Such a presentation would have had a great influence on how the audience experienced the films that had been chosen for a given performance. What he said, and the manner in which he said it, mattered. It also mattered how much attention had been given to the composition of the program, which, after all, consisted of very short films. In other words, it is difficult for us to get a sense of the experience that the audience for silent films must have had. The complexity inherent in some types of non-fiction films would have to have been explained by the presenter, so that all the members of the audience could understand what went on in the picture. Many people around the turn of the century were illiterate. Additionally, the narrative techniques of the film media were changing rapidly, which might well have confused the average cinemagoer.[24] Sometimes the presenter also explained the more creative aspects of the films — for instance, flashbacks and flash forwards by means of time-lapse sequences, camera position and the continuity that was created by means of the editing process.

After 1908–09, some cinemas added sound effects to the pictures. Some theaters used a sound ensemble, consisting of one or more people who stood behind the screen. Waves were accompanied by a roaring sound, and horses were accompanied by sounds of trampling hooves. There were diverging opinions concerning the positive and or negative effects of these sounds. Frederick Talbot, the author of *Moving Pictures: How They Are Made and Work* (1912), admits that he gets irritated when a scene showing a horse galloping on the ground is accompanied by a sound which is not only out of step with the hooves on the screen, but which sounds as if the ground consisted of copped stones. He also mentions the disharmony that occurs when a battle set in the Middle Ages is accompanied by a clattering that sounds like the burst of a machine gun.[25]

In somewhat more advanced cinemas, the "sound people" working behind the screen were superseded by a machine that could imitate several sounds. The machine was called Allefex and was invented by A. H. Moorhouse. The Allefex was supposed to be able to imitate the sounds of about 50 different things — e.g., a tempest, a waterfall, a barking dog and a bird twittering. The machine was operated by a single individual.

This entire spectrum of intended sounds which accompanied the films must be included in our appreciation of what it must have been like to watch films in the silent film period. In addition, it may provide us with a better understanding of why otherwise simple films were able to remain popular until the 1910s.

Eadweard Muybridge

Eadweard Muybridge is a kind of bridge builder between photography and film, and his main focus was the movement patterns of animals. For this reason the description of Muybridge will create a natural transition, or indeed introduction, to the first period. Muybridge was born in Kingston upon Thames, but left England as a very young man and went to America where he began working in a book shop. In America he became interested in photography, which made him return to England in 1860 in order to learn more about this topic. Around 1865 he went back to America with his recently acquired knowledge, and over the next 5 years he took over 2000 pictures of the American West. He later sold these under the pseudonym of "Helios."

Eadweard Muybridge (1830–1904).

By 1872, Muybridge's reputation as a photographer was widespread, and it was in this year that he began wondering how to answer this vexing question: Are all four legs of a galloping horse ever off the ground simultaneously?*

The question had been posed to him by the horse breeder and former governor Leland Standford. Muybridge worked on the solution to the problem for a couple of years, but was interrupted by problems in his private life. He was accused of having murdered his wife's lover, but was finally acquitted due to the nature of his "motive" (i.e., jealousy). Muybridge and Standford may have found the answer to the question long before these personal problems set in, but we have no photographic evidence of this. The two men continued their work once Muybridge had recovered from the trial, and the earliest proofs that are still in existence stem from 1878, when they used a more sophisticated method than they had attempted earlier.

Muybridge's talent for sequence photography meant that he earned much recognition, even in scientific circles, and he was eventually offered a lucrative deal with the University of Pennsylvania, where he began studying the locomotive patterns of people and animals. While in Pennsylvania he took more than 20,000 photographs, of which 781 are reproduced in his book *Animal Locomotion* (1899).

Muybridge had at his disposal the most advanced camera equipment of the day, and used set-ups where the cameras could photograph the movements the subject made when it passed before the lens. One of the basic set-ups consisted of 12 cameras placed at each end of the direction of motion, and 24 cameras placed along the direction of motion. The cameras were released by an automatic electro-photographic cable which activated each camera as the subject touched the electric thread. For rapid movements, the shutter speed could be as fast as 1/6000 seconds (i.e., 100 pictures/second). The pictures were taken as either a special study or in zoological gardens, but Muybridge wished that it had been possible to photograph the animals in their natural habitat. He writes:

> It would have been desirable, however, to have photographed many of the animals while they were enjoying more freedom of movement than afforded by the gardens of a Zoological Society, but the difficulties attending a satisfactory investigation under their natural conditions of life were, at the time, too great to be surmounted [Muybridge 1899, 257].

As a matter of form, I ought to mention that a galloping horse does, at one point, have all four legs off the ground simultaneously.

Muybridge's wish to reproduce the locomotive patterns of the animal kingdom by means of continuously recorded images could be said to be an early form of nature film. But since they were not shown as films, they must continue to be defined as photographs (albeit taken very quickly after one another).[26]

---

*Bordwell and Thompson write 1878 and Hill and Herbert write 1872 and so does Coe.

1895–1902
First Attempts to Make Nature Films

The following pages give an account of the historical background of wildlife and wilderness films. The text has been divided into chapters dealing with a specific time period (1895–1902, 1903–1906, 1907–1910, 1911–1921, and 1922–1928), and each chapter has a similar structure. First there is a description of the general development characterizing the period — i.e., information regarding cameras, lenses, exhibition venues, and various technical developments. These descriptions will primarily be concerned with aspects that may have had an influence on the production of nature films (technical or otherwise).

After this general introduction, a historical examination of the wildlife and wilderness film genre follows — i.e., a depiction of its sub-genres, special sub-genres and cinematographers. Sometimes the description of a cinematographer will take up an entire section. This naturally depends on the individual cinematographer's significance for the genre of wildlife and wilderness film in general, but also on how much material it has been possible to retrieve about the person. The long sections concerning a particular cinematographer all have the same structure: 1. a description of how they began working in the non-fiction film genre; 2. the development of their careers; 3. their work within nature film; and finally, 4. the films they made. Unfortunately, it has sometimes been impossible to find sufficient source material concerning even very important people within the development of wildlife and wilderness film. In these cases I have had to leave out certain subsections.

Technical Development

The period 1895–1902 is characterized by the fact that films mostly consisted of one shot, the duration of which was between 45 and 75 seconds. The films were shown by touring lecturers who gave talks in venues such as music halls, vaudeville theaters, lecture halls, and amusement parks.

Box Cameras

Like the other cameras of the time — e.g., the early Prestwich (1899), the Darling, the Ernemann and the Moy cameras — Lumière's Cinématographe and the Williamson camera were simple, rectangular wooden boxes.[1] The Williamson model came into being in 1904.

Left: A wooden box camera: Ernemann Camera, 1904. *Right:* Ernemann cameras were made in Dresden, Germany (photographs by author).

The camera offered an extraordinary film capacity — namely, 400 feet. In addition, it was possible to adjust the field of vision, thereby increasing the sharpness of the picture. However, this could only be done between shots, which meant that you had to switch to a film with a special transparent focus strip. It was no doubt a nuisance, but this particular feature of the camera must be considered a positive development because now the focus could actually be adjusted (this was not always the case with other types of cameras). Moreover, the owner of a Williamson camera could profitably mark the focus with which he had become familiar. In those situations — when the cinematographer could estimate the distance — such a mark could be used, and the cinematographer could avoid the complicated switching of films.

Due to the fact that the viewfinder was not particularly trustworthy, it was difficult for cinematographers of the time to frame the subject. Still, we must assume that it became routine to assess the framing of the finished picture.[2] The Danish director Peter Elfelt's film *Svaner i Sortedamssøen* (*The Swans of the Sortedam Lake*) (1897) is a good example of how difficult it was for the cinematographers of those days to frame their compositions. In the background we see a crowd of people who are looking at the swans. The swans are in the foreground, but they are only visible from the neck upwards. Seventeen to twenty swans have been squeezed into a wired enclosure. A man grabs hold of a swan and drags it out of the picture. The framing is very dense, has no focus and seems accidental.

Editing Technique

More often than not, the films of this period were not edited, but consisted of a single shot which had a length of up to 75 seconds. The use of films made out of several shots commenced in France and England in 1899. George A. Smith was one of the pioneers of this technique. In his film *Grandma's Reading Glass* (1900), for instance, he edited scenes into several shots and used innovative close-ups. Many years were to pass before these technical editing methods became part of the mainstream practice. From around 1903 there was an increase in the number of films consisting of several shots, but more than half of the existing films made before 1906 still feature only one shot.

The films of this period did not use intertitles. In fact, before 1905, very few films exploited the possibility of adding text in between the pictures.

Lenses

At this time (1895–1902) cameras had no lens attachments, and if a photographer wished to change lenses, he had to have a special device made for his camera. Lens attachments are very important to the wilderness cinematographer, and many cinematographers actually did acquire attachments so that they could switch between different focal lengths. The lenses of those days could not accommodate the high speed that we are used to today. During the first decade of film history, the maximum diaphragm was f4.5–5.6. This meant that you needed quite a significant amount of light in order to ensure a good result.

The Tripod

Since most of the moving picture cameras of the period used a crank handle, they could not be operated without a solid tripod; but the first tripods were very heavy. They were connected in such a way that the two parts seemed to be fused with one another, and the actual tightening of the camera took place on the top of the tripod—a construction that was very clumsy and which did not encourage camera movements. According to film historian Barry Salt, the tripod top for panorama shots was developed by Robert W. Paul in 1897 for a special assignment; and by the following year, Paul had already begun selling this type of tripod. Nevertheless, these "real" tripod pannings were rarely used before 1900, and only after 1903 did they become popular.

As previously mentioned, in the early days of cine-technical history, such constructions were quite heavy. It was not unusual for a tripod and camera to weigh some 99 to 110 pounds. The tripod itself made up most of this weight. Such clumsy and heavy equipment made the work of the wildlife and wilderness cinematographer very difficult.[3]

Exhibition Venues

During this period, films were mostly shown by touring presenters at market places and in village halls—at least with regards to presentations in small villages and towns. In major towns and cities, films formed part of the entertainment offered at vaudeville theaters and in meeting halls. To begin with, it was places like these that brought the first filmic experiences to a public audience. At first the films were a minor part of the shows; later they became much more dominant. But the business of showing films to the public quickly became the domain of touring film exhibitors and lecturers.[4]

Landscape Films

In this section I will demonstrate how films with nature themes helped sow the seeds of actual wilderness films. I arrange these early films into landscape films, travelogues, expedition films and animal films. For their part, landscape films have been divided into wave films, waterfall films, and panorama films. Animal films have been divided into zoo films, park films and wildlife films.

Landscape films constitute a sub-genre which I will define as movies consisting of shots of visually beautiful landscapes. These films feature one or more shots of a landscape, with no added intertitles — never becoming more than filmic picture postcards.

Despite the fact that landscape films were produced over a long period of time, they are mentioned here under one heading because this makes the matter clearer, and because this type of film did not change much over the years.

Wave Films

My compiled film list contains 11 wave films, but many more were made. Wave films are films which depict waves, be they beating against a dike or a gangway (or something similar), or breaking into foam. Wave films appeared between 1896 and 1912, but the most productive phase within this sub-genre seems to be 1896 to 1900. The year after the first films were being shown to a paying audience, the first wave films began appearing in many different countries simultaneously.

Despite its simplicity, English director Birt Acres' film *Rough Sea at Dover* (1896) fascinated the novice audience. The film, which consists of one shot, captures the movement of waves toward the coast. As is evident from several contemporary reviews of the film, English audiences were spellbound by the experience:

> But the final slide — a study of waves breaking on a stone pier — was simply wonderful in its realistic effect. We all know how beautiful ordinary instantaneous effects of breaking waves appear on the screen, but when the actual movement of nature is reproduced in addition, the result is little short of marvellous [*The Era*, April 25, 1896, 17].

This quotation refers to the reaction of the audience at the Royal Photographic Society after the film's first showing in London. On this occasion, *Rough Sea at Dover* competed with films such as *Boxing Match*, *Dancing Girls* and *Derby of 1895* (1896) — films that would probably appeal more to us today than *Rough Sea at Dover*. But at that time, the wave film attracted the most attention, and several wave films were to appear over the following years. Indeed, the wave film was to become the first special genre, representing the pure nature film; and despite competition from other early films, it was incredibly popular.

Today it can be difficult to understand this popularity. Film historian John Barnes believes that Acres shot his films at 40 frames per second and showed them at a speed of 15 frames per second.[5] The effect would have been slow-motion, and this would have given the waves a dreamlike quality — whereas other films, like *Derby of 1895*, might simply have seemed slow and unnatural. This is mere speculation, but it seems plausible that waves will appear more life-like in slow-motion than galloping horses. According to this contemporary review, the waves seemed very natural:

> Another scene showed a stormy day at the seaside. The waves dashed against the breakwater, the spray seemed to start out of the picture and those who stood near the screen appeared to be in imminent danger of being wetted. A few people were observed dodging the flying foam [*The Morning*, February 29, 1896, 1].

Thus, the attraction of this particular film may reside in technical finesse, but this does not explain the attraction of wave films in general. Indeed, Birt Acres became aware of the effect of showing the film in slow-motion. He corrected this, but the wave film remained popular.

In the summer of 1896, one of the film crews of producer R. W. Paul went to Spain and Portugal for five weeks to shoot new films for public exhibition. These films were shown without the slow-motion effect; and still the wave film *A Sea Cave Near Lisbon* received very flattering reviews. The films were shown for the first time on 22 October 1896, in the Alhambra Theatre in London. On 31 October a reviewer of the magazine *The Era* wrote:

> A cave on the coast of Galicia, one of the most beautiful realisations of the sea that we have ever witnessed. The foam-crested waves rush into the recesses of the rocks, clouds of spray are hurled into space, and the grandeur of the scenes are remarkable [*The Era*, October 31, 1896, 19].

The film, *A Sea Cave Near Lisbon*, was one of 14 motion pictures that the Paul film crew had shot on the trip to the Iberian Peninsula, and the wave film became the most popular of the 14. Its popularity continued for many years, and the film was still part of R.W. Paul's catalogue seven years later. In the sales catalogue it said: "This famous film has never been equalled as a portrayal of fine wave effects."

Wave Films Become a Mass Produced Special Genre

Today the director George Méliès (1861–1938) is chiefly remembered for his trick films. Yet before he began shooting these, he made quite a few non-fiction productions. In 1896 he went to the coast of Trouville and Le Havre to film waves beating against the shore. He shot on location for two days during the best season for wave films, and thus managed to film the stormy weather he was looking for.

Méliès' camera only held 20 feet of film at a time, and the reel could only be changed in complete darkness. Thus Méliès wandered back and forth between the beach and the photographic dealer in town — each time carrying all his equipment, as he was alone and did not dare leave anything out of his sight. In his autobiography, Méliès writes that up to 20 times a day he wandered several miles through heavy sand, and that he sometimes walked in sand to the knees due to the heavy weight of the equipment.*

Two of Edison's film people, James White and Frederick Blechynden, saw to it that America got her own wave film — *Surf at Monterey*. Around 5 September 1897, they were filming the coastline near Monterey in California. There is only one shot in the film. We see two rocks in the foreground, and the

George Méliès (1861–1938) — the one without a hat — about 1897 (The Danish Film Institute, Stills and Poster Archive).

*George Méliès also claims he was the first person to make wave films, which — the wave film of Birt Acres documents — is incorrect.

waves crash down on them, sometimes completely covering them in water and foam. Presumably, the film premiered late in 1897 or early in 1898.

If people were to watch wave films today, they would no doubt find them incredibly boring. Despite the fact that they rarely last longer than one minute, the films seem interminable because they have no action and no people appear in them. Of course, the audiences in those days were much easier to please, as film represented a completely new form of entertainment. Yet what is surprising is that wave films were able to compete with motion pictures of a much more dramatic nature—films about bull fighting or trains—and that wave films were actually quite "the thing" for at least half a decade. This tells us something about the attraction of nature scenery at a very early age in the history of film. Nature presented on the screen had a special effect on people, which is evident in the following quotation of inventor Thomas Armat, who describes the reception of *Rough Sea at Dover*, which premiered in New York on 28 April 1896, at the Koster and Bial Music-Hall:

> A scene that was totally unlike anything an audience had ever seen in a theater. When it was thrown upon the screen the house went wild; there were calls from all over the house for "Edison." "Edison," "speech," "speech" [*Journal of the Society of Motion Picture Engineers*, Vol. 24, March 1935].

The fascination with wave films may be explained by the fact that they represented something completely new. Not only did they bring nature indoors, they did it in a realistic and dynamic manner. For centuries the theater had been the home of dramatic art, but never before had nature been brought indoors quite like this. A quotation from George Méliès' autobiography, in which he mentions his own wave film, may give us a hint as to why these motion pictures were so successful at that time: "The ones who were familiar with the sea exclaimed, 'That's it exactly!' and the ones who had never seen the sea felt they were standing on its shore" (Macdonald & Cousins, 1996, 11).

For many years to come, the wave film became increasingly popular. In 1898 the innovator G.A. Smith, a well known name in film history, released his motion picture *Waves and Spray*, representing a rough sea, the waves of which are beating against a stone wall. In 1903, C. Hepworth also tried his hand at this special genre with the film *Breaking Waves*; and seven years later, in 1910, the film *Gigantic Waves* was released by Gaumont Film. A review in *The Moving Picture World* (*TMPW*) shows that wave films could still impress the audience: "Another of the successful ocean pictures.... So well is the technical work done in this instance that one can almost imagine that the huge waves are going to roll off the screen and over the audience" (May 21, 1910, 832).

My compiled list of films does not contain any wave films produced later than 1910. After 1910, the sea merely forms part of more complex films, and thus these no longer fall within the wave film definition.

Panorama Films

Panorama films are motion pictures depicting a landscape that moves — e.g., films produced during a journey by train, car or boat. These films premiered between 1896 and 1914, but the panorama film as a genre saw its most productive phase between 1896 and 1907.

In 1896, one of the operators for the Lumière brothers, Alexandre Promio, added innovative movement to one of his landscape shots of Venice. He did this by placing the tripod in a gondola and filming while it was sailing. Promio might well have been the first person to use the movements of the actual camera to depict a beautiful landscape during a "travelling shot." Such panoramas of nature soon became common in landscape films — it became popular to place the camera on a car, a train, a boat or other moveable foundations. This is seen in films like *View from an Engine Front* (1898), *View from Train on a Mountain Side* (1901) and *Panorama View Between Pallisider and Field, B.C.* (1902). The latter was filmed during a train journey on a mountain slope, whereas the middle film contains at least four shots from the same train journey. Most likely the cinematographer turned the hand wheel when the landscape was particularly beautiful and stopped when it appeared less so.

Waterfall Films

Thirty waterfall films, all depicting waterfalls, water rapids or geysers, have been registered. All these films include some sort of falling water. They premiered at regular intervals from 1896 to 1916, though one of them was made in 1928.

The first filming of Niagara Falls was probably done by the Latham brothers in 1896. The shots were meant to be shown with their Eidoloscope projector. In early June of the same year, one of Edison's crews filmed the waterfalls from various angles. These motion pictures were shown individually. The visual quality was very bad, and for this reason the films were quickly replaced by a new series, shot in December 1896. Before that, in September 1896, the Lumière brothers had sent their cameraman Alexandre Promio to the waterfalls. One of Edison's first Niagara films may have been inspired by Promio, who, as has been mentioned previously, had shot a film from a sailing gondola in Venice.

Niagara Falls/View from Gorge Railroad (1896) depicts a panoramic view over the Niagara canyon, as well as the whirlpool, which Edison's cameraman, William Heise, filmed from the back end of a slow-moving train. The seven new Niagara films that the Edison crew filmed in December 1896 were superior in quality to those of June the same year. This was due to a new and better grade of film. One of the pictures, *Horseshoe Falls — from Table Rock* (1897), is described in this manner in the catalogue: "This is the best general view of the Horse Shoe Falls and shows nearly a mile of the setting rapids above this point. The picture is sharp and clear" (*Edison's Film*, January 20, 1897, 5).

Edison's Niagara movies were made by the same cameraman responsible for the films shot in May, William Heise. They had a standard length of approximately 49 feet and were shot from various angles.

One of Edison's film crews was in Yellowstone National Park between 19 July and 25 July 1897, shooting five films.[6] Two were about waterfalls, two represented geysers and one was unusual as it depicted a wild bear. The waterfalls that were filmed in Yellowstone — the Upper Falls and the Lower Falls — are some of the most spectacular in America. The two geysers filmed in the national park of Wyoming are Old Faithful and Riverside Geyser. In Edison's film catalogue, the following comments were made about *Upper Falls of the Yellowstone* (1897): "This picture shows this celebrated spectacle of nature in the highest state of its grandeur" (1901, 12).

Among the various waterfall films are R. W. Paul's series from Norway. A film of 82 feet called *Laatifoss Falls* is included in Paul's catalogue. The first shot is a long-shot of the entire waterfall. Then follows a shot of the lower part of the waterfall, including its bottom lake into which the water crashes, creating many whirlpools. In the last shot of *Laatifoss*

Upper Falls, Yellowstone (photograph by author).

Falls we see the fast moving streams of the waterfall carrying the water away from the fall's bottom lake.[7]

Waterfall films were simple and uncomplicated, but they sold well due to their depiction of beautiful natural scenery.

A Film Shot of a Geyser

Around the turn of the century, Anton Nöggerath, Sr. (1859–1908) was the owner of one of the most popular music halls of Amsterdam, the Flora Theatre. In 1897, Nöggerath Sr. sent his son, Nöggerath Jr. (1880–1947), to England to study the film trade as an apprentice at Maguire & Baucus. Nöggerath Jr. remained in England until 1906, and worked as a cinematographer and dark room assistant mainly at Maguire & Baucus, which in the meantime had been renamed The Warwick Trading Company. Nöggerath Jr. was to make films for Warwick all over Europe, and in 1901 his work brought him to Iceland. The shots that he took during his visit there were catalogued by Warwick in April of 1902 under the collective name *Iceland Trailer Series*. Among other things, the series depicted men working on their fishing boats, and women rinsing fish and doing the laundry in a hot spring. As noted in his autobiography, Nöggerath Jr. also shot films of Stora Geysir during his visit to Iceland: "I placed my camera on the edge of the Geyser, in order to take a shot of the crater ... in which one saw water boiling. And we nearly lost our lives due to our curiosity" (Blom 1999, 273).

They did get their shots, but something must have happened to the films because they were never catalogued by Warwick. The films may have been developed incorrectly, or may

Stora Geysir, Iceland. Just imagine (photograph by author).

not have been of a high enough quality. This must have been a bitter experience for Nöggerath Jr., since he had gone through quite a few difficulties to obtain these shots. In his memoirs he states:

> Because right at the moment when we had filmed the crater and interior, we suddenly heard a terrible rumbling, and my guide yelled: "Quickly, away from here." Carrying my camera on my shoulders, we ran as fast as we could, escaping just in time! [Blom 1999, 273].

Merely getting to the geyser had been difficult. First he had to travel for two days to get to Stora Geyser, and afterwards he waited for hours for the geyser to erupt. When it finally did, he nearly lost his life. Yet for him, such an experience was merely an occupational hazard. He writes: "Then all of a sudden the Geyser went up again at full speed, and spurted; we hadn't left a second too early. The risk of the film-cameraman.... But I had archived my goal: the Big Geyser had been filmed" (Blom 1999, 273).

Indeed, the geyser had been filmed, but the film was never catalogued, and the question is whether it was a complete failure.

Nöggerath Jr. became self-employed sometime in 1906, but the news of his father's death in 1908 made him return to Amsterdam, where he took over his father's business.[8]

Tourism in Iceland (photograph by author).

Landscape Films as Advertisements for Tourists

From the beginning, promotion of countries or areas as tourist attractions was an essential feature of the film industry. When the Warwick Trading Company sent Nöggerath Jr. to Iceland in 1901, an article in a local Icelandic newspaper, *Thjodolfur*, claimed that the filmmaker had arrived too late. In other words, he had missed not only the whaling but also a group of visiting tourists.[9] Nonetheless, the newspaper concluded that even without these important elements, the films would have a positive influence on Iceland's tourism.

As advertisements for tourism, wilderness films probably also gave rise to a general interest in nature. At least this is evident from the answer to a question posed in an article by Cedric Belfrage: "How, for example, was the Scottish film tackled? It had to make people want to go to Scotland" (Belfrage 1931, 1155). The solution was to film wild salmon on their migration to the spawning area. On the way, the film crew had ample opportunity to film the beautiful natural landscape. By implication, such an advertisement for Scotland was also an advertisement for nature itself.

In Sweden, however, things were not as easy as that. In the 1910s, filmmakers tried to tempt the Swedes to go out into nature by showing them films depicting the natural beauty of the Swedish landscape; but according to Carl Julius Anrick, this proved quite difficult. "We thought the images of nature would tempt people to spend time in nature—but we were clearly mistaken."[10]

Films from Travels and Expeditions

Only very few of the early lecturers' films are still in existence today — probably because these films were only seldom put into circulation, and merely formed part of the travelogue show of the individual lecturer. Lecturers who used *laterna magica*, and who lectured about distant countries and exotic journeys, have existed for over 200 years, and nature was an essential feature of their lectures. As soon as the film camera appeared on the market, people began filming sceneries from nature, and for many people in the countryside the films shown by the various lecturers were their first and only meeting with the film media.

The lecturers offered many forms of entertainment, but film was to become the most important one. The lecturers also used slide shows, photographs and various exotic objects that were passed around the room among the audience. Moreover, the lecture hall might be decorated with pictures and objects for people to look at.[11] A very important element of the travelogue was the ability of the lecturer to spellbind his audience through his rhetoric capability. In fact, his enthusiasm and personal appearance was more important for the success of the show than the quality of the film. In 1910 *The Moving Picture World* published an article that criticizes the general state of the travelogue:

> And after all, much depends upon the man who talks. The management may be good, the pictures excellent, but if the man who is to stand up and talk to these people has not personality and magnetism enough, your travel talk or travelogue is likely to fall very flat, indeed. It is not exactly what the talker says; it is the way in which he says it [Feb. 19, 1910, 249].

The article commended Elias Burton Holmes for his rhetorical skills. In the following sections Holmes, Martin Johnson, the Kolb brothers, Edwin Hadley and Lowell Thomas will be described. It was people like these who, with their travelogues, brought nature scenes and stories to people.

Elias Burton Holmes

Elias Burton Holmes (1870–1958) was born into a life of relative prosperity, as his parents belonged to a wealthy Chicago family. Already as a child, Holmes dreamt of performing in front of an audience, and during his boyhood he put together a conjuring show in his parents' basement, a show which he performed in front of his family and neighbors. From early on Holmes was fascinated by travel, as well as by photography, and when he was 16 years old he set out on his very first journey. He travelled with his grandmother and took a Kodak camera with him. Four years later, in 1890, Holmes travelled alone to Europe. He took a number of slides on this trip, which formed the beginning of a long and prosperous career as a lecturer.[12] Not until the season of 1898-

Elias Burton Holmes.

99, however, did Holmes use film as part of his lectures, and it was not until 1904 that he used the term "travelogue," an expression that captured the unique mixture of film and lecture that characterized his talks.*

The films that Burton Holmes used in his show were shot by his assistant, O. B. Depue, who used a Demery 60mm camera, a camera that Holmes did not replace until immediately prior to the pair's trip to Scandinavia in 1902. At that time it was difficult to get hold of 60mm film, as 35mm was the most common format. The new camera that Holmes and Depue began using was a Bioscope from the Warwick Trading Company, which was far more modern. During their journey to Scandinavia they filmed, among other things, what may be considered small wildlife films: *Bird Rock, Nordland, Norway, Deer in the Wild Park* and *Gothenberg, Sweden* (1902).

Some of the subjects in the films of Holmes and Depue were the beautiful landscape scenery of places like Yellowstone, the Grand Canyon and the fjords of Norway. Holmes and Depue toured all over the world with their show, and naturally chose those subjects they assumed would capture the attention of the audience at hand. They usually included films that depicted beautiful scenery, but they also strove to present the strangeness of the cultures they had encountered. They mostly travelled by train, ship or car, and stayed at comfortable hotels. Yet, when going to locations famous for their spectacular scenery, Holmes and Depue did sometimes expose themselves to somewhat harder modes of travel. When they were to film the waterfalls on Iguacû, for instance, they first went to Buenos Aires and then took an extensive boat trip up the river Rio de la Plata. After 11 days on the river, a paddle steamer brought them further in the direction of the waterfalls, but the last 34 miles had to be covered in a horse carriage along a jungle road.[13]

The pair also filmed landscape scenery during their journeys in Yosemite (1903), Alaska and Switzerland (1904), Russia and Japan (1905), Austria (1909) and South America (1911).[14]

Martin Johnson

Martin Johnson (1884–1937) was to become one of the major cinematographers of wildlife films, which makes his background as a lecturer especially interesting. For this reason he will be described in greater detail than the other included cinematographers. I will describe his youth here, and in the 1922–1928 chapter I will cover his adult life.

Johnson grew up in Lincoln, Kansas. From early on he had a close relationship to nature. As a child he spent a lot of time outdoors and took care of many different animals. The back garden was transformed into a regular cemetery, for it was here that young Johnson buried squirrels, turtles, mice, sparrows and pigeons. It is said that he once beat up another boy for having killed an adder.

Johnson's father, John, was a goldsmith and owned a shop in Lincoln, but hard times befell the city, and the family left for Independence, Kansas. Here John expanded his shop to include cameras and various film accessories from Eastman Kodak, which gave his son the opportunity to become acquainted with the latest equipment.[15]

Johnson's school experience in Independence went terribly wrong. He devised a series of photos of the teachers and manipulated them, making it look as if the teachers were

---

*Barber writes from the season of 1898-99 (1933, p. 78), Brownlow writes from the season of 1897-98 (1978, p. 420).

Charmian London, Jack London, Martin Johnson, and Herbert Stoltz (Martin and Osa Johnson Safari Museum).

engaged in some rather embarrassing situations. He was expelled, and decided to try his luck in the job market. He chose to leave Independence and went to the city of Chicago. Yet Chicago proved to be merely a stop-over in what turned out to be a very long journey. One day during a friendly dispute with some of his colleagues in Chicago, Johnson claimed that he could travel around in Europe for only $4.25. A colleague challenged him to make a bet, and shortly afterwards Johnson left for New York, where he found employment on a ship. Thus, as a 20-year-old, he left for Europe, where he ended up visiting Sweden, Great Britain, France and Belgium.

The information concerning the following years of Johnson's life is sparse, but we may safely assume that he drifted around the cities of Europe, working here and there, and lived under pretty awful conditions. According to the memoirs of his wife, Osa Johnson, *I Married Adventure,* Johnson lived the life of a regular vagrant for about four years.

Johnson was to profit greatly from his photography skills. The first time photography changed the course of his life was when the author Jack London advertised for a ship's boy to go on a long and adventurous voyage on the Pacific Ocean. Onboard London's ship, *Snark,* the most important chore of the ship's boy was to cook; and Johnson got the job primarily because of his knowledge of photography — and his largely fictitious cooking skills. *Snark* departed on 21 April 1907, and Johnson brought with him four cameras and various developing equipment.[16]

The second time that he profited from his photography skills was on the Solomon

Islands in 1908. A film team from Pathé Frères had arrived in the capital city of Penduffryn to film the natural scenery and the local population — especially the exotic cannibal tribes. The crew got into difficulties, and Johnson stepped to assist and advise them on the use of developing fluids. In gratitude, they invited him to join them during the shoot. According to film historian Kevin Brownlow, Johnson is supposed to have been behind the camera in 1908, but this seems unlikely, as it has never been confirmed by other sources. It may have been on the Solomon Islands, however, that Johnson became interested in making films himself.[17]

After having wandered like this for another 3 years, Johnson settled down in America again. He went to Independence, where, with the intention of setting up a movie house, he became the partner of a businessman, Charles Kerr. They named the movie house *Snark* after London's ship, and at this venue Johnson performed a travelogue show which became a great success. The 340 seats in the cinema were often sold out. The success continued, and they opened two more cinemas, *Snark 1* and *Snark 2*; but gradually the cinemas were challenged by competition from a nearby variety theater that offered a live female singer. Johnson and Kerr's countermove was to incorporate a female singer into their travelogues, and in this way Johnson met the then 16-year-old Osa Leighty. After a short period of time, the two married.[18]

After their wedding, Johnson and Osa went on a tour of North America with a show in which Johnson presented his travelogue, and Osa, wearing a grass skirt, sang Hawaiian

Martin Johnson onboard the *Snark* in the South Seas (Martin and Osa Johnson Safari Museum).

Osa and Martin Johnson ready to tour with their travelogue show (Martin and Osa Johnson Safari Museum).

songs. Included in Johnson's lecture were a series of slides that he had taken on the journey to the South Seas, and later Jack London sent him a number of his own slides from that same journey. Johnson also acquired Pathé Frères' film shot in the Solomon and other Pacific islands. All of this material was hand-colored, which added an extra degree of professionalism to the show.

According to the dates mentioned in Osa's autobiography, *I Married Adventure*, the travelogue tour must have commenced in the summer of 1911, taking them through Colorado, the Western part of Canada and all the way to New York. Osa and Martin Johnson's show not only made ends meet, it paid off large debts Martin owed to, among others, the London family; but the pair were never to be rich. Nonetheless, after 11 months on the road, they had managed to save $4000, but this was mainly due to the fact that they had secured a good contract for themselves for the last five months of their tour.*

After six years of performing travelogue shows, Johnson's enthusiasm for travel swelled again, and he decided to bring film equipment with him on the road. Johnson persuaded Osa to go with him to the Solomon Islands, but in order for them to afford both equipment and travel expenses, they had to use all their savings, and even had to sell some of their belongings. Yet they received financial support from a group of Boston investors who sensed the lucrative potential of such a film venture.

*The dates have been calculated from dates and descriptions made by Osa Johnson (Johnson 1947, p. 72–83).

Along the Colorado river in a rowboat, the daring Kolb brothers did everything to get the right photograph (photograph by Kolb Brothers).

The Kolb Brothers

The films made by the Kolb brothers were not distributed. Rather, the brothers used them for their travelogues in which they also told stories about their experiences and adventures on the journeys. They made their first film in 1911 while travelling from Wyoming to Mexico along the Colorado River. The roaring waters rushing through the Grand Canyon caused them many difficulties, as they were travelling in a rowboat, and the film equipment went overboard several times. Down in the canyon the brothers devised a wood construction that made it possible to look down into gorges and out over beautiful landscapes from interesting perspectives.

After having performed their travelogue show for a number of years, the brothers continued to make films into the early 1920s — e.g., *The Valley of 10,000 Smokes*, which was filmed with an Akeley camera during a trip to Alaska.[19]

Edwin J. Hadley

Edwin J. Hadley (1857–1937) is another example of a travelling lecturer. He toured with his lectures and films from 1897 until 1912. In the beginning, Hadley's show consisted of small actuality films that covered all kinds of topics, but his selection of topics changed over the years, and he began to focus more exclusively on films about exotic countries. Initially, the film medium itself was the attraction in his show. Eventually it became the journey, as well as the exotic and strange quality of the destinations portrayed in the films, that attracted the audience. In this manner Hadley's lectures took on the air of a travelogue show.[20]

Lowell Thomas

Lowell Thomas (1892–1981) was a cinematographer who used his own films in his travelogues. These motion pictures gave people an opportunity to see desolate areas and districts not usually accessible to ordinary travellers. Thomas paved the way for the transition between the holiday-inspired destinations of Burton Holmes and the expedition films of Cooper and Schoedsack, whose motion pictures were the length of actual feature films.

The travelling lecturer brought strange animals, exotic nature scenery and different civilizations to small and isolated societies whose audiences got to experience a nature and wildlife they had only read about but never seen.

The structure of the traditional landscape films was fairly simple. They consisted of individual pictures that had been put together without any intention of continuity. Despite the fact that the films maintained this simplicity, they continued to be popular until the 1920s and 1930s — maybe due to the natural (and exotic) beauty they depicted. Louis Reeves tried to account for the popularity even in 1912: "We hunger to see other parts of the earth, possibly from keen curiosity, probably for the purpose of making discoveries in general as to what is going on in lives and conditions remote from our own" (Reeves 1912, 21).

Landscape films did not make use of elaborate artistic maneuvers or dramatic action, but merely endeavored to depict the scenery from its most attractive angle. In this way the films became a cost effective and energy saving tool for the audience — a substitute for the actual journey. The viewer became an "armchair traveller," and presumably this was the major attraction of these films.

Early Expedition Films

In 1898 the zoologist Alfred Cord Haddon went to the Torres Strait, situated between Australia and New Guinea. Haddon wanted to document the distinctive quality of this part of the Pacific Ocean. He was an original thinker and wished to use the film media as a kind of documentary "note pad" or "drawing block." A little later, film gradually became a scientific tool for anthropology.[21]

Walter Baldwin Spencer (1860–1929) was born in England, but worked as an anthropologist and professor of biology at Melbourne University from 1887 to 1929. Spencer spent a year studying the territory of an aboriginal tribe called Never Never, and for this purpose he had brought with him a Warwick Cine-

Walter Baldwin Spencer (1860–1929).

matograph film camera. Without any previous moviemaking experience, Spencer and his friend Francis Gillen filmed their experiences of 1901. What came out of their efforts is the world's first film depicting an aboriginal tribe's ceremonies and ritual dances. Whether natural scenery and wildlife scenes were part of the film, I cannot say, but it seems very likely that such scenes would have been included.[22]

Animals on Film

Zoo Films

Zoo films are motion pictures of animals living in zoological gardens. Twenty-eight such films have been included in my compiled list. Zoo films were produced from 1895 to 1926, with the greatest number being made in the period between 1897 and 1916.

In the early history of filmmaking, shots of wild animals were rare. The easiest solution for the cinematographer was to film animals behind bars, as a number of Zoo films did. This is evident in the film *Lion* (1895), which depicts a lion walking back and forth in his cage, and *Feeding the Tiger*, showing an animal keeper feeding a tiger. The Danish filmmaker Peter Elfelt's film *Dyregruppe i Zoologisk Have* (*Group of Animals in a Zoological Garden*) (1901) belongs to this category.

Park Films

At the same time as zoo films began to appear, another type of nature film developed, in which the animals lived in their natural habitat but were used to people, like in city parks and harbors. Elfelt, for instance, made a film of animals living in the city, *Svaner i Sortedamssøen* (1901). These early animal films, which took place outside the zoos but within the confines of the city, I shall call "park films."

I have found seven such films — all made between 1896 and 1905. They were somewhat more difficult to shoot than zoo films, but still much easier to make than actual wildlife films. The accessibility of the park and the fact that the animals were used to people made the work a lot easier. Other examples of "park films" are *Feeding the Swans* (1896), *Feeding the Seagulls* (1898), *Feeding Pigeons* (1899) and *Seagulls Following Fishing Boats* (1902).

In the early years of film history, many zoo films (e.g., depicting large exotic animals behind bars) and park films (e.g., depicting the feeding of birds) were produced, but according to my definition of nature films, such films have a rather low priority. In fact, I consider them to be interesting only in light of the childhood of filmmaking, and to be merely the foundation for later wilderness films.

Wildlife Films

Films of wild animals depicted in their natural habitat I designate as "wildlife films." This type of motion picture will be discussed for each of the time periods. For the period 1895–1902 only 5 such films have been found: *Pelicans* (1896), *Bird Rock, Nordland* (1902), *Deer in a Wild Park* (1902) and two other films that will be described below.

In 1897, when an Edison film crew was in Yellowstone National Park to film waterfalls and geysers, they also made a wildlife film: *Wild Bear in Yellowstone*— a little curiosity which is believed to have been filmed by Frederick Blechynden. The Edison catalogue describes the film this way:

Here he is fresh from his forest lair, devouring the carcass of his prey. At first he looks in dumb astonishment at the machine that is taking his picture, then growling fiercely he seizes a large bone, rises to his hind feet, pivots around and trots off to the woods in the background [*Edison's Film*, July 1901, 12].

In September of 1897, Blechynden shot yet another wildlife film. The film was shot close to the present site of the Golden Gate Bridge in San Francisco and depicts a colony of sea lions on a rock. The picture lasts for about 50 seconds, and was shot from a rowboat just opposite the rock. The catalogue text issued by the Edison Company states that you can see the sea lions both in the water and on the rock. It points out that the sea lions have been depicted in their natural environment. The name of the film is *The Sea Lion's Home*, and judging from the blurred copy I watched at the Library of Congress, it must have suffered quite a bit of damage over the years. It seems that the film consists of two shots, but the first one is impossible to decipher. The second shot depicts a rock and some sea lions resting on it. Some of the sea lions glide into the water. The focus is shaky because the camera moves on the tripod, which gives the impression of small, twitching movements. Moreover, the waves and the rocking of the boat transmit a sense of movement to the picture.

Frederick Blechynden was probably the first man to film wild animals in their natural environment, which makes him especially interesting, but my investigations into his background and life in general led me to conclude that he remains a blank page in the history of film.

The audiences were fascinated by the way moving pictures could represent nature. Photography had existed since the 1820s, and the photography itself was not so impressive anymore. A film like Birt Acres' *Rough Sea at Dover*, however, managed to capture its audience in spite of its simplicity and inactivity. The success of the early nature films may be explained by the fact that the theater had been part of peoples' lives for centuries, and thus watching drama on the screen did not really represent any profound change. Yet the powers of nature — e.g., moving waves or waterfalls — had never previously been reproduced photographically. Audiences found this fascinating and were spellbound by the exoticism and strangeness represented by the animals, people and scenery from other parts of the world. This might be countries, animals or plants that most people had never seen or heard of, and merely read about.

Judging from the first period (1895–1902), I conclude that already before the turn of the century there were films that endeavored to depict wilderness scenes and wildlife. These films provided the audiences with beautiful or exciting experiences, and sometimes functioned as sheer tourist propaganda, but they also widened the horizons of the people who watched them. When all is said and done, these films placed a greater focus on nature itself and paved the way for future nature films.

At the same time, we must remember that this was a time when the development of nature films was held in check by the limitations of the equipment. It was heavy. It was not unusual for the equipment to weight 100 to 110 pounds. The lenses were not particularly light sensitive and had small focal lengths that made it difficult to get close to wild animals and film them when they were most active (in the morning and in the evening). Nature films had other limitations too. In this period, cinematographers did not edit the various scenes together, and it was difficult to tell a story.

1903–1906
Nature and Wildlife Films Take— and Make Use of— Form

During this period some important developments in nature and wildlife filmmaking occurred. Some nature and wildlife films began including more shots, and some nature films began incorporating narrative techniques. This happened at about the same time as the first viable, permanent cinemas appeared and as the rental of films was systemized.

Charles Urban was the focal personality of the period. His interest in nature films took the genre in new directions. He helped Martin-Duncan to make the world's first nature film series in 1903, a series that was to mark the beginning of the educational nature films.

The Development of the Period

Between 1903 and 1906 some important technical advances were made, advances that had an enormous importance for wildlife films. Colored films became common, as did lenses with focal lengths of up to 100 or 150 mm (5.9 inches). Additionally, a portable development tank was invented, making it possible to develop films anywhere in the world.

Colored Film

Film historian John Barnes claims that Robert W. Paul was the first person to color a film. The picture was supposedly shown on 8 April 1896. Yet, according to another film historian, Paolo C. Usai, the Edison Kinescope Company produced tinted color films as early as 1895. Moreover, he mentions that the Lumière brothers made a hand-colored film in 1896. These colored films were exceptions, however, as it was not until the 1900s that the coloring of film became so profitable that it became widespread.[1]

The first public screening in which a new color system, Kinemacolor, was used took place at the Palace Theatre of Varities in London on 26 February, 1906. The program included, among other films, *Waves and Sprays* and *Sweet Flowers* (a wave film and a flora film). With their colorful subjects, they made good use of Kinemacolor's rich colors. They were short films that achieved an extraordinary beauty due to the coloring. In the following years the Kinemacolor system was introduced in a number of countries, and experienced relative success in Great Britain. The system ultimately proved not to be functional enough, however, and by 1916 it had disappeared.*

The Kinemacolor system was one of five color systems — yet the other four (hand coloring, toning, tinting and coloring by stencil) were not patented. The cinematographer Oliver G. Pike's second film, which was shot on the Farne Islands in 1909, had stencil color provided by Pathé Frères in Paris. Pike visited the place where the color was printed onto the film, and recalls the result in these words: "It was not

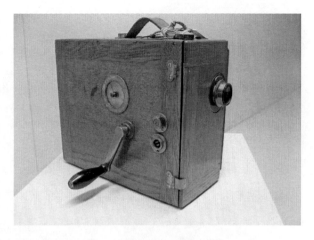

Pathé 35mm box-camera (photograph by author).

color photography to be sure, but the results were remarkably true to nature" (Pike 1946, 117). By 1907 almost all films were colored.[2]

Lenses and Narrative Technique

Bigger focal lengths appeared on the market, and, according to Salt, focal lengths between 100 and 150mm already existed in this period.[3] In the period between 1903 and 1906 it was common for a film to last between 36 seconds and 6 minutes 22 seconds.[4] Major breakthroughs in narrative techniques were made during this period. From 1902, more directors began matching time and space between the cuts. *Rescued by Rover* (1905) was one of the first films that demonstrated a conscious use of the continuity of movement towards a goal. Around 1903 there was an increase in the number of long films with several focuses (yet it must be remembered that more than half of the existing films made before 1906 still consisted of a single shot). Before 1905, only a few films used intertitles. According to Bordwell and Thompson, cross-cutting between scenes divided by space was used from 1906 onwards; but according to Salt, cross-cutting between parallel narrative lines did not reach a high technical standard until around 1907 and 1908.[5]

Developing Equipment

According to Burton Holmes' photographer, Depue, a film had to be developed as quickly as possible — otherwise the quality of the picture would be greatly reduced. Had the film been exposed to light, the contact with oxygen could slowly damage and remove the print that the exposure had left on the film. Depue describes an experience he once had in which a film was not developed until two years after the exposure. This experience led him to conclude that film starts to lose the exposed emulsion from the moment it is shot, and that it should be developed as quickly as possibly.[6] For this reason, it was necessary to bring developing equipment on long field trips and expeditions.

One such piece of equipment was Williamson's portable development machine. It

---

*Kinemacolor was unable to catch on in the rest of Europe and in North America. Yet this is a disputed fact. Salt disagrees with Neal. Salt believes that Kinemacolor was a success in the major cities from 1908 to 1915.

could develop film with an average speed of 500 pictures per minute, depending on the type of negative and its sensitivity to light. Williamson's portable development machine was devised in such a way that it saved developing fluid — and this was a great advantage on those occasions when it had to be transported over great distances. For the development of 75 feet of film, approximately 0.53 gallons of fluid was used, and the same fluid could then be used several times. The developing apparatus was a little over 3 feet high, 25 inches broad and 10 inches deep, which made the machine acceptable for major expeditions. The machine was used by Herbert Ponting on Scott's polar expedition.[7]

Venues

From 1898, several people tried opening cinemas in Copenhagen, but all of these venues shut down within a few months. Not until 1904 did Copenhagen get a viable cinema. In other countries, profitable cinemas were established earlier. Thus, Canada got its first viable cinema in 1902. The cinema, *The Electric*, was situated in Vancouver and charged an admission fee of 5 cents. In London, Paris and Marseille similar electric palaces, built solely for the purpose of showing films, opened in the seasons of 1902 and 1903.[8]

Almost simultaneously in the western world, a new kind of cinema was introduced: exhibition venues with a permanent location that showed nothing but films. In Europe, as well as in the USA, the new cinemas were mostly established in empty depots, warehouses or, if the rent was sufficiently low, shops. Their design was quite simple, and they were named "shop cinemas"—a name that recalled the previous function of the locality. The windows were covered with sheets and the room filled with wooden chairs. Comfort was not an issue here, and the same film was shown over and over again. According to film historian Talbot, a film might be shown from 12 A.M. to midnight. In the beginning, a show cost about 1 penny in England and 5 cents in America.[9]

Harwich Electric Palace, built in 1911 (Great Britain).

In America, the so-called "shop cinema" was introduced by the vaudeville entrepreneur Harry Davies, who opened a small permanent cinema in Pittsburgh on 19 June 1905. The admission fee was 5 cents for a 15 to 20 minute show. Since a 5-cent piece was called a "nickel" and "Odeon" is the Greek word for "theater," in America the cinemas became known as "Nickelodeons." These shop cinemas spread all over the United States.

Denmark had witnessed a similar development. Three men played an important role in this context. The first great entrepreneur was Constantin Philipsen (1859–1925), who opened 26 Kosmorama cinemas in Denmark between 1904 and 1906. He was succeeded by Søren Nielsen and Thomas Hermansen, who began establishing cinema venues around the same time. In France, from 1905, more and more touring film operators began settling down and establishing permanent cinemas in locations with audiences big enough to support the venues.[10]

Electric Palaces, village halls, amusement parks, and shop cinemas attracted separate clienteles, and as time progressed there were venues for every taste and income.

Distribution

In the early years of the film industry, the showmen bought the films directly from the producers or the importers, and then exchanged the films with other showmen. There were no fixed prices, and negotiations were conducted in a manner not unlike a market place shortly before closing time. The situation was out of control, and those unfortunate showmen who had been overcharged were obviously dissatisfied, which in turn led to illegal copying. Other showmen bought copies of films collectively and shared them among themselves. The copy was distributed among them by a delivery boy, and the same copy might be shown in four different locations in a city on the same evening. In 1906, steps were taken to insure a system of distribution. The system was introduced by producer and distributor George Kleine, who set up branches in the USA and Canada in which the films were not for sale, but could be rented. Slowly this practice spread all over the world.

Charles Urban Leads the Way

The Road to Nature Films

Charles Urban (1867–1942) grew up in Cincinnati, Ohio. Before he entered the film business, he was a travelling salesman. He sold books, typewriters and office equipment, like the Edison Phonograph (an early version of a dictaphone), which played an important role in any professional office. Urban also became acquainted with other Edison products — e.g., the Kinetoscope and Kinotograph — and gradually he began moving in the direction of the film business.[11]

In 1897, when Charles Urban moved from America to London, it was as manager of Edison's film agent company Maguire & Baucus. The company was successful and soon expanded (thus Nöggerath Sr. received the negotiation rights to the films of the company in countries like Holland, Denmark and Norway).[12]

Around 1898, Charles Urban reorganized the company and changed its name to Warwick Trading Company (WTC) due to the location of the offices in Warwick Court. Urban then began producing films. This proved to be a good idea, and in time he built up his own team of cameramen and directors. Moreover, Urban began distributing films on behalf of innovative directors in Europe, the most important of whom were Lumière and Méliès in France, and George Smith and James Williamson in Great Britain.[13]

Charles Urban was a leader that people counted on, and his vision, foresight and eye for talent meant that he became a defining factor in the development of the nature film genre. From very early on, Urban recognized the potential of educational nature films, and arranged several film expeditions that brought scenes from exotic locations to his audiences.

Expedition Films

From 1902, American Mutoscope had the sole rights of sale for the films of Warwick Trading Company in the United States. It was also in the year of 1902 that WTC sent an expedition to the Alps, led by F. Ormiston-Smith. The film crew actually climbed Mont Blanc and Schreckhorn, which was not only an enormous achievement, but also a somewhat daring venture, considering the heavy equipment and the lack of proper mountaineering gear.[14]

Charles Urban left WTC early in 1903 to build his own film company, the Charles Urban Trading Company (CUTC). Many of WTC's cinematographers left the old company and began working for Urban.* One of them was the aforementioned Ormiston-Smith, who continued to shoot films of the Alps. The innovative directors George Smith and James Williamson also began working for CUTC. Williamson had taken up cinematography in 1896 when he became acquainted with its existence during a laterna lecture.[15]

CUTC carried out a number of adventure/globetrotter expeditions in the year 1903. One of these was an expedition to Borneo, which was filmed by H.M. Lomas. Another example was an expedition — the Urban Mountaineering Expedition — launched on 28 September of the same year. It consisted of two climbs in Switzerland, one from Zermatt to the top of the Matterhorn, and the second from Interlaken to the top of the Jungfrau. Out of this expedition came a number of short films, several of which incorporated true wilderness elements. There were depictions of landscape scenery in *Soft Snow on the Mönch-Joch*, *A Winter Fairyland* and *Panorama from the Summit* (1905). The latter exists in two different versions — one of the Jungfrau and one of the Matterhorn.

Entrepreneur Charles Urban (Luke McKernan).

*Warwick Trading Company continued but was merged with Autoscope Company, managed by Will Barker, in 1906.

Educational Films

On 9 January 1905, Charles Urban introduced a series of teaching matinees at London's Alhambra Theatre. The matinees were called *Urbanora* and were structured around the many educational pictures that Urban Films had made during the two previous years. The matinees were meant to be educational shows for children. In November 1905, a similar matinee show opened in Newcastle, the first provincial city to offer this kind of show.[16]

In June 1905, the Charles Urban Trading Company published the Urban film catalogue, which shows what products the distribution company was offering its customers at this moment in time. The catalogue claims that the films have both educational and scientific value — a claim which must be taken with a grain of salt. One of the films is entitled *Educated Monkey in Costume*, and depicts a chimpanzee wearing clothes who is set to do various human chores. I doubt that the film enhanced any understanding of the theory of evolution, but the texts in the catalogue indicate that from early on, the English market put a considerable amount of weight on the educational effect of films. CUTC's catalogue shows to what extent the company tried to establish the basis of an educational film program. The Urban Film catalogue of 1905 includes a number of slides, the topics of which fell within the fields of biology and natural history. The educational shows were often a mixture of films and slide shows.

Already in 1905, the Charles Urban Trading Company was aware that purely educational films were considered boring and unappealing by the majority of potential viewers. In the June catalogue they therefore try to forestall this resentment with a slogan, claiming that *their* educational films were also quite entertaining: "To entertain and amuse is good, To do both and instruct is better."

Urban's educational films were collected under the title *Urban-Duncan Bioscope* (UDB). UDB included film series such as *The Unseen World*, *Natural History* and *Denizens of the Deep*. These series had been created through collaboration between F. Martin-Duncan and Charles Urban.

Francis Martin-Duncan

Francis Martin-Duncan (1873–1961) was the leader of CUTC's scientific and educational film department. He was a zoologist and a great nature lover. Before the film media experienced its breakthrough, Martin-Duncan had experimented with the same type of sequence photography as Muybridge. Charles Urban heard of Duncan's work with microscopes and photography, got in touch with him, and began a fruitful collaboration that later led to the Urban-Duncan Bioscope.

Martin-Duncan never doubted the advantages of using films in a teaching environment: "Modern educational methods all prove the importance of teaching through the agency of the eye as well as the ear. A lecture or lesson demonstrated by a graphic series of pictures remains vividly impressed on the mind" (Herbert 2000, 86).

On 17 August 1903, the Alhambra Theatre in London introduced a number of films from the series *The Unseen World* and *Natural History*. The press and the public were intrigued by this new way of using the film media. According to the theater manager, Douglas Cox, the shows were a great success, but he admitted having been skeptical in the beginning:

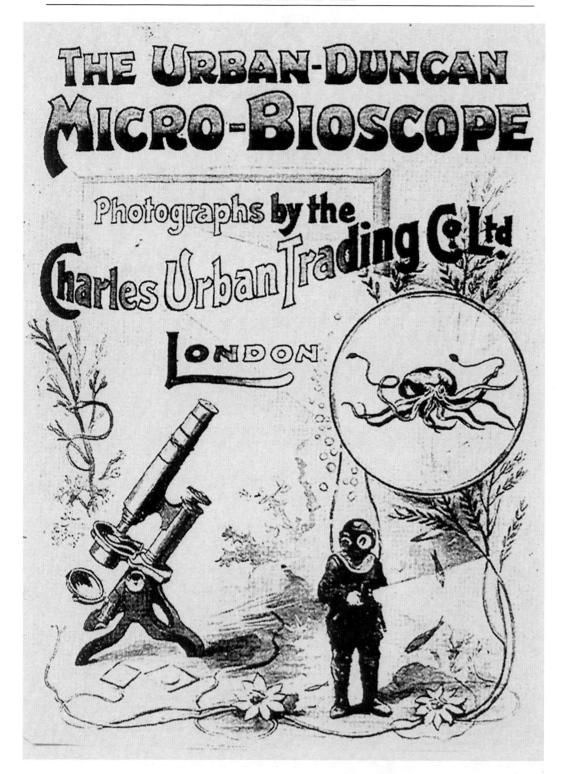

The Urban-Duncan catalogue front page.

"I was a little in doubt," says Mr. Cox, "as to whether they would appeal to the public at large. But from the very first night they were a huge success. They ran for two months, and we have now replaced them by a series entitled *Denizens of the Deep*" [Herbert 2000, 90].

The Series: *Denizens of the Deep*

Denizens of the Deep is a series of films illustrating life under the water's surface. The series includes films about lobsters, cuttlefish, sand fleas and crayfish. According to Urban's film catalogue from 1905, this series consists of 22 films. Neither the titles nor the descriptions reveal much, but most likely films like *The Lobster* (1904) simply depicted a lobster from various angles. The "main characters" were filmed in an aquarium. Life under water could be depicted relatively easily in a realistic manner, and you could obtain decent shots of the animals in question. Real underwater shots were still impossible to make, and quite some time would pass before such shots appeared in nature films.

In my compiled film list, only those titles that fit into my nature definition have been included, and for this reason some of the films in this particular series have been left out.

The Series: *The Unseen World*

The series *The Unseen World* dealt with subjects that could only be seen under a microscope. The films depicted microscopic creatures magnified between 22 and 28 million times their natural size. Sometimes the microscopic subject was represented by means of connecting time and space. According to film historians Bordwell and Thompson, more and more directors began matching time and space between the individual scenes, and thus some nature films clearly went with the times.[17] This is evident in the description of catalogue film no. 2501 of *The Unseen World* series, called *Cheese Mites* (1903). According to the catalogue text, the film depicts a man who looks at a slice of toast and discovers something on it. He examines it through a magnifying glass, and to his dismay finds it to be full of life. Only very few nature films, however, had such a narrative structure. In comparison, *The Amoebe the Beginning of Life* (1903) is much more pedestrian. It simply shows an enlargement of the movements of an amoeba and its splitting into two organisms.*

I have seen one of the films from *The Unseen World* series, *Water Fleas and Rotifers* (1903), at the British Film Institute. The film lasts for 39 seconds and merely shows some unclear microscope shots of various organisms from lakes and village ponds. The film is only worth seeing if you remember what novelty the medium held for people back then. Most likely, the blurred and indistinct images are caused by the natural ageing of the film. The shots made me think of abstract art, as well as the nature films of Jean Painlevé; indeed, it was impossible for me to judge the actual qualities of the film.

The Series: *Natural History*

The *Natural History* series is the last of the educational series produced by Urban-Duncan Bioscope. The films in this series were shot by F. Martin-Duncan and depict mammals, reptiles, insects and birds. Filming was done under controlled conditions — i.e., at the London Zoo or at farms, usually while the animals were being fed (in other words, at that

---

*The title makes you wonder if Darwin's evolutionary theory was commonly known amongst people — presumably not!

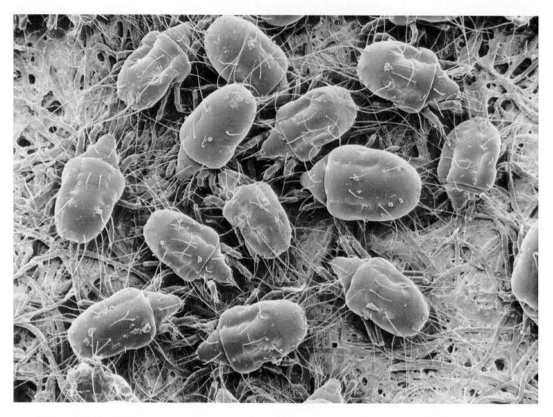

Micro-bioscopic films were F. Martin-Duncan's speciality. Cheese mites (United States Department of Agriculture).

time of day when the animals are most active and, from a filmic point of view, most interesting).

Catalogue film no. 2003, *Feeding Pelicans* (1905), is a good example of how the films in the series were introduced in the catalogue: "This is a splendid and most humorous subject, full of laughable incident and animation. The pelicans rush from their pen and plunge into the well-stocked fish pond, tossing their heads, jostling each other, fighting over the fish, etc." The description is typical; many of the other films in the series are described as funny and humorous. It could be a conscious attempt to make simple and non-dramatic films sell well. In addition, most of the other films in the *Natural History* series are also described as educational. They do not appear to have any narrative features, but some descriptions do hint at staged, dramatic and narrative depictions. This is the case with *The Boa Constrictor and the Rat* (1905) and *The Spider and the Fly* (1905). The description of the latter is as follows:

> A beautiful picture of the web of the large garden spider, with the spider awaiting the prey. The victims fall into the meshes of the wonderfully constructed web, and are at once attacked by the spider, overcome, and swathed in silk. So rich is the harvest, that a great spider of a neighboring web is attracted upon the scene, rushes on to the web, and fights and drives off the rightful owner, who beats a hasty and ignominious retreat. During the scuffle for the booty, the web is badly damaged and torn asunder.

Judging from the above description, we might be inclined to think that *The Spider and the Fly* incorporated some element of suspense; but, sadly, it has not been possible to get hold of it. Of course, the generation of suspense is highly unlikely, as, according to Bordwell and Thompson, cross-cutting between scenes was not used until 1906.[18] Still, the description of *The Monkeys of Borneo* (1903) is rather dramatic and even a bit sanguinary: "They have long and very strong arms, and can pull a man to pieces." This kind of "verbal trailer" might even remind us of the cinema trailer spots of today.[19]

Special equipment was developed for the Urban-Duncan Bioscope series, and it took over two years to record all the material. The series must have required a great amount of work, considering the heavy and cumbersome equipment. The series might be said to have been inventive in regards to narrative techniques, and innovative in its use of aquariums, microscopes, staging and topics. In other areas, the films were quite conventional. The series never gave the audience an understanding of how the animals lived in their natural environment. It may have been possible to see the habits and lives of captivate animals, but the films never depicted the normal behavior of the animals living in their natural habitat. Despite the fact that the films represented captivate creatures, they must have fascinated the audience. Not many village people had visited a zoo, and not many city dwellers had been to a farm. The films depicted strange worlds and gave the audience an opportunity to see captured animals involved in various activities. While very few of the films from this period depicted animals in their natural environment, some did, and we will turn to these in the next section.

Wildlife and Hunting Films

Wildlife Films

My compiled film list includes four wildlife films from this period. Two of these were made by Urban-Duncan Bioscope — namely, *The Monkeys of Borneo* (1903) and *Elephant in Native Surrounding* (1905).

Urban Films sold a number of small nature films that could not be bought individually, but only came as part of a package. The package contained films with a combined length of some 40 minutes. A package cost £50 and was sold under the heading *Wild Beasts, Birds and Reptiles*. I identified a number of Martin-Duncan films in the package, but other cinematographers were also represented (e.g., Joseph Rosenthal, H. M. Lomas and J. G. Avery). Most of the films in the package were shot in zoological gardens, and its advertising is somewhat misleading in claiming that the package contains authentic depictions of animals, as well as noting, "Realistic and life-like pictures of wild Animal Life are the admiration of all who have the good fortune to behold them."

The majority of the films were not shot in the animals' natural environment. This is actually indicated in both the titles and descriptions of the individual films. These descriptions include words like "zoo," "grotto," "animal keeper," and "enclosure"—words that indicate the real locations of the films. Moreover, the descriptions emphasize that the films show the lives and habits of wild animals, and have been made without disturbing them. They point out that the cinematographers have had to overcome many difficulties, and have shown great patience during the shooting of the films: "In obtaining this unique series of Natural

History Films, many long hours and even days have had to be spent in patient waiting, ere the characteristic picture could be procured."

Naturally, we must take this emphasis on the unique form and creative process with a grain of salt, but we must also keep in mind that the conditions of production were very different back then, and that the technical equipment was much heavier than that available to future filmmakers. The only titles of the package that indicate somewhat natural and authentic surroundings are *Elephant with Native Surrounding* and *The Monkeys of Borneo*. Nonetheless, it is difficult to accept these two motion pictures as "wildlife films," as the information available suggests that the films depict working elephants and a monkey on a leash, respectively. The films were shot in Borneo, which gives them an air of wildness and authenticity; and despite the lack of naturalness, I believe the films to be a step in the "right" direction — at least if we compare these two titles with aquarium films or zoo films.

The next special sub-genre is more authentic and gives a more realistic depiction of the animals.

The Establishment of the Hunting Film

It might seem strange to include hunting films in a book about wildlife filmmaking, for in hunting films it is the hunter and not the animals or nature that is important. Yet, hunting films often take place in a wild and unspoiled natural environment, and depict animals in their natural surroundings. It is a shame, however, that the animals in hunting films are never photographed when they are at peace. In a sense, it is a little grotesque that we hardly ever see the hunted animal alive, but only after it has been killed by the hunter. Hunting films are motion pictures that focus on the killing of a wild animal. My compiled film list contains only six such titles, but many more were made — all produced between 1903 and 1906.

There are many explanations as to the appearance and later successful mass production of the hunting film. The hunting film had entertainment potential. At the beginning of the 20th century, innovative filmmakers developed narrative techniques and editing methods that were to pave the way for more complex film narratives. In the period between 1903 and 1906, hunting films and other similar pictures helped develop and refine editing methods, creating continuity from shot to shot. Among others, fiction films like *Desperate Poaching Affray* (1903) and *Rescued by Rover* (1905) laid the groundwork for this development through the use of chase scenes. The degree to which the hunting film made use of this method differs from title to title, but the hunting film was in a good position to utilize these contemporary developments. They had a progressive story line, a natural sense of drama and a logical conclusion — a clearly defined goal and a natural climax (namely, the bringing down of the animal).

The first hunting film was probably *Une Chasse à l'ours blanc*, which premiered in America in 1903. It was a short film that showed the hunting of a polar bear. After the premiere of the film, nothing much happened within the sub-genre for almost two years. In other words, the hunting film did not materialize as a sub-genre overnight; but around 1905 or 1906, more hunting films appeared — for instance *A Devonshire Badger Hunt* (1906) and *Moose Hunt in New Brunswick* (1906).

Polar bear hunt in Greenland (Library of Congress, LC-USZ62-62343).

Change of Production Mode Within the Film Industry

The Change from Non-Fiction to Fiction Films

> Within a few years in the early part of the 20th century, film production turned into a regular industry, and in this process, the depiction of reality was invaded by the models of fiction represented by the theater. This combination proved to have an ever-expanding market [Larsen 1990, 49 — my translation].

The quotation above was made by film theorist Peter Harms Larsen, and describes very well what happened. In a relatively short time span the film industry went from producing non-fiction to producing fiction films. This is easy to see by looking at the production figures: According to Richard Sanderson, non-fiction films were the most important films in North America in 1897, making up 73.8 percent of the entire production.[20] In the following years, narrative fiction films began appearing, and in 1905 its two main categories, comedy and drama, had reached 45 percent of the total production (comedy representing 30 percent and drama representing 15 percent). For comparison, I have looked at the figures offered by Marguerite Engberg on Nordisk Films for 1906, and it appears that the company's production of comedies represented 14 percent and drama 24 percent, with the remainder of the productions consisting of non-fiction titles.

The supply of films available to the American market was to change completely in favor of fiction. In the season of 1907-1908, fiction films had reached 96 percent of the total number of productions. At Nordisk Films no such drastic change is evident. In Denmark, the share of non-fiction was 54 percent in 1908, but that number went down by 10 percent the following year — and this tendency continued over subsequent years.[21]

Explanation: Supply/Demand or Cost/Benefit

Film historians have often tried to explain the change from non-fiction to fiction as a result of the supply-and-demand principle. According to this theory, the audiences had grown tired of non-fiction and wanted pure entertainment. Thus, Hampton states, "The short-film program system was banished very quickly from leading screens.... Within two years it was difficult for fans to remember that features had not always been their entertainment" (Hampton 1970, 123).

Bordwell and Thompson agree with this viewpoint: "Moreover, audiences seemed to prefer story films" (Bordwell and Thompson 1994, 24). Such comments are mild when compared to some of the more categorical explanations of other film historians explaining the falling popularity of the non-fiction genre. Roger Manvell suggests:

> Classed at the worst as highbrow and educational, at the best as "travelogue" or "interest," during which an audience could change its seats and buy its chocolate, documentary got little headway as a whole in commercial programmes [Manvell 1944, 108].

Robert C. Allen has another theory, however. He believes that the tendency to move away from non-fiction was caused by the technical advantages offered by narrative films. It was a lot easier to estimate the logistics and control them during production, and in many cases the price could be arranged beforehand.[22] When writing about early Danish film history, Casper Tybjerg describes the gradual takeover of fiction, and he uses the same argument as Allen. Indeed, the theory finds many supporters today — for instance, Charles Musser and Richard Abel, who write about English and French film history, respectively. They believe that the narrative fiction films were easier to both produce and systematize. Abel writes: "The cost-effectiveness, along with the desire to increase and regularize production as well as extend the 'shelf life' of a film's distribution, undoubtedly fuelled the overall shift from actualities to story film during the period" (Abel 1994, 23).

Allen supports his hypothesis with a number of articles in contemporary magazines that describe the extent to which people missed non-fiction films. Allen quotes a review in *The New York Herald*, which is particularly interesting in relation to wildlife films: "The five cent audience is interested in wild animal life and in historical views much more than in the ridiculous comedies" (Allen 1980, 216).

I have found yet another quote that supports Allen's argument. It is from Frederick Talbot's early work on film history: "In spite of the fact that the programme of the average picture palace of today is chiefly occupied with filmplays, nevertheless the greatest attraction is undoubtedly the 'topical picture'" (Talbot 1912, 116).*

Abel deems the French change from non-fiction to narrative films to have occurred between 1902 and 1907. As for America, I rely on the studies of Sanderson, Musser and Allen, and I will limit the years of transition in the States to between 1904 and 1907. In

---

*Topical Film. Film that depicts an event which might have a certain news value, and for this reason, actuality and sport are also part of the category. It might have been more correct, had Sanderson mentioned the earliest films as actualities. These are films in which movement is of primary importance and in which the invention is the main focus.

Denmark the transition was not as dramatic as in other countries. Well into the 1910s, non-fiction films still had an impressive share of the total production at Nordisk Films.[23]

Explanations Relevant to Landscape Films

If we look more closely at landscape films, the cost/benefit theory offers little foundation. The most expensive part of the production was transportation to the beautiful locations. The films were mostly produced by a single cameraman who just had to find a beautiful location, put the camera on its tripod, and turn the handle. The camera and the landscape did the rest. According to Canadian film historian Colin Browne, landscape films were quite cheap to make:

> Apparently all one had to do was journey to Banff on the CPR, film in the Rockies for a week or so, and, with luck, obtain enough footage for a good scenic short, replete with wildlife, mountains, alpine lakes, titanic glaciers, and attractive young women hikers [Browne 1979, 4].

Mostly, these films were produced during a trip to a specific area of natural beauty where there would be plenty of panoramic views and other attractive natural phenomena. The films had a simple structure and were probably cheap to make. Kevin Brownlow suggests that the films were also cheap to buy: "Scenics were often thrown in by exchanges as part of a program, costing exhibitors virtually nothing" (Brownlow 1978, 418).

As demonstrated earlier, these films remained popular for a surprisingly long time. In fact, they appeared in their simple form until the 1920s. Yet, in time, people did become critical of them — as is evident in an article from 1919 in which the Swede Gustaf Berg comments on what I call landscape films:

> Some people go there, claiming that they would visit the cinema even if there were only nature films on the program.... Others — the majority —... "Aren't the waterfall films finished soon," you can hear from the cinema vestibules, "so that we can get to see some action." No doubt, the number of people who are downright annoyed with the nature films are an exception, but the fact is that the majority of cinemagoers consider these as something one has to endure in order to get what one really wants [Berg 1919, 3 — my translation].

Berg's concluding remark brings us back to the discussion regarding the transition from non-fiction to fiction films. I have previously mentioned the cost/benefit and supply/demand explanations, but an additional explanation should be included as well. If you look at the films, it is clear that the landscape films were slow to make use of chronology. Indeed, non-fiction motion pictures were slow at picking up on the general development of the film media. As Barsam writes, "They make little effort to approach their subject from a creative or dramatic point of view" (Barsam 1973, 11).

The Emotional Landscape

Between 1901 and 1904, landscape films did begin to incorporate elements of fiction. Charles Musser has examined Edwin S. Porter's mixture of fiction and non-fiction. Porter used shots of beautiful landscape scenery, panorama films and elements of comedy in a number of pictures from 1903 and 1904 — e.g., *Ruby and Mandy at Coney Island* (1903), *European Rest Cure* (1903), and *Romance of the Rail* (1903).* These films take place in beau-

---

*A film which might have been inspired by Zecca's *Flirt en Chemin de Fer* (1901).

tiful surroundings and consist of small episodes that embody a touch of love and romance. The backdrop is always a pretty landscape, and the foreground shows a man and a woman. Together, these elements create a special atmosphere connoting romantic love. These small attempts at using fiction were further developed and refined in the following years. Thus, in 1912 an Italian film called *Tra le Pinete di Rodi* appeared. The film was shot on the lovely island of Rhodos, and in most of the scenes we see a pair of lovers. Both the scenery and the couple may be understood in the context of romantic love — and even sexual passion.

Movement on the Journey

An important sub-genre, which used landscape or panorama shots for new purposes, was embodied by the *Phantom Rite* or *Hale's Tour*— an experience for all the senses. George C. Hale, a former chief fire officer, had a special train wagon made for the Expo-exhibition in St. Louis in 1902. The wagon was turned into a small cinema that had only one window, through which the audience could see beautiful landscape scenery pass by outside. What the "passengers" looked at was a film on a screen, a film that had put together various shots from trains in motion. For the sake of authenticity, the "train journey" was accompanied by whistle sounds and flashing lights, just as the wagon itself rocked from side to side. A great number of people became "passengers" of such illusory train journeys that toured Europe, Australia and the USA in the years following 1902.[24]

Up until 1906, nature films made only sparse use of creativity and drama, elements that might otherwise have made the content much more interesting and exciting. Yet soon nature films would develop more variety — perhaps depicting a person on a journey through the landscape, or using intertitles that could explain things and create interest. These were developments that gave the films more structure and content. Films with nature or animals would become better at telling stories, and would find new methods, securing the attractiveness of the genre for showmen and audiences alike.

Nature films made from 1903 until 1906 did attempt to incorporate narrative elements, thereby strengthening the narrative structures, but often it was only the catalogue descriptions that indicated suspense, tension and humor. These consciously attempted to give the impression that the films were entertaining — which naturally made them easier to sell.

From very early on, the Charles Urban Film Company helped develop knowledge-imparting films that dealt with various aspects of natural history.

Apart from hunting films, it was still rare for wildlife films to be shot in authentic locations. The filming usually took place under controlled conditions, such as film studios with aquariums or microscopes, or in zoological gardens, parks or farms.

1907–1910
Exploring Borderlines

The period 1907–1910 experienced a boom in the number of cinemas. Moreover, the film industry became much more organized. This led to an increased demand for motion pictures, which led to the establishment of many new film companies. The period was also characterized by significant technical improvements in regard to both lenses and cameras. This will be discussed in the following sections.

The Development of the Period

The Pathé Camera

The Pathé Company manufactured their own film camera, which was used by, among others, Oliver G. Pike for his bird films. I have not been able to ascertain exactly when the camera went into production, but we must assume that this happened in the late 1800s. Sources suggest that between 1910 and 1915 the qualities of the Pathé camera were widely recognized, and many people bought it for this very reason. Moreover, the price (£ 70) was reasonable, making it an attractive buy for semi-professionals.

The advantage of the Pathé camera was that the ocular, the buttons, the handle and the film reel were placed in such a way that you could work the camera from behind, which was not standard procedure at the time. This was a major advantage when the camera was to be used in a shelter that had little room for the camera and the cinematographer. The camera's feeding device had a severe problem, though. From time to time it would produce electric sparks. One such spark could leave static-electric marks all over the contents of the film reel. If this happened, all you could do was to throw out the entire 400 feet of film that the camera could contain.

According to nature cinematographer Oliver Pike, who commissioned a special camera from the company, the Pathé camera was much better than cine-cameras produced in Britain around 1910. From 1914, it was the preferred choice among several film companies in London.[1]

Lenses

Although the author of *Wildlife Films*, Derek Bousé, claims that telephoto lenses were not used until the 1920s, many other sources prove him wrong. Small telephoto lenses were

Herbert G. Ponting filming in the Antarctic with a long lens in 1911.

used by non-fiction cinematographers during the first decade of the 20th century. Bigger telephoto lenses (i.e., over 300 mm) were used during the First World War (1914–1918). It is very likely that long lenses of around 230mm were used in animal shots in 1907, for in this year Oliver G. Pike is said to have used a 230mm f 6.8 Goerz Celor lens.[2]

Exhibition Venues

In the season of 1907-8 the competition between the Nickelodeons and the Variety Theaters in the United States increased, and at the same time the American market experienced a minor crisis, brought about by a panic on the stock exchange in 1907, which led to a decrease in wages. Some variety theaters responded to the crisis by reducing their entry fees. Thus, one variety theater in New York reduced its prices from 50 to 30 cents. The competition for the audience became increasingly tough, and the counter-move of the Nickelodeons (shop cinemas) was to clean up and decorate their venues. Some of them also began introducing small song and dance acts in keeping with the Variety Theater tradition. Due to the economic situation, the Nickelodeons ultimately proved to be the more attractive form of entertainment because the price was still only 5 or 10 cents.

Shop cinemas had been established in most reasonably sized cities. To the average family, film had become an everyday form of entertainment. According to Barry Salt, there were 3000 Nickelodeons in America around 1907.[3] Shop cinemas had up to 200 seats, were cheaply furnished, and their film programs were short. The films were accompanied by a

Admission 5 cents. Toronto's Auditorium Theatre, a Nickelodeon that opened in 1908 (photograph by William James, City of Toronto Archives, Fonds 1244, Item 320C).

second-rate pianist.* Barry Hampton estimates that there were between eight and ten thousand Nickelodeons in America in 1909.[4] Hampton describes their atmosphere thus:

> In the crowded, poorly ventilated nickelodeons, patrician youngsters sat with commoners and their offspring, democratically munching peanuts as they unconsciously created the great army of film fans that later was to dominate the screens of the world [Hampton 1970, 47].

With the opening of the Omnie-Pathé on 15 December 1906, France experienced a boom in the establishment of new cinemas. This cinema, which accommodated 300 people, was the first of many to be built by Pathé Frerès and the Bennoit-Levy company. Other cinema entrepreneurs followed, and by the summer of 1907 there were 50 cinemas in Paris. Many of these were situated in shopping or entertainment areas, and consisted of new buildings, converted lecture halls, concert halls, theaters or even churches. Already two years later, in 1909, the number of cinemas had reached over 100.

*Bordwell and Thompson 1994, p. 31. They write that the Nickelodeons had room for fewer than 200 people. Allen, 1980, estimates that they had room for about 100.

Film Distribution

The Pathé Frerès Company was progressive in many ways. From 1906, they began buying the theaters that were to show the films the company produced. Thus, they were the first film company to practice vertical integration, meaning that a single company controlled production, distribution and exhibition venues. Moreover, Pathé Frerès changed their distribution system so that their films were for rent rather than for sale. The producer and distributor George Kleine made similar changes in several of his branches in America and Canada.[5]

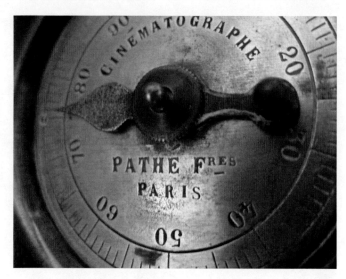

Pathé Frerès (photograph by author).

In December 1908, a number of film producers formed the Motion Picture Patent Company, and after a few years they established the General Film Company. The General Film Company was meant to safeguard the producers' rights as well as establish common rules of distribution. The purpose of the new distribution system was to achieve order. The exhibition venues were ranked according to the strength of their location, and film rentals were charged accordingly. In the new standardized system, the rental of the same film sometimes varied between $15 and $125.[6]

Knowledge-Imparting Films

Establishing what exactly constitutes a "knowledge-imparting film" is rather difficult, for most motion pictures might be said to fall under such a category. Director and writer Paul Rotha once made this excellent observation regarding "instructional films":

> The instructional film does not dramatize but describes, not for the sake of creating emotional effect, but for the strict purpose of imparting knowledge. In most cases, the second aim does not require creative skill, but is well served by capable craftsmanship [Rotha 1936, 109].

Rotha's definition of instructional films, however, is too narrow within this context. For my purposes the term "knowledge-imparting films" is better, for this designation does not exclude drama or creativity. I define it as films that communicate knowledge about nature, animals and natural phenomena with all the means available within the boundaries of the documentary.

For a long time many film historians believed that knowledge-imparting films were not widely made until the 1920s. Thus in 1931 film historian Benjamin Hampton made the following observation: "Not until 1929–30 had there been anything further than pioneer work in this important direction" (Hampton 1970, 419). It should be clear from the earlier section on Charles Urban, however, that such claims are much too categorical — unless, of course, Hampton's understanding of "pioneer work" differs greatly from my own.

Author Charles Guggisberg follows in the footsteps of Hampton, yet his observations made in the 1970s are not as unequivocal as Hampton's. Guggisberg writes, "There probably was little actual experimentation during the first years of the century" (Guggisberg 1977, 67). Even as late as 1990, the claim had not yet been dismissed: "Not until the 1920s and 1930s do filmmakers take serious advantage of the possibilities of using film for education and conscious ideological influence" (Larsen 1990, 49 — my translation).

Presumably, the institutions wishing to use the film media for propaganda and other ideological effect only did so from around 1920. However, film had been used to educate, instruct and encourage tourism long before this. Charles Urban and Martin-Duncan were among the pioneers within this field, but other enthusiasts continued to further develop and refine this kind of film. Already in 1907, Urban wrote the following in *The Moving Picture World*:

> The entertainer has hitherto monopolized the cinematograph for exhibition purposes, but movement in more serious directions has become imperative, and our object is to prove that the cinematograph must be recognized as a national instrument by ... every institution of training, teaching, demonstration and research [324].

Not many years passed before Urban's hopes began to be realized. The Urban Film Company was not the only one in Britain to work on the production of knowledge-imparting films.

France, Educational Films and Anthropomorphic Intertitles

Around 1907 intertitles began to be seen in educational films or knowledge-imparting films. They were used to create drama and provide information, as well as for pure entertainment.

From early on, French film companies attempted to produce films for educational use; indeed, Pathé Frères and the three other major French companies, Gaumont, Éclair and Eclipse, each had their own departments for educational and scientific productions. The films were made in order to illustrate scientific principles and were supervised by teachers of high rank within the French educational system. Already from the 1910s, French film companies had established departments for educational use, which may have given France the lead in the use of film in this context. Around 1913–1914, French schools were making regular use of film for educational purposes.[7]

Pathé Frères was quick to perceive the importance of using film for the purpose of general education. In 1908 they commenced a collaboration with the Englishmen Oliver G. Pike and the Frenchman Jean Comandon. Pathé Frères offered Comandon a laboratory that belonged to their department for scientific films. It was here that Comandon carried out the cinematographic microscope experiments that were presented to the Académie des Sciences in November 1909.[8] Comandon kept his film laboratory well into the 1920s, and continued to make natural history films. They became more popular and were shown in cinemas all over the world.

In addition, Pathé Frères made a number of films which formed part of a package that included teaching material for school use. The material consisted of all the intertitles of the film in question, general information about the topic, suggestions for relevant questions that the teacher could ask the students, and, finally, references to where one could find more information. Examples include Pathé Freres' *Ants: Nature's Craftsmen* (191?), which was part of the series *Plant and Animal World*. Judging from the teaching material that accompanied the film, it appears that the picture contained 37 intertitles. Nr. 35 reads like this: "Not only are ants wonderful workers but the greatest students of them tell us that they are really fond of what we can tell by no other name than athletics and *play*. Watch this clever gymnastic performer" (Ellis and Thornborough 1923, 186). It would have taken some time for the audience to read an intertitle of this length, but the anthropomorphic and entertaining juxtapositions make the text easy to read. The other intertitles are not quite as anthropomorphic as this one, but they are just as entertaining.

Anthropomorphism ascribes to animals abilities and social conditions that are otherwise only applicable and relevant to human beings. In literature, this is evident in the animal fables of Aesop and La Fontaine. The most famous animal fables were written by Aesop, who lived 600 years before Christ and who inspired La Fontaine (1621–1695). The animal fables reflect the human universe; and over the years the stories have helped establish supposed characteristics of, and prejudices about, many common animal species, like wolves, owls, tigers, elephants and bears. Many of these characteristics are very well known (e.g., the wolf is evil, the bear is friendly, etc.).

Britain, P.O.V. and Narrative Continuity

In 1908, the Williamson Kineto Company produced *Nature's Hidden Beauties—Pond Life*. The copy I have seen has a length of 7 minutes, contains 20 scenes and 10 intertitles, and forms part of the series *Hidden Wonders of Nature*. The film begins with a man fishing in a pond with a net. He catches something, which he puts into a glass. The second shot depicts (in p.o.v.) what he sees in the glass. The next shot shows the man in a laboratory, and in the following shot we see how he gets ready to look into a microscope. In this, the fourth shot, the cinematographer uses p.o.v. to show what the man actually sees — microscopic animals. In between most of the following shots, intertitles explain which of the small animals the viewer should pay attention to. They give us the name of the species in question but nothing more. The last two shots depict the blood circulation of a tadpole and the sap circulation of some leaves of Saragossa grass. *Nature's Hidden Beauties—Pond Life* displays a conscious perception of the principle of continuity, and makes use of the simple identification effects of p.o.v.

Yet not all English nature films were informative or innovative. In 1910, Warwick Trading Company sent out *Nature's Children in Their Native Haunts*. The copy I saw at the British Film Institute (BFI) is only 86 seconds long and consists of 5 shots. One shot lasts for 27 seconds and shows an elephant walking towards the camera, carrying two people on its back; another shot depicts two elephants walking from left to right. The latter shot has a length of 18 seconds. Between them, these two shots take up more than half the total length of the film. What remains are two shots of bears and a panoramic camera movement that follows an elephant eating in a lake. The panning is impressive, but the actual shots — not to mention the less-than-inspiring intertitles: "The Elephant" and "The Bear" — do not represent anything new, nor do they contain any sense of narrative continuity.

USA: The Spreading of Ideas and Informative Intertitles

I have seen *Insect Pond Life* (191?) at the Library of Congress in Washington, D.C. The film's structure is similar to that of the previously mentioned English nature film *Nature's Hidden Beauties — Pond Life*. Both films begin with a man drawing a fish net through the water of a lake. In the following shot he pours the content of the net into a glass, and we then see the animals — either under a microscope or in an aquarium. In *Insect Pond Life* we see a common backswimmer, a dragon fly larva, and an aquatic beetle. The shots have been taken from the side of the aquarium or from above it. The intertitles are informative and prosaic: "The Dobson lives under stones in streams. It is often used as fish bait."

In addition to the similarity of the two films' contents, they are almost of the same length (seven and eight minutes, respectively), they have the same number of shots and intertitles, and both give a fairly objective description of insect life in fresh water. It is safe to say that the producer of *Insect Pond Life* had been unusually inspired by its English predecessor.

Intertitles were used in nature film from around 1907, and made it possible for even landscape films to impart knowledge. An example is *A Trip Through the Yellowstone Park, USA* (1907). The film lasts for 4½ minutes, and contains 11 shots and 7 intertitles that give a prosaic description of the next shot. Containing shots of waterfalls, geysers and water rapids, the film, which was produced by Edison, follows in the footsteps of the waterfall films and helped develop this sub-genre.

The educational films produced by the National Non-Theatrical Motion Pictures company were more text-oriented. The motion pictures they produced did not offer the same amount of educational material as did the educational films of Pathé Frerès. However, the films came with a poster and graphic maps, and their intertitles were long and ponderous. For instance, the film *Alaska* (191?) included 55 intertitles, which took up two entire film reels. This corresponds to two texts per minute, which is quite a lot. The content of these texts was very informative, prosaic and factual. A good example is text number 5: "Its land area is nearly 6,000,000 square miles, one sixth that of the United States proper" (Ellis and Thornborough 1923, 189).

National Non-Theatrical Motion Pictures also made other nature films — for example, *The American Fish Hawk* and *Wild Animals and Their Young* (190?). They are also text-oriented films.

Denmark Lags Behind

In Denmark, a few fiery souls advocated the use of film in the classroom. Many attempts were made, but they rarely lasted long. A few shows for children were in existence from around 1907, but the use of film in schools is not documented until 1912, when a teacher named Hansen from the Oehlenschlägergade School in Copenhagen used film as an adjunct to his regular slide shows. Mostly, these films were about foreign countries or natural history, and they were accompanied by the teacher's own comments.

A more official sanction of the use of film within the public school system occurred in 1913 at the Forchammervej Community School.[9] In May 1913 there was an article in a Danish newspaper, *Politiken*, about a new company that rented out films and projectors. The director of the company (Dansk Skolefilm A/S) was an art publisher named V. Müller.

Bison in Yellowstone National Park (photograph by author).

The article states, "In America, England, Germany, Sweden, yes even in Spain, films are frequently used in schools" (*Politiken*, May 25, 1913 — my translation). In all probability, the success of the company did not last long, but it may have inspired the external examiner Anton Nicolaisen to show films during the war years at the La Courvejen's School. Nicolaisen later established The Schools' Film Library (Skolernes Filmcentral). It definitely existed in

1921 and continued until 1935, when the government took over the rental of films to schools. In an article in the newspaper *Nationaltidende* from 1921, Nicolaisen explained his interest in using films for educational purposes: "It was partly the beautiful pictures of nature sceneries and partly the major historical films that made me interested in working towards this development" (August 8, 1921 — my translation).

It was not merely the above mentioned countries that realized the inherent educational value of knowledge-imparting films. In Australia in 1913 the Department of External Affairs set up a special division dealing with photography and film.[10]

Authenticity and Wildlife Films

Fictional Films

In this period there were still no consistent conventions — within the realm of film — regarding the difference between fiction and non-fiction. Anything that was possible was considered a valid opportunity. In the early days, one used the artistic effects available — and films about wildlife and wilderness in general were no exception.

Apparently William Selig had heard of President Theodore Roosevelt's forthcoming expedition to Africa in the autumn of 1908, and it seems that he obtained permission from Roosevelt to film it. Things turned out differently, however. In consultation with the president, the Smithsonian Institution, which led the expedition, decided to hire another cameraman, and whatever Roosevelt had promised Selig fell through. Instead, Selig, who refused to miss out on what would obviously be a commercial success, made his *own* African expedition. The filming took place in his own studio, decorated to look like an African jungle and savannah. According to Terry Ramsaye, Selig bought a lion for the occasion, and apparently made a bargain — the stuffed creature was full of mothballs, and Selig paid "only" $400 for the poor thing. The film featured a couple of Afro-Americans from Chicago and an actor who was famous for his variety show imitation of Roosevelt. The film was made ready for promotion and put away in storage. As soon as the news arrived from Africa that Roosevelt had shot his first lion, Selig's film *Big Game in Africa* was released (1909). Selig avoided all mentioning of Roosevelt, but no doubt the audience was able to make the desired connection.[*11]

The *authentic* Roosevelt film, *Roosevelt in Africa* (1910), was distributed by Motion Picture Patent Company from 18 April, 1910. The version consists of 36 shots and deals with Roosevelt's official visit. Among other things, the film contains a scene in which Roosevelt plants a tree and another in which he watches a performance of a war dance. The animals in the film include a group of giraffes, hippopotamuses and a cerval cat, and it depicts the mating dances of various birds.

It must be assumed, however, that the public was more interested in action, and they clearly preferred the dramatic scenes that Selig had created for *his* Roosevelt expedition, for this film was a much bigger financial success than the non-fiction version. According to an

---

*Guggisberg's explanation and description of *Roosevelt in Africa* is completely different and contrasts with some of the situations depicted by the two others. Yet Guggisberg makes no use of source references, and I choose to believe that his observations are not well researched (Guggisberg 1977).

Roosevelt in Africa, probably 1909 (photograph by Edward van Altena. Library of Congress, LC-US262-131443).

article in *The Moving Picture World*, "Roosevelt in Africa" only depicted dead animals, and the picture caused the film industry to become skeptical about hunting films taking place in Africa: "They were so disappointed with the Roosevelt pictures that they have looked with suspicion ever since upon anything of the kind pertaining to Africa" (Feb. 25, 1911, 404).

Nordisk Film Kompagni produced several fictional hunting films between 1906 and 1908. The first picture, made by Ole Olsen (1863–1943), was 1907's *Isbjørnejagten* (*The Polar Bear Hunt*). During the winter of 1906, the channel between Denmark and Sweden was frozen solid, and Olsen used the opportunity to make an arctic hunting film. *Isbjørnejagten* was a success and sold 191 copies on the international market.

This success no doubt encouraged Olsen, and his follow-up film, *Løvejagten* (*The Lion Hunt*, 1907), sold 259 copies. For the production of *Løvejagten* Olsen bought two worn-out lions from Hagenbeck's Animal Park in Hamburg; and to boost the authenticity of the project, the film also featured a black man.

Already-existing shots of zebras and hippopotamuses were inserted. These animals were filmed in the Copenhagen Zoo, and in order to avoid showing the cages, the shots were taken from a bird's-eye view. The lions were released onto a small Danish island in Roskilde Fjord, Elleore, and a hunting expedition set out after them.

Nordisk Films Kompagni produced a third hunting film, *Bjørnejagten i Rusland* (*Bear Hunt in Russia*, 1908), but it was not as successful as the other two. The success of the previous films indicated that the audience longed for drama as well as continuity. They wanted to see films that incorporated plot and action.

Demand for Wildlife Films

Films made between 1907 and 1910 with shots of wildlife and wilderness are still not very well represented in my compiled list. This may be because the titles and or films have disappeared or have not yet been rediscovered. For instance, I have been unable to find several of the motion pictures made by Oliver G. Pike and Cherry and Richard Kearton. The list of films contains at least 20 titles produced between 1907 and 1910 which must be assumed to contain shots of animals in wild nature (comprising hunting films, expedition films and other wildlife films). Ten of the titles are hunting films.

The 1909 review in *The Moving Picture World* of *Big Game in Africa* may well have led to the production of more films depicting wild nature and wild animals:

> There is no doubt about this lion ... enabling an audience to realize how a lion would look, not on a war path, but peaceably ambling about among natural surroundings. Your captive lion in a zoological park does not do too much prowling about except in a small cage. This part of the film attracted very great attention ... an encouragement to Mr. Selig and his merry men to cultivate the production of moving pictures of animal life [May 29, 1909, 712].

The film magazine encouraged the production of films that contain authentic shots of wild animals — not shots taken in zoos, but in their natural surroundings.

Five months later, in October 1909, there arose a keen interest in expedition and exploration films. The editors of *The Moving Picture World*, Chalmers and Bedding, regretted that the animal photographer, Arthur Radclyffe Dugmore, did not shoot live pictures during his expeditions in East Africa, and they also emphasized the value of the film material from Shackleton's Antarctic expedition: "It now remains for the private individual, the travelling photographer, explorer, geographer and the like never to undertake his journey without a moving picture camera" (Chalmers and Bedding 1909, 519).

Despite the flattering words in *The Moving Picture World*, William Selig had no intention of making authentic films of wild animals, or indeed expedition films. But he was aware of the lucrative potential of this particular field, and so dramatic fictional nature films became one of the specialities of the Selig Film Studios.

Selig developed his own idiosyncratic "thriller" template featuring animals from his own zoo, which held predators for the purpose of featuring in his films. The films incorporated tigers, lions, wolves, and bears, and usually depicted how Selig's female star, Kathlyn Williams, managed to escape the claws of these "wild" beasts.[12]

The methods of Selig and Olsen created much debate within the film business: Was it morally acceptable to abuse animals in this way — not to mention tricking the audience? The magazine *Kinematograph and Lantern Weekly* criticised Ole Olsen and his film *Løvejagten*: "Because a Danish manufacturer sees fit to degrade himself in securing a disgusting film subject, ... Olsen, the manufacturer in question ... can hardly be a desirable member of the trade" (Aug. 29, 1907, 242).

The method and topic aside, the audience was remarkably interested in the films, and the sales figures were impressive. The fictional, dramatic motion pictures sold really well —

a fact that most film companies could not ignore, and both Selig and Olsen may well have regained the respect of the film business over the following years.

There were others who included shots of real wild animals in a more acceptable and recognized manner — in the name of nature preservation. In 1907, Stephen Leek filmed the migration of the wapiti deer through a beautiful area called Jackson Hole in Wyoming. Later, he used the film to bring the situation of this particular deer to the attention of the public. In 1910, again in the name of nature preservation, Leek filmed wapiti deer that were starving to death. When people saw these pictures they were upset and came to understand the importance of helping suffering animals.

Cherry Kearton

The Road to Nature Film

Cherry Kearton (1871–1940) was born in Yorkshire, England. Both his father and grandfather were respected ornithologists, and they had ample opportunity to influence him. When Cherry was 14 years old his father died, which meant that Cherry had to work to help support his family. As soon as he had saved enough money, he bought a camera, and by 1892 his abilities as a photographer had reached such heights that his brother Richard Kearton (1862–1928) recognized his talent and foresaw great possibilities for himself and his younger sibling. During a visit to some mutual friends in Enfield, Cherry had taken pictures of a song thrush lying in its nest. The pictures were so good that Richard, who was an avid amateur ornithologist, suggested that the two of them should collaborate on a book about birds, the illustrations of which should consist of Cherry's pictures. This was quite unusual, since books on wildlife in those days relied on drawings, not photographs. In 1898, their book, *British Birds' Nests*, was ready — a book that was to become "required reading" in courses on English birds.

From about 1905 the Kearton brothers started to film birds. It has not been possible to retrieve reliable source material about the content and style of these motion pictures — apart from the fact that some of the shots depicted the common white throat. It *can* be documented, however, that already in 1907 the two brothers were widely recognized for their bird films.[13] This is evident from newspaper and magazine quotes — for instance, *The London Times*: "It has been known for some time that he and his brother, whose photographs of birds are known all over the world, had been experimenting with the bioscope.... The results are astounding" (Aug. 17, 1907).

Among other birds, the films showed young broods of pipits, bullfinches, spotted flycatchers and wrynecks, but also a series of shots from the Farne Islands with cormorants and terns. Their films were supposed to be very special:

> The results are astounding. The photographers have chiefly been busy with young broods. The first series showed pipits ... in each case the parents being engaged feeding the young. You could follow every movement of the bird.... The waving of the grass, the ruffling of the feathers, were quite distinct. The audience could not forbear a cheer when the sedge warbler, finding his mate on the nest, passed on the food, which she in turn passed on to the young [*The London Times*, Aug. 17, 1907].

This early notice goes on to indicate that there were other bird films before the Keartons, but they were not shot in the wild. So far I have found no trace of these American films: "But Mr. Kearton kept a climax. At the end we were shown a sparrow hawk feeding its young. Nothing comparable with this photograph has been hitherto approached, even by the American 'fakers,' recently attacked by Mr. Roosevelt" [Ibid].

After having made quite a few bird films in England, Cherry Kearton went abroad, and as the years passed he experienced incredible things and exposed himself to many dangerous situations. He made a living by writing books and articles about his adventures. During a stay in Africa, Kearton shot a film and made money on writing about the events that he experienced. Among other things, Kearton described a lion attack, and the power of his prose reveals his gift for drama:

> He came slowly at first, biting at stinging spears, tearing up the ground in monstrous big gashes, and roaring the roar that strikes one in the chest and vibrates out of the back. Then he charged, right into the thick of them. I have it on film, but it is silent there, and one can gain no idea at all of the awful tumult [Steele 1913, 332].

On another occasion his depiction was no less dramatic:

> The animal snarled fiercely and showed his great yellow teeth. My heart thumped painfully. And I believe I perspired. Nevertheless, I remained perfectly still and steadfastly returned his stare. He growled "Gnaeum-eugh!" I stood as stone. What did "Gnaeum-eugh" mean? [Kearton 1923, 233].

I will not comment on the inherent truth of the above quotations, but the entertainment value is self-evident, and Kearton *did* write to earn a living.

Cherry Kearton filming crocodiles in India.

The Career Progresses

Almost from the beginning, Cherry Kearton made use of a cine-camera during his travels abroad. According to his own memoirs, he filmed in Borneo in 1908 in a warm, dense jungle with high humidity. He obtained shots of, for example, a hornbill, but I have not been able to verify his statements through other sources. It is certain, however, that in 1909 Kearton accompanied James L. Clark from the American Museum of Natural History on a trip to Kenya. In East Africa he filmed the material for *Native Lion Hunt, African Animals* and *Theodore Roosevelt's Africa Expedition* (1909).* According to Kearton's own memoirs, he filmed kingfishers, non-passerine birds, chameleons, hippopotamuses, lions, jackals, marabous, vultures, colobus monkeys, buffaloes, and Jackson's dancing birds; and he is also supposed to have filmed a war dance of the Masai people.

The Library of Congress has a film entitled *African Animals* that the archive assumes stems from 1909. The copy may be one of Kearton's films, but I have no definite proof. The copy is a fragment of a longer film, and lasts a mere 23 seconds. The first shot depicts a hippopotamus walking in the water close to a riverbank. This is followed by an intertitle reading: "Having a damp fine time." Three other shots follow, all showing hippos splashing in water. The final shot of the fragment depicts a rhinoceros eating leaves from a bush. All the shots are of a very high quality. They are long shots, and I think the cinematographer used a small telephoto lens with a maximum of four inches. Whether or not the film is one of Kearton's is impossible to say for certain at this point. It is remarkable though that the animals filmed in the little fragment have been shot on location — in Africa — and that they display a behavior that seems quite natural. There is no indication that the animals are being hunted — they show absolutely no awareness that they are being watched. They seem at peace, which indicates that the film may well have been shot by Kearton. Other indications of a connection to Kearton are the title, year and the animals being in Africa.

When Roosevelt and Cherry Kearton met in Nairobi in 1909, Kearton had filmed groups of animals on the plains of Athi near Nairobi, as well as a group of lions from a distance of merely 100 feet. Roosevelt saw these shots during their meeting, but he was already familiar with the work of the Kearton brothers. In 1908, Richard Kearton had been invited to the White House to give a lecture and show some of the bird films that he and Cherry had made. Consequently, Roosevelt already had great admiration for Kearton's authentic shots of wild animals — in fact, he praised them in public, which occurred during an introduction to one of the brothers' bird films:

> "A number of years ago," said Colonel Roosevelt when he secured quiet, "my attention was attracted to some very remarkable work that was being done in taking moving pictures of live birds and animals by the Kearton brothers. I was so much impressed by it that I got Mr. Kearton's brother to come over and give an exhibition in the White House" [*TMPW*, March 1, 1913, 868].

Colonel C. J. Buffalo Jones was a 67-year-old cowboy from Nebraska who accompanied two couples, the Means and the Lovelesses, on a hunting trip to Africa. Cherry Kearton was their cinematographer. Buffalo Jones' hunting expedition began immediately after Roosevelt's return to America, and was unusual in the way it was conducted. From a review of

---

*The Roosevelt film was shot when the two met in Africa 29 August 1909 (Kearton 1914, pp. 105–106).

the film *Lassoing Wild Animals in Africa* (1911), it appears that Kearton shot 40,255 feet of film and that the finished picture had a length of 2000 feet. The film is described in some detail in *The Moving Picture World* (25 February 1911), and from this description it appears that Cherry Kearton filmed how Americans caught wild rhinoceroses, giraffes, cerval cats and cheetahs with a lasso. (These are merely examples, for the members of the expedition caught lots of other animals too, but they always released them afterwards, which in those days was a remarkable display of "nature preservation.")

Kearton was not completely satisfied with his working conditions, or, indeed, with the expedition itself. This East Africa expedition was very cumbersome and slow, and disturbed the wildlife. This is visible in the shots: the animals depicted are clearly frightened, stressed and not at peace, running contrary to Kearton's usual trademark. But lasso hunting provided ample opportunities for creating dramatic scenes — especially the rhinoceros hunting.

From very early on, Cherry Kearton documented the wildlife of many impassable countries. Thus, in 1911 he filmed orangutans in Borneo, and tigers, wild dogs, butterflies and elephants in India. Kearton described India as a fiasco, film-wise. The jungle was too dense and the view of the animals appalling. After 20 days in India, Kearton had given up on getting shots of tigers; but when he least expected it, he got the chance. A few miles outside a small village he discovered the traces of a tiger, and succeeded in tracking down the animal. With the help of a noisy crowd, Kearton managed to drive both the tiger and a number of wild elephants out of the dark jungle, and was thus able to film them.[14] After the trip to India, Kearton went to Borneo to film under very difficult conditions — humidity, rain and the density of the jungle made the process almost impossible. Still, Kearton managed to film an orangutan and a nesting hornbill.

In 1912, Kearton was on yet another adventure/globetrotting expedition — this time a trip through Canada and the American Northwest — the most important purpose of which was to film the Canadian elk. This he achieved, and he also obtained shots of fish hawks on Long Island. In Yellowstone National Park he filmed pelicans, black bear and bison.

Around 1912 a coincidental meeting between James Barnes and Cherry Kearton led to the Kearton-Barnes expedition to Africa in 1913. For a whole year they journeyed across the African continent from Kenya to the source of the Congo. On this journey Kearton filmed the Grevy zebra, the weaver bird and the Beisa oryx, but his greatest wish was to film the then newly-discovered species the okapi. Unfortunately, this did not happen. It was around this time, however, that Kearton filmed the Masai people during a lion hunt. However, I have not been able to verify if this event took place during this expedition.

In 1914, Kearton returned to Africa with the sportsman and nature enthusiast F. C. Selous. This journey was to last for four years, and the two went through many hazardous experiences in the African wilderness. It was a journey into a wild animal kingdom, and Kearton got many fine shots of animals — especially those taken close to riverbanks. He filmed impalas, oryxes, baboons, ostriches, leopards, chimpanzees and elephants. When he returned to England he discovered that he had caught both malaria and dysentery, but this did not put an end to his wanderlust or indeed his work. In 1921, Kearton went to Africa again — from the Cape through Rhodesia and the Congo to Cairo. It was during this trip that he saw the adelie penguins for the first time, and it was also on this trip that he managed to film the white rhinoceroses in Zululand. Towards the end of the 1920s Kearton filmed adelie penguins just beyond the coast of mainland Africa — on the island of Dassan. The resulting motion picture was named after the island, *Dassan* (1930). Kearton stayed several months on the island, where he studied the lives of these amazing animals. He gently mocks them, and appears himself in the film several times. *Dassan* was Kearton's first tone film, and he handled the new medium quite well. Ingeniously, he has the penguin eggs hatching to the melody "Pop Goes the Weasel." The sound of honking car horns accompanies an amusing scene in which a large number of penguins wander one after the other toward the ocean in single file. The music composed for *Dassan* is happy, sad or dramatic by turns — and almost always evocative.

The film begins with Cherry Kearton sailing from Cape Town to Dassan. We then see a map of the island and are told that 5 million adelie penguins live here. Kearton introduces himself and takes his hat off to the penguins. He introduces us to some of the animals, such as the "Minister of War" and "Frank and Flora Flatfeed." He pokes fun at the penguins, but also at himself—"an Englishman far from civilization." We are given some information about the lives and behavior of the animals, but this is done rather anthropomorphically. Thus, Kearton suggests that married couples mate for life, but that some of them flirt a bit on the side—like Frank Flatfeed—and that this always leads to trouble. The next picture shows three penguins fighting with each other, with the fight presented as if it were a boxing match. The sound of a bell informs us as to the number of rounds, and when one of the penguins tumbles down, it takes the count. This is made plain by a shot in which a penguin beats one of its wings against the ground, with the shot repeated over and over again — "1, 2, 3..." The voice-over is entertaining rather than informative: "Shy little things. It takes a long time to come out of their shells, but once out you can't get them back in again."

Dassan does contain elements of natural history, as it presents the laying of eggs, and the brooding and hatching of the eggs, but humor remains the very foundation of the film. As mentioned earlier, *Dassan* depicts a "penguin parade." Each animal is accompanied by the honking of a particular brand of car that fits the individual walking style of the penguins: Rolls-Royce, Ford, etc. At one point we are told that the penguins have gone to the mainland, which gives Kearton the opportunity to introduce us to a number of safari animals, as well as showing a staged fight between a mongoose and a cobra.

In the late 1920s and early 1930s Kearton shot scenes for his second great Africa film: *Tembi*. Kearton did not limit himself to the typical, popular species. Over the years he filmed small animals like tree frogs, cororants, mantises and termites. From the descriptions in his book *In the Land of the Lion* (1929), it appears that he filmed several kinds of insects (e.g., grasshoppers and white ants). He also filmed reptiles (e.g., chameleons and iguanas), rodents (e.g., hares and rock rabbits), and birds (e.g., the crowned crane, the fish hawk, the secretary bird and the great bustard). He also mentions a dwarf civet, which he claims is a rare species.[15]

The Work with Wildlife Film

Cherry Kearton gradually developed a combination of patience, knowledge of nature, and composition skills, and he eventually became a very good cinematographer. His admirable patience was evident when he was filming on location: "At one water-hole, I waited in hiding for my 'sitters' exactly thirty days, and the picture I show on the screen does not occupy more than thirty seconds" (Kearton 1914, 213).

Kearton's patience was also evident during the time when he was shooting a film about

Cherry Kearton walking on the island of Dassan amidst the adelie penguins.

butterflies. He spent four years securing a scene of a caterpillar entering the chrysalis stage. The wait did pay off and he got the shot, but the sequence only lasts some 40 seconds. Similarly, Kearton spent years on a film showing a butterfly coming out of its cocoon. This time he did not succeed, however, and the picture was never finished.[16]

First and foremost, Kearton was an expert in camouflage and finding himself a decent hiding place. Among other things, he discovered how he could avoid disturbing elephants. His hiding places were constructed with natural materials, and for each stage in the construction process, wet sand was strewn over it. The sand was crucial, as it removed the human scent, to which elephants are very sensitive. Already when the Kearton brothers made their bird films they had developed stake-out and camouflage techniques. When filming birds, they used artificial rocks, tree trunks and stuffed sheep and cows, and they learned how they could build hiding places of stone or camouflage a tent with plants that grew naturally in the area.[17]

Richard Kearton in a hiding place.

There were aspects of the film business that Kearton mastered less well, however. During his 1914 trip to Africa, Kearton was shooting scenes of a wild leopard eating the carcass of a hippopotamus. "I continued to turn the handle until I had used up all the film I had in the machine. Even then we remained watching him for some time longer" (Kearton 1923, 119). Unfortunately, Kearton was less than brilliant when it came to darkrooms and chemical processes, and it so happened that the leopard shots were ruined. This was indeed a blunder, as the experienced Clark, who had been on quite a few safaris before and who had watched the leopard with Kearton, had never seen a leopard in an open landscape before. On a different occasion, in Borneo in 1911, Kearton also ruined a film because his darkroom was not completely dark.[18]

In the beginning, Cherry Kearton used a Kinemascope film camera, but around 1911 he switched to an Aeroscope. On several occasions the Kinamascope camera turned out to be a clumsy device and had a tendency to upset the objective, which meant that what you saw in the viewfinder was not what you saw on the finished film. During his visit to East Africa in 1909, Kearton had the opportunity to film a group of Masai warriors hunting down a rhinoceros, but he later stated:

> I would have given a great deal to have secured a photographic record of it; but the moving picture camera of those days was very different from my spring camera of to-day. It was distinctly an awkward and unwieldy affair, and by the time you had it on its legs an interesting incident was often finished [Kearton 1923, 119].

The combination of a heavy tripod, an awkward camera and a pending wildlife shot was not always a happy one. The change to the Aeroscope camera no doubt made Kearton's job a lot easier, and led to superior results, for this equipment was better suited to nature cinematography.[19] Nonetheless, it was far from perfect. Kearton had to give up filming mountain goats in the Rocky Mountains in 1912 because the camera was too heavy (40 pounds).

Kearton's finished films are beautifully created compositions and — more importantly — are authentic. This is only possible to achieve if one has patience, a certain insight into the behavior of the animals, and a knowledge of camouflage and the construction of hiding places. In a review of *Lassoing Wild Animals in Africa*, the reviewer acknowledges the work of Kearton: "The photography, on the whole is excellent, clear, bright and distinct. The excitement at times is almost hair raising, as these three American cowboys perform their wonderful stunts with their lasso" (*TMPW*, February 25, 1911, 405). President Roosevelt and the press were likewise enthusiastic, and the material that I have been privileged to see clearly demonstrates that Cherry Kearton was one of the best cinematographers of his day.

The Films

Among other films, I have seen *With Cherry Kearton in the Jungle* (1926) at the British Film Institute. It is an incomplete copy, lasting 2 minutes 52 seconds, which I assume has been pieced together from several earlier films. The short abstract from *With Cherry Kearton in the Jungle* indicated that Kearton was a very capable animal cinematographer who mastered the use of big telephoto lenses. Judging by the compression of both foreground and background, I believe that Kearton used lenses with a minimum of 300 mm in some of the shots. The copy consists of 34 shots and depicts various large animals. Not all of these are from the jungle, as the title might otherwise indicate. Towards the end, for example, we see a number of shots of adelie penguins. These shots display a convincing photographic sharpness and give a beautiful impression in contrasting shades of grey; the images are of an unusual aesthetic quality even for today. Cherry Kearton appears in several of the shots, mostly behind the camera, working intensely on filming the animals that we see immediately afterwards on the screen.

Shots 7, 19 and 20 deserve special mention. They all depict close-ups of male lions. The shots have great density and are very beautiful. The last shot shows a lion drinking water, cut in such a way that we only see his mane. While he drinks, he stares directly into the camera. The mood of that shot is so intense that the audience actually might feel the presence of the animal.

Nature Perception

In the preface to *Photographing Wild Life Across the World*, Kearton writes that he noticed a decrease in the number of animals on the African savannah, a decrease that occurred over a period of only 12 years (from his first visit in 1909 to his last visit in 1921–22). Although he points out that he shoots with a camera and not a rifle, there are certain animals for whose existence Kearton cannot find any justification. He believes, for instance, that crocodiles and snakes ought to be killed at any given opportunity: "They are enemies of all living things" (Kearton 1923, 46–7). He feels the same way about the hyena. In 1929, Kearton made the following disturbing observation:

> I like neither the look of him, nor the smell of him, not his habits, nor the sound of him. He is a pest and a particularly evil one at that. He is the kind of creature on whom men do not waste good bullets, because poisoned food is both more effective and more appropriate [Kearton 1929, 197].

Yet Kearton also expressed a sense of sadness and vexation about the fact that so many wild animals were being destroyed. For instance, he lamented the fact that the beaver in Canada was on the brink of extinction, "with no one to raise a protest until it was almost too late."

Kearton was not fond of the Native Americans, though. In his opinion they deserved to die:

> The Red Indian had to go of course. He belongs to one of those races which cannot thrive side by side with the white man. No amount of legislation or care would have preserved him for long. Really, he was out of date. Doomed when the first settler began to build his log hut. But the game was different [Kearton 1923, 278–9].

No doubt this personal view of Kearton's was one that he shared with many imperialists. In a sense, the Indian is placed among crocodiles and poisonous snakes, whereas the existence of more cuddly and noble animals — lions, beavers and rhinos — is justified as a matter of course.

In many ways, Kearton knew much more about animals and nature than he knew about indigenous peoples. The following descriptions of the gorilla and the penguin put his view of the "Red Indians" in a somewhat grotesque light: "An entirely unjustified reputation for fierceness ... it is in fact that the gorilla is a very harmless and peaceable animal" (Kearton 1929, 138).

Hyenas have never been popular. Cherry Kearton hated them (photograph by author).

Kearton was not a hunter, but he was not against hunting per se. He writes, "During the last twenty-five years I have had many expeditions into this country [Africa] and always my object has been, not to kill animals, but to study and to photograph them" (Kearton 1929, 16). Once again Kearton's personality seems complex. He knows that the zebra herds of Africa are suffering a terrible fate at the hands of white people, but nowhere does he suggest that the white man's hunting of this animal should be stopped. He merely states, "The zebra is regarded as the settler's worst enemy, and in my opinion it is only a matter of time before this beautiful animal which now appears common will become practically extinct" (Kearton 1929, 213).

The aboriginals' hunting of the zebra and selling its skin offends him, however. He is sympathetic neither towards their need for meat nor towards their financial situation. "I condemn the local residents who shoot a zebra because he can get the sum of five shillings for its skin" (Kearton 1929, 213).

As mentioned earlier, *Dassan*, the film about the adelie penguins, has a very humorous undertone, gently poking fun at the penguins. In his book about his stay on Dassan, Kearton apologizes for this approach: "I hope I wasn't unfair against them, for — like most people — I laugh at them — but I love them too" (Kearton 1931, 12).

In the 1930s Kearton visited the Australian continent, but by then his health had begun to deteriorate. He went back to Britain and settled down permanently in Surrey, where he had spent his youth and childhood.[20]

Oliver G. Pike

Oliver G. Pike (1877–1963) made over 80 nature films, primarily about birds. Like many of the very best cinematographers, Pike took a naturalistic approach to his work. He did not approve of sports hunters — indeed, he despised them. The following shows just how much:

> Sportsmen, as they called themselves ... fire load after load of shot into the packed mass of birds, leaving hundreds dead, and still more dying of their wounds.... After an hour or so of this slaughter, called sport, the people sailed away, leaving a picture of destruction and desolation [Pike 1949, 129].

Comments like these more than indicate that Oliver G. Pike was an honorable representative and defender of the animal kingdom from which he made his living. He labelled his own "hunting" with the camera as "Hunt without Hurt" (Pike 1949, 129).

The Road to Nature Film

Oliver Pike's interest in birds and photography began as early as 1891. A local portrait photographer, whose shop lay midway between Pike's home and school (Enfield Grammar School), displayed various bird pictures in his show window, and these captured the young man's attention.[21]

Oliver Pike received his first cine camera in 1905.* By this time he was already a recognized still photographer with years of experience. His first film camera was a portable box camera that was easy to master and which recorded the exposed film on a circular glass plate. Pike later recalled that the camera was very noisy, both during the shooting and the showing. The noise proved to be a problem when Pike attempted to film in his own garden for the first time. As soon as he started shooting, the noise began and the birds immediately took flight. Pike attempted to wrap a blanket around the camera, but the noise was still audible. He had another idea: He filled a tin can with small stones and shook it continuously. He did this for a few days, and gradually the birds got used to the sound and returned to the garden, completely ignoring the racket coming from the camera. In this way Pike got his first bird shots.

Very soon Pike realized that the box camera, with its atypical film format, was outdated and insufficient. He therefore borrowed a 35mm camera that used film reels of about 300 feet.† Pike learned an important lesson using this camera. During his first outing he recorded an entire film reel of black-headed gulls. Not surprisingly, the result was a shot that lasted for about five minutes. This was incredibly boring, and gradually Pike learned that a 40-second shot was usually enough.[22]

Around the end of 1905, Pike took the camera out into nature, filming forests, fields and coastlines. The work was painstakingly slow, but after two years, a 10-minute nature film appeared. The film was called *In Birdland,* and was first presented to the press at the Palace Theatre in London on 29 August 1907. The press material accompanying the film stated that *In Birdland* was made "by that well-known naturalist Oliver G. Pike, who has penetrated into the actual homes of wild birds and with his camera has secured lasting records of the feathered denizens of the country" (Pike 1946, 17).

---

*This has been calculated from a premiere date, August 29, 1907, from which two years of production time have been detracted. Pike 1946, pp. 14–17. See also Hosking 1947, p. 102.

†No available information regarding the type of camera.

Pike believed that never before had such a film been made, but this must be considered a naïve or self-promoting viewpoint.[23] According to Pike himself, the papers were full of positive reviews — and this may have enhanced the popularity of the film. *In Birdland* was shown at the Palace Theatre for over a month. According to Pike, its fame spread throughout the entire country, and over 100 copies were sold.

I have seen dozens of papers published in London during the days when *In Birdland* premiered. I have read copies of *The Standard* and *The Times* published between 29 August and 6 September 1907, and none of them mention the release of this film or the press meeting accompanying it. *Kinematograph and Lantern Weekly* mentions the event, but their wording is not particularly flattering: "We were sorry to find in so many instances that the technical quality of the films did not please us; some being much underexposed and consequently wanting in detail" (Sept. 5, 1907, 265). Moreover, the review mentions the latest bird film of the Kearton brothers, and describes this as the more beautiful and successful of the two:

> Altogether Messrs. Pike and Sanders have some interesting examples of wild bird life. We do not think however, that their results thus far can be said to approach in excellence and comprehensiveness the series obtained by their contemporaries, Messrs Richard and Cherry Kearton [Ibid, 267].

Considering these comments, it is difficult to believe a word Pike writes. Nonetheless, maintaining a healthy skepticism regarding superlatives, I believe that *In Birdland* was fairly successful. It certainly brought Pike so much money that he was able to commission a special cine-camera based on his own specifications. The camera was smaller than the others, it was portable and made less noise. Most important was the special socket which made it possible for Pike to change lenses and so use various focal lengths for the same subject. He received his new camera in 1908, and over his long career he filmed with over 12 other types of camera.

The Career Takes Shape

Pathé Frères were quick to sense the financial opportunities and educational values inherent in Oliver Pike's bird films. Already in 1908 the company began distributing Pike's films, and they continued to do so over a 10-year period. All in all, they distributed about 12 of his pictures.

The islands of St. Kilda just off the Scottish west coast are a paradise for birds, and during his first visit in 1908, Oliver Pike filmed the inhabitants of the island, both human and avian. The result was the film *St. Kilda, Its People and Birds* (1908).

A cinematographer — especially a wildlife cinematographer — must possess almost inhuman patience, and he must be willing to expose himself to dangerous situations that most people would consider foolish. During the filming on St. Kilda, Pike made good use of his patience and also experienced a number of dangerous situations. Here follows a dramatic quote by Pike:

> At last, with torn clothes, and tired limbs we found ourselves half way down, and rested on a narrow ledge crowded with talkative guillemots. "There's worse to come," said my guide. "Just round the corner there's quite a dangerous place" [Pike 1946, 178].

Pike made his way to the bird colonies on the steep coastal rocks. There was a terrible stench, and the place was pandemonium, where fulmars, puffins, guillemot and gannets fought for attention. Pike's quote continues:

When I saw the leading climber creep round the corner with practically nothing between him and the sea, I wondered if I should succeed in getting down. The foot holes of our feet were exceedingly small, some only an inch in width, and there seemed to be hardly a niche in which to place our fingers, taking the equipment from my back, and even any projecting things from my pockets, I essayed to follow, and after the most exciting but shortest climb of my life, I found myself once again on a firm foothold [Pike 1946, 196].

Arriving on his first visit to the islands, Pike was met by rain and tremendous gusts of wind; the storm was such a wild experience that he forgot to bring his film equipment with him in the confusion, and he saw the ship disappear with the 2000 feet of film that he was supposed to use during his stay. He managed to scrape together bits and pieces of film and ended up with 850 feet at his disposal. This seems incredible — Pike's finished film ran to 800 feet, so if this story is true, he must have been incredibly economical with his film stock.[24]

The first thing I noticed when I watched the film was the length of each shot. One of these depicts a colony of fulmars on a rock. The distance between the camera and the rock is so great that it is difficult to spot the individual details. Nonetheless, the shot lasts for 22 seconds. The next shot lasts 20 seconds, but this feels acceptable because we see a long shot of a female bird placing herself on her egg. In other words, something actually happens in the shot. Moreover, the film illustrates how the people of the island catch birds with nets, and it also shows us colonies of jackdaws and gulls.[25]

According to Pike, *St. Kilda, Its People and Birds* was a huge success. With obvious exaggeration, he writes the following about the circulation of the film: "[It was] shown in almost every town where there were cinemas, all over the continent, America and the colonies" (Pike 1946, 196).

Pike's film work came to a virtual standstill during the First World War, and not until 1919 was he again able to continue. By then, his desire to shoot films of animals and nature had become an urgent issue for him. His camera was now a Pathé camera, and he took it into nature to make a small film about grebes called *The Stream* (1919).

Three years later he began working for British Instructional Films — a collaboration that may well have started when he befriended Bruce Woolfe, who had established the company and who was the prime mover on *Secrets of Nature*. Nineteen twenty-two was also the year Pike made his first film using the slow-motion technique. The film is called *Nature's Gliders* (1922) and is, as far as I can tell, one of the first motion pictures to be shot on panchromatic film.

Oliver Pike was to work for British Instructional Films (BIF) for the next 25 or 30 years.* Pike and his wife made a number of nature films for BIF — all shot in Hertfordshire, where they lived. Among others, they filmed *Polly All Alone, Two Little Orphans* and *We Are Seven* (192?). They also made *Babes in the Wood* (192?), which they filmed on their own beautiful grounds. This picture featured various young animals, and the shots were mixed together with shots from the forest situated close by. Several of Pike's films took advantage of man's inherent sympathy for young animals and people in distress, and so the films thrived on the emotionally charged effect to which such scenes would inevitably give rise.

---

*BIF later changed its name to Gaumont British Instructional Films.

Work with Bird Films

Pike must be remembered as one of the absolute pioneers within the area of bird photography and especially bird cinematography. He stretched the possibilities of the equipment to the limit, and had a fine technical ability. One of his technically most memorable films is the slow-motion picture *Nature's Gliders*. It was filmed with a Debrie camera fitted with a 100mm (4 inch) lens and shot on Kodak SS panchromatic film. Filmed on St. Kilda, the gliding of the gannets appears both graceful and beautiful.[26]

Pike had a steady hand and a natural ability to handle large telephoto lenses, which he used for, among other films, *Nursery Island*. This is evident from the compressed field of vision — Pike probably used a lens of 500mm (20 inches).

In collaboration with the famous ornithologist Edgar Chance, Pike made an important discovery about the life of the cuckoo, and the two men set out to communicate their newfound knowledge in a film shot on the Worcestershire Common.* Pike had 12 assistants observe the movements of a pair of cuckoos during the day. The knowledge of Edgar Chance made it possible to estimate which nest the cuckoo would use. Chance believed that the cuckoo would probably choose the nest of a meadow pipit because the bird had herself hatched in a nest belonging to such a species. The team found 13 meadow pipit nests on the ground. Chance knew that when the cuckoo was ready to lay her egg, she would find a nest where the meadow pipit had laid her own eggs a few days earlier. Pike and his assistants consequently destroyed the contents of all but one of the meadow pipit nests. This way they were certain which nest the cuckoo would choose. The plan worked out, and Pike managed to set up his camera by the right nest. The shots proved that the cuckoo lays her eggs directly in another bird's nest, and not, as previously thought, by laying it on the ground and subsequently carrying it to the nest in her beak. The experience of documenting this discovery was one of the greatest moments in Pike's career as a cinematographer.

At least two films exist that reveal the "secret" of the cuckoo: *The Story of the Cuckoo* (1922) and *The Cuckoo's Secret* (1922). Both films are over 1000 feet but do not contain the same shots. Nonetheless, the structures of the two films are similar. They both begin with a group of people arriving at some kind of nature resort. They erect a hiding place and go inside it. Afterwards we see some birds in a nest, and we see how the cuckoo places her egg in the other bird's nest. The eggs hatch and the nestlings grow steadily. It is obvious that the young cuckoo is much bigger than the other nestlings.

The Story of the Cuckoo differs from *The Cuckoo's Secret* in that it has slow-motion sequences. One of these shows the cuckoo choosing the nest she wishes to use, and another shows how the foster mother feeds the young cuckoo. After the slow-motion sequence a couple of picture frames are tinted amber, but this lasts only a few split seconds. The final version was probably tinted all the way through, but this had not been done in the version I saw. Both films include intertitles, but the ones that appear in *The Cuckoo's Secret* are much longer and more scientific. The effect of this is that the message of the film becomes much clearer. The editing and intertitles compliment each other well. One of the shots is especially fascinating. It depicts how the young cuckoo pushes both eggs and newborn birds out of the nest in order to get all the food for itself. *The Cuckoo's Secret* was produced by

*Already in 1913, Pike is supposed to have filmed a cuckoo that pushes out a lark from its nest in order to use it itself.

Edgar Chance, which does not appear to be the case with *The Story of the Cuckoo*. Chance's ornithological expertise may have brought about a more comprehensible version in *The Cuckoo's Secret*.

Production of Sound Films

The nightingale was one of the species that presented a challenge to early filmmakers. One of Pike's films about this bird was called *Singing While You Work* (1932). It was shot on the improved Kodak Plus X-film. A sound version of the film was produced by Mary Field, who retitled it *The Nightingale*. *Singing While You Work* was made at a time when adding sound to a motion picture was still very difficult. The speaker had to record the commentary while an orchestra played the required background music. This process occurred while they watched the film on a screen; and during it all, a sound recording was made that was later added to the film. During this complicated process for *The Nightingale*, Mary Field happened to notice a sequence in which it looked as if the nightingale was dancing. They quickly decided to capitalize on this "optical illusion" by prolonging and repeating it. The planned commentary was dropped, and a piece of music, especially composed for the occasion, was coordinated with the movements of the bird. This way it looks like the nightingale is indeed dancing — as if it listens to the music and follows its rhythms. This is a very early example of "Mickey Mousing" in a nature film.

Pike began looking for this type of scene, and the same technique was applied to *Nursery Island* (1936), which deals with the bird life on the Farne Islands. Music and sound is synchronized in a scene depicting a young arctic tern desperately seeking its mother. The scene took hours to create in the editing room, and has nothing to do with reality. Pike's comment, "So whenever I saw a shot that would link up with the scene I had in mind" (Pike 1946, 128), indicates that Pike would construct a scene in his head, then simply wander around trying to find suitable footage. By so doing, he staged reality from several independent fragments that he would later edit together and fit into the plot of the film.

Micro- and Time-Lapse Cinematography

The filming of microscopic animals had been employed in the Urban-Duncan Bioscope series from 1903, but not until the end of the decade was this technique used in an advanced and technically satisfying manner. My compiled list of film contains 29 motion pictures that in all probability used micro-cinematography. These appeared between 1907 and 1919.

Micro-cinematography is done by connecting the lens-socket of the camera to a microscope or some other mechanism that will enlarge the chosen subject. If we compare the natural size of the objects to their size on the screen, enlargements somewhere between 2000 and 76 million times were not uncommon during this period.[27]

The period in question offered some technical and optical problems related to micro-cinematography, and a director had to take certain precautions. One of these was that even the slightest vibration from the surroundings would transmit themselves onto the subject, and due to the quite significant enlargement, such vibrations would appear enormous in the finished film.

Moreover, the optical construction of the microscope caused a lack in the depth of

focus. This means that the filmed subject was not able to move an inch ver-
tically without the shot losing focus.
To avoid this, the director would give
the subject as little room for movement
as possible. The limit was reached if
the subject was jammed or dead,
which, of course, was not the intention
at all, since the whole idea was to
depict *movement*. Sometimes the solution was to use a tiny transparent container filled with water. The container
limited the vertical movements of the
subject but allowed it to move horizontally.[28]

I know of only two people who
may have played a part in the development of micro-cinematography during
this period: the Russian Ladislas Starewitch and the British F. Percy Smith.
The only films of Starewitch that I am
familiar with are *The Beautiful Stag-
Beetle* (1910) and *The Cicada and the
Ant* (1927). Starewitch is supposed to
have been an insect enthusiast as well

Flowers have been popular subjects for micro-
cinematography (photograph by author).

as a filmmaker. According to film historian Lefebvre, the motion pictures that Starewitch
made indicate that he was able to balance an objective, scientific approach with a somewhat
subjective, cartoon-like tone.[29]

In my compiled list of films, 13 deal with flowers. I presume that most of these contain
sequences applying the time-lapse technique. I doubt that the first one mentioned, *Sweet
Flower* (1906), used time-lapse, but between 1909 and 1914 six films certainly did. There is
a break of some 12 years with no registered plant films, after which the series *Secrets of
Nature* begins and takes up the time-lapse technique.

Nordisk Films Kompagni's *Moderkærlighed Blandt Dyrene* (*Mother Love in the Animal
Kingdom*, 1908) show young animals that have been filmed in zoological gardens and on a
farm. The shots are very brief and portray the relationship between a mother and her young.
The following species are represented: ducks, turkeys, cats, dogs, pigs, goats, reindeer, horses
and zebras. The most significant scene in the film is a time-lapse sequence of a hen's egg
hatching. This is one of the first ever time-lapse scenes in a nature film. The film is especially
good because it combines the use of aquarium shots with other locations, and it incorporates
time-lapse sequences.

Film-release by automatic electric ignition has been around since 1888 when it was
invented at the Marey Institute in France. Later, the scientist Lucien Bull (1876–1972)
developed the method further, so that by 1904 a camera could take 1200 images per second.
The method has been described in detail by author Frederick A. Talbot, who in his early

work on film production devotes an entire section to a description of it.[30] Very briefly, it is an external electric activation of the winding within a camera. Such a mechanism is useful when you want to film the development of a flower from seed to grown plant. If, for instance, you want to film the development of a lily, you must take a picture each and every 20 minutes, day and night, for up to three months. In such a situation an automatic release is not only useful but necessary.[31]

The electronic release mechanism was used for filming a fly in *The Actual Travels of a Fly as Caught by a Moving Picture Camera* (1911).* Not surprisingly, the film is about a housefly flying past a camera. To make sure that the animal would fly in the right direction, the director used the knowledge that insects will always fly towards strong light. The small size of the fly meant that its course past the lens had to be very precise. This was sorted out in the following manner: A long glass tube was placed at the same level as the lens. The fly was placed at the end of the glass tube and was half anesthetized by a light electric current. When the fly was released and flew towards the light at the end of the tube, it activated an electrode that in turn activated the release mechanism of the camera. They placed a light source at the same level as the camera and the tube in such a way that the fly would be filmed as it flew towards the light. This was an ingenious experimental technique constructed for the specific purpose of filming an insect flying in midair.[32]

Despite the invention of the electric release mechanism, there were many examples of "Gyro Gearloose" constructions. Percy Smith made a see-saw construction where the end of one side consisted of a tin can and the other end consisted of an object of a similar weight. At a certain speed, water would drip into the can; when it reached a certain weight the can would fall off and (through a clever construction that involved a hook and a toothed wheel) release the shutter. This was yet another ingenious device used to make a film about the life of a flower, as well as a film about a growing seed. These two films were shown around 1911, with the monochrome color process of the Kinemacolors. One of them, *Birth of a Flower* (1910), follows the hyacinth flower from the first germination of the seed until the crown bursts open. The result was so beautiful that it remained popular for a long time. As late as 1915 there was a review of the film in *The Independent*.[33]

Other similar, strange constructions were developed and used, but the First World War put an end to the work within this field — and for a long time, too. In 1922, Harry Bruce Woolfe took up the work with plant cinematography again, when establishing the series *Secrets of Nature*.[34]

Working Conditions Caused by the Time-Lapse Technique

Many things can go wrong during time-lapse filming. This is mainly due to the time involved — from hours to weeks and, in extreme cases, even months. For this reason it took (and still takes) some experience in calculating the picture frequency when making time-lapse films. In a film following the hatching of a hen's egg, Smith made a schedule from which he could calculate how many pictures he should take in order to obtain the best result. This meant that over 21 days, a shot was taken every third minute — day and night. If projected at a speed of 20 frames a second, this would result in one minute of film for

*I assume that the film Talbot mentions is this film — a review of which occurs in *The Moving Picture World* June 12 (1911): 1898. It might also be *The Strength and Agility of Insects* (1911) that was made by Percy Smith.

every two-and-a-half days. Consequently, the picture must have lasted for over 8 minutes. This may seem a long time, but in 1934 the producers Field and Smith calculated that a botanical time-lapse film could well last for 8 or 9 minutes.[35]

Many other things could go wrong during time-lapse filming. Insects sitting on the plant during the activation of the closing mechanism could ruin the continuity of the film; spiders spinning webs might ruin the view; the plant could grow out of the picture frame; electronic devices could break or glow lamps burn down. You also had to be aware of potential operational difficulties with the camera. The studios were always very warm — not unlike hothouses — and variable humidity could create problems for the optics of the camera, which might steam up.

Another equally annoying problem was that the subject might not behave in the way you had anticipated. In the 1910s, a film studio used the time-lapse technique to photograph a caterpillar transforming into a butterfly. The studio had worked on the film for a year and a half, and the second the chrysalis opened, a light cannon exploded and 18 months of work literally went up in smoke.[36]

Percy Smith managed to overcome some of these problems. He devised, for instance, an alarm bell warning him about any hindrances that might jeopardize his film work.[37]

F. Percy Smith

When a nature film expert praises a competitor, the latter is either dead or incredibly good. F. Percy Smith (1880–1945) is a case in point. Oliver G. Pike lauded him to the skies — and Smith was not only dead, he had also been a fantastic cinematographer. Pike wrote, "He produced amazingly clever nature films which have unfolded to botanists many hidden secrets" (Pike 1946, 214).

Percy Smith's first profession was as a principal in a government office. He spent his free time researching and microscoping, and he also edited a magazine called *Quekett Microscopical Club*. In addition, he was busy taking pictures of living organisms. In a continuation of his hobbies, he lectured frequently and attended a number of lectures himself. It was during one of these lectures that he became aware of "optic projection." He attended a film demonstration held by Martin-Duncan, and he realized that this medium could be used in education.[38]

Smith was one of the first film people to specialize himself within popular science nature films, and he became affiliated with the Charles Urban Trading Company in 1908. At an early stage he and Charles Urban tried to convince various public bodies of the qualities the film media had in relation to scientific work, but to no avail. Smith produced a number of popular science films on his own, and these were distributed by Kineto at the beginning of the 1910s. Smith chose a wide variety of topics for his films, but concentrated especially on microbes and plants. He achieved extraordinary results through his dazzling technical inventions and admirable patience. He adapted old equipment — and invented new devices — for his own special purposes, usually with only one assistant to help him.

Some of Smith's early films were about flies — e.g., *The Strength and Agility of Insects* (1911). The film contains shots of flies doing all sorts of "impossible" things. One fly carries a cork while sitting in a miniature chair. Another one is depicted inside a Ferris wheel. The wheel turns because the fly walks within the inner "staircase." Smith made a similar film about the bluebottle. Naturally, the flies were impossible to direct, and it took weeks to obtain the shots.

Percy Smith was one of the first people to film the opening of a flower bud. This was done by means of time-lapses. Percy shot a number of different plants, and his first time-lapse film probably depicted the opening of a hyacinth. Because it had been shot in time intervals of about 15 minutes, what you saw on the screen in fast-motion was how a plant develops a flower bud that eventually bursts open. To a contemporary audience, this was an amaz-

F. Percy Smith behind the camera, fully concentrating while standing in a pool of water (Science Museum/SSPL).

ing sight. Smith first produced a few series in black and white, but when Kinemacolor came on the market, Smith immediately understood the advantages this technique would have in the context of a flower film. Using the Kinemacolor system, he made a series of color films that premiered at the Scala Theatre under the title *Bud to Blossom*. Not until later did Kineto Ltd. release Smith's black and white films *The Birth of a Flower* and *The Germination and Plants*. It is difficult to say when these films were made, but judging from the various sources at my disposal, I believe they were produced in 1910 or 1911.

During the First World War, Smith did not produce any films on natural history. Instead, he came to work for the Royal Air Force, where he made a film about special "mystery ships" that controlled planes landing or taking off from vessels.[39]

The films that Smith produced before the war had already given him a lot of experience as well as a good reputation. For these reasons he was hired in 1925 to work as a specialist on the *Secrets of Nature* series. This was a series produced by British Instructional Film, and Smith was assigned to their department of micro-cinematography. Over the years he was to make the majority of the *Secrets of Nature* films that dealt with plant or underwater cinematography. It was a friend of Smith's, John Avery, who put him in touch with the director of *Secrets of Nature*, Harry Bruce Woolfe. Thanks to this meeting, Smith was able to make a living out of nature films.[40]

Working Conditions

In a 16-page article originally appearing in *International Review of Educational Cinematography* in 1931, Smith gives a detailed description of his methods of shooting time-lapse films and of conducting micro-cinematography. Many of the problems he encountered in his work still, according to *Oxford Scientific Films*, presented problems to cinematographers in the 1960s and '70s. For instance, Smith writes how cinematographers

> have short exposures, intense illumination and difficulties arising from the fact that by increasing amplification we correspondingly reduce the light upon the film, magnify movement and consequently exaggerate any trace of vibration. Added to this the intense light necessary for our

purpose is often distasteful, injurious or even fateful to many of the organisms whose movements we desire to record [Smith 1931, 1000].

Smith also made knowledge-imparting films. For instance, he made a motion picture about the adder, a film that was shot in a Sussex forest. Using many visual details, the film showed the teeth of the snake, how it attacked, how to handle it, and how *not* to handle it. For the purpose of illustrating the latter situation, Smith had sedated the adder with chloroform. Unfortunately, the dose was not sufficient, and the snake woke up during Smith's demonstration. It bit him, and it took weeks before he completely recovered.[41]

Smith died during the Second World War. Oliver Pike said of Smith: "The beauty of the films he has produced are a fit reward for his untiring efforts, and a lasting monument to a man who has devoted the best part of his life to revealing with the cine camera those secrets of nature" (Pike 1946, 214).

Adventure-Globetrotter Films and Hunting Films

Alfred Machin and Adam David

In 1907, the zoologist Dr. Adam David from Basel in Switzerland went to Africa as an expedition leader. He took a number of photographs during this trip. When he showed his pictures of wild animals to a gathering back in Basel, someone suggested to him that motion

From *La chasse à la panthère* (1909) (Iconothèque de la Cinémathèque française).

pictures of the animals would have been much more interesting. David quickly contacted the film company Pathé Frerès in Paris, and in December of that year he arrived in the Sudan with a loaded gun, a film camera and the cinematographer Alfred Machin, who supposedly was interested in filming wild animals. Alfred Machin (1877–1929) had begun working for Pathé Frerès the same year, and this film expedition was probably his first job for the company. Before then Machin had been a photo reporter for the weekly magazine *L'illustration*. As a young man, Machin had grown up in France, in Pas-de-Calais, or Westhove, situated close to Blendecques. Here he must have acquired the technical skills in handling a camera that later gave him a job within the world of photography.

Adam David and Machin travelled through Egypt along the Nile to the Sudan. Along the Dinder River in Sudan they filmed and hunted for five months and did not return to Europe until August 1908. During the expedition, Machin had problems with the film equipment, which was not geared for the humidity and heat of the tropic climate. The wild animals, the insects and various illnesses plagued Machin. He held out, but much of the film was destroyed, and he only brought back a few bits and pieces.

The film depicts Adam David's experiences in Africa — their trip to the Sudan, life in the camp and the big-game hunting. Among other things, it depicts how vultures and marabou storks fight over a dead body, and how a kite steals food from the camp. The big game is filmed from great distances and always during hunting events. Keeping in mind the long distances and small telephoto lenses, the animals are merely small dots on the screen.[42]

The film cannot have been a total disaster, however, for Pathé Frerès sent David and Machin on yet another hunting trip that lasted from January to August 1909. This time Machin was the director, and he had a cinematographer with him, Julien Doux. On this trip they shot more film, and the result was much better than the first

Adam David with a fleshy skull and tusks.

time around—mainly due to the fact that the film was stored in wooden boxes that were insulated with ashes. This way the film was protected against high temperatures and humidity. On the last expedition—the destination of which was East Africa, the Nile, Fachoda and Victoria lake—they hunted and filmed elephants (among other animals).[43] Among other film they made were *Dans l'Ouganda: Chasse à la Giraffe* and *La chasse à la panthère* (1909).

Alfred Machin made many more films later on—both colony films and documentaries about Holland, as well as a large number of feature films. He had developed a passion for animals, though, and in the early 1920s he made a number of brief comedies that included animals. They were dressed up in human clothes and were part of the melodrama of the films.[44]

Francis Birtles

Writing about Francis Birtles (1882–1941) is not an easy task, as little information about him exists. He was born 7 November 1882, in Melbourne, Australia. After having finished his education at South Wandin Primary School, he began an adventurous life. When he was 17 years old he had already sailed around the world twice, and was soon to be involved in the Boer War in Zululand. Around 1907 he returned to Australia, but the adventure bug was still in his system. For this reason Birtles went on a number of bicycle and car tours in his native country. They were long, tough trips without much comfort, and after Birtles had made several trips that lasted for months, the Gaumont Film Company realized the commercial value of what he was doing. In 1911 Gaumont sent a cinematographer to film one of Birtles' bicycle trips. Richard Primmer received the assignment of filming Birtles' bicycle trip from Sydney to Darwin, and Gaumont had told him to film "moving pictures of interesting scenes, incidents, studies of native life, habits and customs, kangaroo and crocodile hunting, and in fact anything of interest" (*Australia's Photo-Review* 1911, p. 295).

Apparently, the finished film incorporated a number of fictional suspense scenes. For instance, the film includes fighting scenes between a kangaroo and a dog, and between a leguana and a snake. But it also contained more authentic nature scenes, such as the shot of an emu running across the Australian plains. The

Francis Birtles was an adventurous and restless person. Here he's pictured in Arnhem Land, Australia (National Library of Australia, nla.pic-vn 3301801).

film, the length of which was 3000 feet, premiered in Melbourne in May 1912 and was entitled *Across Australia with Francis Birtles*.

Yet this was far from enough for Birtles. In 1914 he took part in a film produced by
Australasian Films Ltd. that was shot by the legendary Frank Hurley. They never managed
to finish their adventure-globetrotter journey, for Hurley received an urgent message request-
ing that he go to Buenos Aires immediately to meet with Ernest Shackleton. For this reason
Birtles and Hurley ended their journey and went to Sydney. By then they had biked 8000
miles through the wilderness of Queensland and the Northern Territory (according to writer
Frank Legg, they supposedly drove a car).

The film made during this trip was released at the beginning of 1915 as *Into Australia's
Unknown*. According to Australian film historian Ina Bertrand, *Into Australia's Unknown*
was supposedly more objective than Birtles' previous film, but as the picture no longer
exists, she judges from the contemporary articles that describe the film. Unfortunately, she
gives no actual source information about these articles. Bertrand believes that *Into Australia's
Unknown* must have included scenes depicting the lives of aboriginal peoples, as well as
scenes of the Australian flora and fauna. The film ran in Sydney and in Melbourne for two
weeks, and later appeared in Brisbane and Adelaide.

More films about the adventures of Francis Birtles were made later on, but we know
very little about these, since they (like many other films) have been lost; and, unfortunately,
I have not been able to unearth any information about their content. The films in question
are entitled *Across Australia in the Track of Burke and Wills* (1915), *Through Australian Wilds:
Across the Track of Ross Smith* (1919) and *Australia's Lonely Lands* (1924).

1911–1921
Concern for Nature Preservation

In the period 1907 to 1910 a new 230mm camera lens came on the market, making it easier for nature cinematographers to obtain high quality wildlife shots. In 1909 the magazine *The Moving Picture World* encouraged cinematographers to make authentic wildlife films as well as motion pictures from foreign parts of the world. This encouragement may well have been prompted by the work of people like William Selig, Cherry Kearton, Oliver Pike and Alfred Machin. With its didactic and enlightening content, the knowledge-imparting film actually developed much earlier than previously thought by film historians, and this period is characterized by major developments and ingenuity within nature film — as is evident especially in the work of F. Percy Smith in the fields of microscope and time-lapse cinematography.

Nineteen-eleven to nineteen-twenty-one was a period in which cinema interiors reached grandiose proportions, in some cases holding several thousand people. Many expedition and hunting films shot in Africa and the Arctic regions were made at this time, but it was also a period of changing attitudes, creating the foundation and need for wildlife and wilderness films that preserved nature — i.e., films that did not display the mere killing of animals or destruction of natural environment, but rather focused directly on the problems facing the environment.

The Development of the Period

Cine-Cameras

The Debrie Parvo camera had been developed in Paris as early as 1908, but it was expensive and not used widely until around 1914 (the same year it was exported to Britain). The Debrie had room for a film magazine containing 400 feet of film and included an automatic winding mechanism. It was the smallest professional camera on the market. The wooden model weighed 15 pounds, whereas the aluminium model weighed 18 pounds. The size made it easy to bring on travels. Moreover, the means of adjusting the focus were fast and easy to use, which made it ideal for wildlife cinematography. The camera's solid construction and ready handle made it especially suited for extreme conditions (for example, polar expeditions where it worked even in temperatures of minus 40 degrees).[1] It should be mentioned, though, that the handle was sometimes a disadvantage because it made it difficult to pan the camera during shooting.

The Debrie camera was well suited to slow-motion cinematography. The cinematographer simply turned the handle two or three times a second, and the camera reached its maximum projection speed of 240 pictures a second. At this time films were usually shown at 16 pictures per second, and thus 4 minutes of shooting at maximum speed was enough for one minute of projection of slow-motion shots.

A reconstructed Debrie Parvo (Danmarks Fotomuseum; photograph by author).

In 1911 a Polish inventor called Kasimir Proszynski invented the Aeroscope-Camera. It was run by a compressor, consisting of a hand or foot pump. The pump, similar to a bicycle pump, supplied air current to a small air-driven motor. The Aeroscope camera was easy to use and came without a handle. One pump was enough to drive the full capacity (450 feet) of the camera reel. The diaphragm was set automatically, and through a peephole you could see the level of the remaining air in the camera. Not only was it easy to use and maintain, the special mechanics of the camera meant that it was fairly quiet too.

The cameras of those days could not be handheld, partly because most of them were operated by means of a handle, and partly because the cinematographer's breathing would be transmitted onto the picture as small, rocking movements. The Aeroscope Camera compensated for all of this. It had a gyroscopic wheel that stabilized the picture when the camera was handheld. The mechanism was termed an "Equilibrator" and made sure that all minor rocking movements were swallowed up by an inner stabilizer — a gyroscopic head inside the camera and the tripod effectively reduced movements. The head also made the camera movements seem softer and smoother. For this reason it was suited to the filming of wild animals. The Warwick Trading Company produced the camera for a few years, until in 1921 a new model arrived on the market. It was produced by Eracam Ltd. and had rechargeable batteries.[2]

The Aeroscope camera of Kasimir Proszynski from 1911.

A Bell & Howell camera was the first to have a battery-driven motor, and the first camera to feature an all-metal body. The camera body was of aluminum construction and weighed 4 pounds. Together with lens and film magazine, it weighed 6 pounds; but the total weight of a Bell & Howell (including all accessories, as well as the tripod) was almost 25 pounds. It cost around $2000 and (probably due to the price) was not widely used until 1914 — two years after it came on the market.

The Bell & Howell camera had the advantage of four lenses with different focal points that could rotate in a carousel. This meant that it was possible to shift between different focal points within a few seconds. This is naturally an advantage when dealing with wild animals when a few seconds can mean everything. Moreover, the large film chambers of the Bell & Howell Camera was advantageous, as it made it possible to film for a long time without changing the reel.

Lenses

According to Barry Salt, short focal point lenses were not marketed until 1912. These were Zeis lenses with focal points of some 35mm; but not until the early days of the sound film were wide-angle lenses (i.e., less than 30mm) marketed. Light-sensitive lens construction was gradually developed in the period between 1914 and 1918, when Zeis Tessar produced a lens with an aperture of f 3.5. Around the First World War, Cooke produced telephoto lenses of 300mm and 430mm.[3]

The Tripod

Akeley's gyroscopic system of connecting tripod and camera was marketed in 1918. This system was also used by other manufacturers from around 1926 when the frictional ball and socket head, True Ball, appeared on the market. It was worked by hand through the use of an extended arm — and this is still the case today. In this way it could perform whatever combination of pans and tilts the cinematographer wished to make. With an inner friction knob one could adjust the speed with which the arm moved; this way the movements became smoother.

Exhibition Venues

In countries like the USA, Great Britain, France and Denmark, the interiors of the exhibition venues became increasingly elaborate. The major venues were called picture palaces, and the interior design of these certainly lived up to the name, for some of them could accommodate an audience of two or three thousand people. Despite the extravagance of these places, heavy competition made sure that the ticket price remained more or less unchanged.

On 29 September 1911, the Gau-

A lens carrousel on the later Bell & Howell Eyemo. This model only had three lenses (Danmarks Fotomuseum; photograph by author).

mont Company opened The Gaumont Palace in Paris — the first really extravagant film theater, which, at the opening, is said to have been the largest in the world, with a seating capacity of 3400.

In America, picture palaces opened all over the country due to the success of the Strand Theatre in New York; and in Denmark, Paladsteatret opened on 17 October 1912. It was beautifully and luxuriously decorated, and accommodated some 2500 people and a 30-piece orchestra, whose music accompanied the films.

This new initiative within show business made life difficult for the shop cinemas in the cities, and they were gradually outflanked by the big venues that could afford the latest attractions and still manage to maintain a cheap entry fee.[4]

Rainey's Hunting Trip and Other Hunting Films

Paul J. Rainey (1877–1923) was a rich businessman and sportsman from Philadelphia who often went big game hunting. You might well call him trigger-happy — during a 35-day safari, he and his party shot 27 lions.

In 1910 Rainey went on an arctic expedition, during which he not only killed animals but brought back live ones: two walruses, six musk oxen and two polar bears. Four months after this expedition, in 1911, Rainey went on yet another hunting trip; the destination this time was Mombassa, and the trip, which was privately financed, cost $250,000. Rainey brought the cinematographer John Hemment with him, who obtained some good shots of animals by leaving bait around in the form of carcasses, and filming the animals when they came to feed. Another method of his was to film the animals when they approached the water holes to drink. Hemment managed to shoot 1640 feet of film, which was used in the production of *Paul J. Rainey's African Hunt* (1912), a picture which incidentally also contains material shot by Carl Akeley during an expedition to East Africa between 1909 and 1910. The film was greeted with interest in the press:

> The photographs are bright and clear, and as good as it is possible to make in the bright tropical sunlight. Moreover the views we get of the various animals are not the short and irritating glimpses that have heretofore characterized wild animal pictures. Each view gives a good, long look at the various animals [*The Moving Picture World*, Apr. 20, 1912, 214].

The importance of this review lies in the fact that it concentrates on the film's representation of wilderness and wildlife, and the fact that the viewer is as interested in the animals themselves as in the hunt. The film consists of eight reels that depict scenes from various stages of the expedition — scenes from camp life and the hunting of lions and rhinos. The most interesting scenes are the ones shot around the water holes. These include fine shots of zebras, rhinoceroses, giraffes, gazelles, elands and boars. The individual shots are long, and I believe that they were shot with a lens with a focal point of 100mm at most. The impressive number of animals that stop by the watering hole is really fascinating, and the reviewer quoted above makes the following remark: "To see all these creatures together on one picture is a remarkable sight; one that will interest any man, woman or child" (*TMPW*, Apr. 20, 1912, 215).

The Films

The focal points of the lenses that Hemment used cannot have been much bigger than 100mm, and this means that he must have been fairly close to the animals, especially the elephants and rhinoceroses (maybe 80 to 100 feet). The film also includes pans of scenery and animals, and these pans are incredibly beautiful.

One dramatic sequence in particular is worth mentioning: A hyena has been caught in a trap, which is obviously a very painful experience. After a while some men arrive with a wooden box. It takes some time, but eventually they manage to get the struggling animal into the box. The scene is quite dramatic — not because of the editing, but because of the situation itself, the hyena fighting for its life.

Paul J. Rainey, a rich hunter (Library of Congress, LC-B2-3126-6).

The mixture of dramatic entertainment, the natural behavior of the animals and a light informative style made *Paul J. Rainey's African Hunt* a box-office hit. Not only did the film bring in money, it also created an enormous interest in the African continent, and *Paul J. Rainey's African Hunt* was to become the best-selling nature film of the entire decade. In New York alone the picture ran in the cinemas for 15 months, and Carl Laemmle, who distributed the film, made half a million dollars on it.[5]

Two years later Paul Rainey made a sequel to his first Africa film, but it was not as successful as the first. *Rainey's African Hunt* (1914) was made during a later big game hunt in Africa, and took up 9 film reels. If you read the contemporary reviews of the film, it seems strange that Rainey's second picture was not as popular as the first one: "His second series, now on exhibition, is more remarkable than the first, for he has got closer to his game" (*The Independent*, Aug. 31, 1914, 313).

The explanation probably lies in its lack of newness. The film crew may have gotten closer to the animals, but summaries of the film indicate that the storyline was the same: setting up the expedition, the water hole, animals attacking, animals being hunted.

Terry Ramsaye praises Rainey's films for paving the way for more elaborate, longer pictures, such as Flaherty's *Nanook of the North* (1922) and Cooper and Schoedsack's *Grass* (1925). Many others have praised the films of Hemment and Rainey.* Thus, Kevin Brownlow writes that "viewing this material, one can see why the Rainey film had so much more of

---

*For more praising comments, see. Dench 1919, p. 119 and Ramsaye 1926, p. 600.

an impact than anything before it" (Brownlow 1978, 406). Apart from their length, however, I do not believe that Rainey's pictures were epoch-making in and of themselves. I believe that Laemmle's marketing led them to be distributed in a manner not previously seen, exposing them to a wider audience.

Many of the shots in Rainey's films were overexposed, the cinematographer having employed long-shots for the majority of the animal scenes, and it is not possible to see the features of the animals (which was often the case with zoo films). There are exceptions, though, like the aforementioned shots of elephants, and also various depictions of animals that are either dead or behind bars. However, Rainey and Hemment really understood the importance of drama. In *Paul J. Rainey's African Hunt* for instance, Rainey lifts up a lion's head, grabbing hold of the animal by the ears. There is also the aforementioned hyena scene, as well as a sequence in which Hemment has moved quite close to a dying rhinoceros, so that the viewer may be able to "enjoy" its final muscle spasms.

Around 1914, people in some circles had become tired of hunting films. They believed that hunting films and other films about animals had become too dominant in the market. This is evident from an article in a German cinema magazine from 1914: "No one wants to see films of lions anymore — at least not if they are paraded as mere show pieces. But the wild animals of regular hunting films have lost some of their charm, too" (*Kino-Variété*, July 25, 1914, 63).

Around this time, the hunting film underwent significant changes — changes that were to become regular conventions within the genre and helped keep the genre alive. Most importantly, the hunting film cinematographers learned to incorporate narrative techniques into their motion pictures so that the excitement and tension of the hunt was evident in the film itself. Naturally, this meant that some of the scenes had to be directed; it also meant that you had to provoke or tease the animals so that they appeared fiery and aggressive in the finished film. The result was that the animal became stressed and was ready to attack.

At this point in time, several conventions of the hunting film genre were falling into place. Using various small tricks was becoming acceptable — for instance, to construct a plot and thus create continuity in the film. In other words, cinematographers would film inauthentic scenes in order to put together a story in the editing room. It had also become standard procedure to provoke the wild animals so that they appeared more threatening than they actually were. This could be done by throwing stones or shouting at them to get their attention. When they started to become irritated or to attack, the hunter made ready to shoot.

Any ethically acceptable reason one could come up with legitimized the killing of the animal. It is well known that some film crews kept animals in large enclosures from which they could not escape. Naturally this stressed the animals and made them likely to attack anything that moved. All this was arranged to create an image of dangerous wild animals and fearless white hunters.

That the animals were being subjected to "artificial" stress is proven beyond doubt both in the films themselves and in the biographies of directors and cinematographers. Naturally, one example is Martin Johnson, but similar accounts are to be found in the books and films of the German director Karl Heinz Boeses. For instance, in the 1926 book *Zum Schneegipfel Afrikas* (*To the Snowy Summit of Africa*), Boeses claims that it is necessary to show the actual killing of the wild animal in order to give the sensation-lusting audience what they want. Boeses even states that to obtain one shot it was necessary to throw stones at a lazy rhinoceros.[6] This helped create a preconceived notion among ordinary people that wild predators were evil, man-eating beasts. Not until well into the 1930s did this attitude towards animals begin to change. It has not completely disappeared, however, as one comes across this attitude even today.

Among the films that helped change this "convention" was Hans Schomburgk's *Das letzte Paradies* (*The Last Paradise*). You might say that a new type of hunting film was invented here — a kind of subgenre to the subgenre — that focused not on the hunt or the killing of an animal, but on the divine beauty of nature. The hunt is still present in the film, but it plays a much smaller role. The same goes for his film *Mensch und Tier im Urwald* (*Man and Animal in the Primeval Forest*). The film contains only two hunting scenes; these have a fine narrative structure, making use of the continuity principle. The rest of the picture depicts the jungle in a much more peaceful manner than had been the case in previous hunting films; here more attention is paid to insects and birdlife, and the overall atmosphere is one of idyll and romance.

Maybe it is no coincidence that around the same time, what we might call the "classic wildlife film" was taking form. The classic nature film was rooted in the educational films of the 1910s; the genre developed steadily through the 20s, and by the 1930s they had become a "convention" in their own right. The camera captured the untouched and undisturbed nature that man had seemingly never been in contact with before and which existed in a world of its own. The frame was the world of the animal — a paradise where noble savages and wildlife roamed free. A classic example is *Urwaldsymphonie* (1931) by Schomburgk.

The Great Polar Cinematographers

Frank Hurley

THE ROAD TO NATURE FILM

According to film historian Ina Bertrand, James Francis (Frank) Hurley (1885–1962) was the most important non-fiction film producer in Australia from 1910 until the outbreak of the Second World War. Frank Hurley grew up in the Sydney suburb of Glebe. His father, Edward Harrison Hurley, was born in England. He worked as a typographer, first at *The Sydney Morning Herald*, and later for the governmental Printing Office. Hurley's home was a typical working class home.

Frank Hurley ran away from home when he was only 13 years old and found a job in a smithy. After a while, he contacted his parents and told them where he was. Afterwards, his father sent him a letter that introduced a motto that was to become a staple in Hurley's life. Edward Hurley wrote, "If you tackle all life's problems with the optimism and determination you have shown recently, there is nothing you might not achieve.... If you can't find a way, make one" (Legg 1966, 6).

As a 17-year-old, Frank Hurley set himself his first goal: he wanted to become a really good photographer. He bought a Kodak box camera. As he did not have enough money, the camera was paid for in instalments, and he decided to learn all the secrets of the camera. He read everything he could find about photography, and practiced as much as he could.

After only one year, he earned his first paying job as a photographer. It was an advertising assignment for the Edison Phonograph Company that was setting up an office in Sydney. Hurley soon developed a good reputation.

One of his early achievements was the expedition film *Home of the Blizzard* (1913). The film was shot during Sir Douglas Mawson's Australian-Antarctica expedition of 1911–1912. Apparently Hurley did not get the assignment due to his qualifications as a photographer, nor to his cinematography skills (of which, as a matter of fact, he had none whatsoever). There were applications from well-qualified people who had experience with both photography and cinematography, but Mawson is supposed to have chosen Hurley because he showed initiative during his interview. When asked if he could cook, Hurley had answered, "I can cook, marsh, pull sledges, sew sails, design clothes, and forge iron" (Legg 1966, 10–1).

Hurley took photographs and filmed during the expedition, but I found few clues as to his subjects. He is supposed to have taken some good pictures of king penguins and elephant seals, but the working conditions were next to impossible. The film camera became stuck all the time and was unfit for the climatic conditions. Indeed, it was not easy to move around with a camera that could only take decent shots when fitted onto a tripod, and which weighed some 80 pounds. Nonetheless, Hurley succeeded in filming some extraordinary shots of an Antarctic tempest — a tempest that he filmed from behind a wall built of snow and stones.

Once Hurley was back from the expedition, the film material was quickly edited, and in August 1913 it was presented at a public showing in Sydney. The film was eventually shown all over the world and achieved much recognition. One of the people who saw it was a famous Brit — Ernest Shackleton — a fact which was to prove significant for Hurley's career.

Frank Hurley, around 1915.

HURLEY AS FILMMAKER

Shortly after his return from Antarctica, Hurley got a job at Australasian Films Ltd., which was to throw new adventures his way: he received the assignment to accompany the adventurer Francis Birtles and to film his experiences in the Northern Territory and the Gulf of Carpentaria. According to the biographer Frank Legg, they travelled around in a Ford, they slept in a tent and cooked their own food. They set out from Sydney on 14 April 1914, and went on a strenuous journey through the Australian wilderness. They were supposed to film aboriginals, but they also filmed thousands of tropical birds, boars, cone-shaped anthills and a crocodile hunt. Hurley is even said to have filmed crocodiles mating. Hurley's trip was cut short when a currier arrived with the message that new adventures lay ahead for the young cinematographer. The message came from Sir Ernest Henry Shackleton (1874–1922), who was leading a new Antarctic expedition. Frank Hurley had been chosen as the official photographer and cinematographer of the expedition, a choice Shackleton had made because a sponsor of the expedition (who had invested £20,000) had seen *Home of the Blizzard* and insisted that Hurley join the expedition. The Francis Birtles film was finished nonetheless. Its title was *Into Australia's Unknown*.

In October 1914 the ship *Endurance* set sail from Buenos Aires for Antarctica. The expedition did not go as planned, however, as the *Endurance* became irretrievably stuck in the inland ice. The crew stayed on the ship for 9 months; and eventually the ship's condition became so bad that the crew had to leave it and set up camp on the ice. Once the ice melted, it smashed the *Endurance* to pieces. But Shackleton was an incredible expedition leader and managed to save his crew through his drive and expertise.

For Frank Hurley, the loss of the *Endurance* was particularly distressful, for most of his film footage was lost. Most of the shots depicted wildlife; among these were some amazing shots of elephant seals. After a legendary rescue, the shipwrecked expedition finally reached civilization. Hurley and the film's sponsor, Perris, edited a first version of the material that had survived the trip, and the film was shown in London in 1916. Hurley was far from satisfied with the result; the wildlife scenes were missing, as were scenes shot from Southern Georgia. Yet, Perris let him go on another trip.

In Southern Georgia Hurley stayed at a whaling station, and using this as his base, he managed to film king penguins, albatrosses, storm petrels and elephant seals. He exposed both still photographs and the moving pictures in the station manager's bathroom. Hurley returned in the summer of 1917, and shortly afterwards the first official film from the expedition was released in England: *In the Grip of the Polar Pack-Ice* (1917). The film was very successful in Britain and Australia, where Hurley went on a lecture tour.[7]

The fact that both *Home of the Blizzard* and *In the Grip of the Polar Pack-Ice* had been filmed in an uninhabited landscape, and in a harsh, inhuman climate, meant that the pictures had an inherent drama and a latent sense of tension. Again and again Hurley returned to situations and places that offered such an inherent tension.

Around 1919, Hurley went on an adventure-globetrotter expedition to Papua New Guinea, which at this time was part of Australian territory. Hurley is supposed to have exaggerated his experiences on this trip in order to attract the attention of the press. He claimed, for instance, that the areas they had travelled through had been completely unexplored, and that he had filmed rituals that had never been seen by any white man before. In reality, he never ventured very far into the jungle. His exaggeration also had to do with the apparent dangers that lurked in the unknown territory. He claimed that cannibals had been a constant source of anxiety. Later, Hurley toured the small islands of the Torres Strait (Moa, Saibai, Boiga, Thursday, etc.) and filmed the lives of native peoples as well as the wildlife of the islands. The film material was extensive — at the end of the trip he had almost 22,000 feet and had taken some 1,200 photographs. He brought a special camera with him that could be used under water. His intention was to film the Japanese pearl-divers.

Hurley had major difficulties with the diving dress that he used during his first underwater filming. He once told the following story:

---

*The film was later renamed *The Endurance*.

Penguins at the wreck of the *Gratitude*, Macquarie Island, 1911 (photograph Frank Hurley).

> A singing in the ears, a suffocating sensation, and I touched the bottom. Impulsively opening the valve for more air, I felt myself growing invisibly larger, my suit inflated, and, like a submerged cork let go, I turned a somersault and sped to the surface head down! The appearance of two feet on the surface provoked much laughter aboard the lugger.

But Hurley did not give up, and after a number of dives he had many wonderful experiences in the undersea coral world, some of which may be seen in *Pearls and Savages*.

All the material from the trip was used to make the film *Pearls and Savages* (1921), a picture that was met with enthusiastic reviews both from critics and the press in general. Andrew Pike has called *Pearls and Savages* Australia's greatest documentary in the 1920s. The film is said to have added both sensation and romance to its main theme, and Hurley's beautiful camera work is said to have been of a much higher quality than most other Australian non-fiction films of this period.[8] Two years later, Hurley added some shots from Fly River and Lake Murray, hand-colored the film, and gave it the new title *With the Head Hunters in Papua*.

Working with Nature Film

Frank Hurley is said to have done most of the work for the films himself— except for the actual editing. This he left to others. At least, this is the impression I have gotten from the sources available to me.

Hurley's photographic speciality was compositions of impressive cloud formations and various subjects placed in direct contrast to a dramatic background He experimented with these motifs by composing two individual pictures in a double exposure (these pictures became popular as postcards). Not until much later in his life, when he became more experienced, did he manage to transfer this technique to the film medium. The visual artist in Frank Hurley had a good understanding of the effects and significance of light in a composition, and he was talented both in regards to technique and composition; but his artistic capabilities rarely shined through in his early films. The focuses in his early films are flat; indeed, they consist of banal compositions that are put together into independent focuses. But he became better at this. In the beginning, Hurley was not good at building narrative in his films, nor was he good at using the continuity principle. This did not matter much when the films were used as part of his lecture tours, however, for Hurley was a very competent lecturer. His dynamic rhetoric added the action and excitement that his films lacked.

According to historian Andrew Pike, Hurley was a self-promoting man who fabricated exciting stories about himself for the public; he often presented himself as a regular daredevil who got into one dramatic or extreme situation after another. Unfortunately, these situations were usually made-up and did not fit with the events mentioned in Hurley's own private diary. His sensational stories drew a lot of attention to his persona in the press, and this way he generated publicity and interest for his films and his later adventure-globetrotter expeditions. Naturally, the premier of *Pearls and Savages* in Sydney was somewhat extraordinary — the film was accompanied by Papua New Guinea songs, and the composer, Emmanuel Aarons, had composed a special piece for the occasion. Hurley gave a lecture during the film — which included a staged attack from a group of cannibals. The Sydney show took up an entire evening and was so successful that Hurley later toured with it, first in Australia and later in both England and the United States. In America, he first toured in 1923; the film was introduced under a new, Americanized title: *The Lost Tribe*. Many Americans were enthusiastic about Hurley's sensationalism, and one reviewer described the show as "the greatest travel film that has ever come to America" (Legg 1966, 130).

AFTER 1928

The films he worked on may not be characterized as wilderness and wildlife films in the purest sense, but they nonetheless incorporated nature and wildlife scenes. Some examples are *The Ross Smith Flight* (1919), which is said to have been very creatively edited, and *Siege of the South* (1930), yet another film from Antarctica. His first sound film was a beautiful depiction of the Isle of Lord Howe in *Jewel of the Pacific* (1931). After having worked for a number of years as a cameraman on feature films, Hurley made the tourist film *Oasis* (1936), as well as another beautiful film called *Treasures of Katoomba* (1937). He also filmed a couple of tourist films for Tasmania, but his most successful and "perfect" film from the 1930s is no doubt *A Nation Is Built* (1938), about Australia. During the Second World War, Hurley filmed in the Middle East, and much of his work became part of *Dessert Victory* (Boulting and McDonald, 1943).

Hurley also directed a feature film, *The Jungle Woman* (1926), a picture which could be called reality's predecessor to *King Kong*. Hurley brought a film crew, including actors, to New Guinea. The leading actress (Grace Savieri) had to go through strange ordeals on the island, coping with the humidity of the jungle, vermin and mosquitoes. During some

A sledge dog pup (photograph by Frank Hurley).

shots, her co-stars were leeches. In other words, the actual shooting took place in a real jungle, which she found very disturbing. Among other things, she had to swim in water full of crocodiles and snakes, and in one scene she had to stand underwater and breathe through a bamboo cane. Everything was shot on location in New Guinea![9]

Hurley had three children — two girls and a boy — but for long stretches of time he did not see much of them. He traveled a lot and remained an active filmmaker until he died.

Herbert George Ponting

THE ROAD TO NATURE FILM

When he was 18 years old, Herbert G. Ponting (1870–1935) tried to follow in his father's footsteps and became a banker, but after only four years he gave up this career and went to the west coast of America instead. He bought a ranch and became partner in a goldmine. In 1895, Ponting married Mary B. Elliot, with whom he had two children, and for a while the family moved back and forth between California and London. In 1904, Ponting left his wife, according to film historian Dennis Lynch, because he was not able to cope with a family *and* at the same time have an artistic career.[10] Ponting's career in photography had commenced in 1900. He won several photography competitions early on, and his eye for composition, as well as his expertise in photography, led to several paid assignments. Apart from a three year stint in Japan, he was sent on assignments all over the world by various American magazines. Thus, he took pictures of the summit of Mont Blanc in

Herbert Ponting in Antarctica.

France, as well as the Jungfrau in Switzerland, and he had some harrowing experiences in Siberia.

During all these travels, Ponting wrote several travel letters that were published in popular magazines. In these, Ponting displayed a talent for evocative descriptions of his dangerous experiences (for example, coming across a group of crocodiles outside Calcutta in 1907).*[11] From 1905, Ponting became a member of the Royal Geographic Society in London.

THE CAREER TAKES SHAPE

Ponting had an amazing understanding of picture composition, and relatively quickly he became a household name within the world of photography. It is said that "he was considered to be the greatest outdoor cameraman in the world." His reputation and his professionalism were no doubt instrumental in getting Ponting on Scott's expedition. Although Ponting was a very capable photographer, he had never laid his hands on a film camera before the deal was signed between himself, Scott and Gaumont Pictures, who were to distribute the film. Before the expedition, Arthur Newman (the camera manufacturer of the Newman-Sinclair) had given Ponting some brief instruction on the use of a film camera. These did not at all frighten Ponting, who later wrote, "I found no difficulty in mastering it, as it was merely a question of applying the technique, gained during the lifetime of the study of photography" (Ponting 1914, 235–6).

On 10 June 1910, the *Terra Nova* set sail from London. On board were the members of Scott's Antarctic expedition. Their first destination was Australia. Ponting brought two film cameras, a Newman-Sinclair model No. 3 and a J.A. Prestwich. Moreover, he brought a number of lenses and a tripod from Theodite. Ponting did not squander any material, for the total amount of film used during the entire expedition was no more than 25,000 feet.[12]

WORKING WITH NATURE FILM

Ponting would risk his life when it came to getting the best possible composition, and in the bitter cold of Antarctica he went through many rough ordeals. On one occasion he lost a piece of his tongue when it touched the icy metal on the camera. On another occasion he got into trouble with a seal: "It suddenly evinced the most determined objections to the proceedings and lunging out at me, it seized hold of my leg, throwing me to the ground. Its teeth went through all my clothes and drew blood" (*Scientific American*, June 21, 1913, 568).

Due to the climate, Ponting had to wear big gloves, and also had to pay acute attention to the "well-being" of the camera. Static electricity was difficult to avoid, and the parts of the camera that used oil often froze. Condensed water was another major problem. In order to avoid condensation getting into the camera house and onto the film, he never put the camera inside the cabin. The finished film that was ready to be exposed had to be gradually acclimated to higher temperatures; likewise, new film from the magazine had to be acclimated to the outdoor temperatures — a process that took about two days. Onboard the ship, Ponting had his own film exposure laboratory, where he used an exposure machine

*This is evident e.g. in the 1908 article "Photographing Alligators" by H. G. Ponting in *Scientific American Supplement* 65, pp. 353–354. I call them crocodiles in my text, as there are no wild alligators in India. Alligators live in Cuba, Southeast USA and in China.

developed by Newman-Sinclair. According to Ponting, it took some 100 hours to expose all the film.

As is well known, the expedition ended in tragedy. First of all, Roald Amundsen beat Scott's expedition to the South Pole, and Scott had to plant the British flag next to the Norwegian one. Secondly, the four members of the expedition who had gone on dog sledge to the Pole (including Scott) died. The last pages of Scott's diary, found next to his body, describe their final days. On the way back from the Pole, the team had to set up camp due to a terrible storm, and Scott knew that this was the end: "Had we lived, I should have had a tale to tell of the hardihood, endurance and courage of my companions which would have stirred the heart of every Englishman. These rough notes and our dead bodies must tell the tale" (Scott 1912).

Ponting was not a part of the team that went to the Pole. Rather, he was to spend his life honoring the dead members of the expedition. Ponting made it back to London unharmed, but already in May 1911, 8000 feet of film had been sent to England, where it was edited into the first official film from the expedition: *With Captain Scott, RN, to the South Pole* (1911).*[13]

In 1913, Ponting's finished film was distributed by Gaumont under the title *The Undying Story of Captain Scott*. The title was meant as a tribute to the expedition leader who had died so tragically in a harsh and inhuman climate. Even before the film was finished, Talbot described it as "possibly the greatest triumph of scenic cinematography" (Talbot 1912, 127). He was probably referring to the fact that no matter the quality, the film would document the expedition and the experiences of the crew members, providing authentic shots from an adventure that had gone terribly wrong.

The year after the release of *The Undying Story of Captain Scott*, Herbert Ponting bought the rights to the film material for £5000. He used the film in his lectures, during which he also showed a number of slides he had taken during the expedition. In 1917 he replaced the early film versions with a re-edited one to which had been added diagrams, drawings and maps depicting an exact reconstruction of the route to the South Pole, as well as the final resting place of the deceased members of the expedition. Kevin Brownlow commented on this version, "The arrival at Ross Island and the kind of life led by the expedition is celebrated by Ponting with a graphic excellence rare in early films of fact" (Brownlow 1978, 433).

FILM MATERIAL FROM THE SCOTT EXPEDITION

It was difficult both for Ponting and the equipment to function in an average temperature of minus 30 degrees. The harsh climatic conditions made the waiting for the best animal scenes a regular trial for Ponting, both physically and psychologically. Nonetheless, he managed to get many shots of Adelie penguins, Weddell seals, killer whales and arctic skuas. The shots detailing the behavior of the penguins are interesting, for they illustrate animal behavior over a long period of time. The film covers, for instance, courting, nesting, the hatching of eggs and skuas stealing penguin eggs. It is obvious from the shots that Ponting was in Antarctica for quite a while; to begin with, we see the Adelie penguin hatching her eggs, and later we see the young ones at their "swimming lessons."

---

*A version that was later changed — the first time this happened was in August 1912 and later in September of the same year.

One of Ponting's stills from Scott's expedition: the *Terra Nova* in an ice-eye.

Sometimes the waiting did become too long, as when Ponting wanted to film a gull stealing a penguin's egg. He waited and waited, and finally felt obliged to step in: "I finally decided that the incident would have to be 'produced'—just as any drama film is produced—and the various characters concerned would have to be made to play their parts" (Ponting 1921, 247). Ponting forced the penguin to leave the nest. Then he waited for the gull to snap up the egg, which it naturally tried to do; but as soon as Ponting started turning the handle, the gull gave up the endeavour and took flight. No doubt, from that point on, Ponting longed for a noiseless camera.

Ponting toured with *The Great White Silence* for many years, but sources suggest that the success of the lectures gradually declined, and only few people turned up in the end. For instance, six lectures in the Philharmonic Hall in London had to be cancelled because not enough tickets were sold. Despite this, Ponting continued his lectures. Indeed, he made two sound versions of the film, the most famous one being *90° South* (1933). Herbert Ponting died in 1935 after many bitter years during which he had suffered severe economic losses.[14]

From Hunting to Nature Preserving Films

My compiled list of films contains eight hunting films from the period 1911 to 1921. Seven of those were made from 1911 to 1915. I have found only five hunting films made in the period 1916 to 1928, which indicates that the popularity of this genre gradually declined. The large number of hunting films produced in the early part of the period (1911–1915) might be seen as a reaction on behalf of filmmakers to the public interest in Roosevelt's hunting expedition to Africa. At any rate, the majority of the hunting films were shot in Africa.

Apart from the already mentioned Paul Rainey, there were a number of other adventurous hunters and cinematographers who were keen to make films about Africa, its wildlife, and themselves (which of these subjects proved to be the strongest motivator, I will not hazard a guess).

J.C. Hemment, who had been the cinematographer for Rainey's Africa film, returned from his own personal African journey towards the end of 1914. Hemment had exposed some 249,343 feet of film on African wildlife and indigenous peoples. Among other things, the film depicted buffaloes and rhinoceroses.[15]

Harold Sintzenich was cinematographer for a rich woman on her hunting expedition to Africa, and this led to *Lady Mackenzie in Africa* (1915). Structurally, it is quite an ordinary hunting film depicting the usual scenes of wildlife being killed (rhinoceroses and lions). Its only unusual feature is the fact that the hunter is a woman.[16]

Hunting films did not all take place in Africa; a number of them were about the Polar regions. *Kleinschmidt: Arctic Hunt* (1911) and *Captain F.E. Kleinschmidt's Arctic Hunt* (1914) are prime examples. However, the typical hunting film soon began to come under severe criticism. More and more people considered the mass killings that took place during these film expeditions to be tasteless and meaningless. For this reason, hunting films which did not actually depict any killings began to appear—but "killing-free" hunting films did incorporate some form of hunt. One example is *Lassoing Wild Animals* (1911), where the lasso was used instead of a rifle. Another example is a series that was produced by Hepworth

Harry Whitney (left) and Paul J. Rainey (right) c. 1910 (Library of Congress, LC-B2-1067-4).

American Film Corporation and launched under the title *Blinkhorn Natural History Travels*. The bloodless films were often marketed as educational pictures full of excitement. *Blinkhorn Natural History Travels* contained all the typical elements of this kind of educational film. What is meant by the word "typical" I will illustrate by the following example: In one film we see a cinematographer being lowered on a rope down a steep rock in order to film a gull colony. This shot is followed by close-ups of a nest and the nestlings inside it, which is followed by shots depicting different stages in their development towards adulthood. This method is repeated with scenes of pelicans and cormorants. In addition, there are shots of seals, sea lions and elephant seals. All of the footage was filmed off the coast of California and Guadalupe. The series also includes a crucial moment of tension. This occurs in a film called *The Capture of a Sea Elephant* (1914). It had been the intention of the filmmakers to kill a sea elephant and bring back its skin, but instead it was decided to catch the animal alive — which, as we know, was in keeping with the spirit of the times. Shooting the sea lion would only take a second, but struggling to catch it alive would take much longer. A critic at *The Moving Picture World* was enthusiastic: "The roping and caging of the big fellow forms one of the most interesting incidents in a film filled with good things.... [It] will do more than entertain any audience. It will instruct" (May 2, 1914, 675).

Other wildlife preservation films followed. Edward A. Salisbury produced *American Animal Pictures*, which differed from the usual hunting films in that the animals were not killed *en masse*. At least one critic at *The Independent* was in favor of this new trend:

The scenes showing the hunting of the mountain lions and the lynx and various species of bear look well on the screen because the author has avoided all wounding or killing of animals and devoted his whole energies to recording their traits and characteristics [June 14, 1915, 484].

Indeed, I have come across a lot of material supporting my argument that people were tired of films about animals being killed for the mere pleasure of the hunter and the camera. When *Captain F. E. Kleinschmidt's Arctic Hunt* was released in 1914, not one word was mentioned about the killing of animals in the reviews I have read. *The Independent* stresses the fact that Kleinschmidt succeeded in showing a number of Arctic animals in their respective biotopes and praises the method: "Is among the most valuable of this class of films because of its sincere and successful effort to show how the animals live" (Oct. 5, 1914, 23). *The Moving Picture World* pointed to similar features of the film: "He has caught caribou and moose and brown deer and bears and porcupines in their native habitats and at close range when they fancied themselves unobserved" (Feb. 21, 1914, 956).

People also draw attention to this film due to its educational value — not only in terms of wildlife, but also in terms of nature and culture. Among other things, the film shows volcanic activities in Alaska, the glaciers, and the government's successful releasing of salmon and reindeer. But most of the film is still about the wildlife, and found here are some of the moments of excitement mentioned earlier. Just like in *Capture of a Sea Elephant*, these scenes depict the capturing of animals by means of a rope.

Denmark — Richard Lund

The Road to Nature Film

When the press became acquainted with a number of new Danish nature films they were immensely impressed. One reviewer from *Kinobladet* commented: "We have had the opportunity to see some of these animal films that have not been released yet, and we do not recall ever having spent more jolly times in front of the screen" (1921, no. 21, 664–5). The majority of the other critics agreed. In *Dansk Arbejde*, a reviewer wrote, "The amount of scenes that director and cinematographer have managed to secure is admirable. The pictures are works of art" (April 1, 1921).

Judging from comments like these, Denmark might well have become one of the major nature film producing countries — maybe even of the same calibre as Britain, America or Sweden, countries that have a strong nature film tradition going back to the beginning of the 20th century. But this was not to be the case. And what films were the critics raving about? Who made them and why did the "fairytale" of Danish nature films end?

Between 1919 and 1932, Filmfabriken Danmark (Film Factory Denmark) produced no fewer than 28 short films about biological topics, as well as 5 ethnographic films. Behind these motion pictures were the director of the company, Kay van der A. A. Kühle, and his friend and employee Richard Lund. The films had been shot by, among others, Ludvig Lippert, Richard Lund and H. F. Rimmen, who had been one of Arctic explorer Knud Rasmussen's cameramen. The zoology student Ingvald Lieberkind acted as advisor. The most important person was no doubt Richard Lund, as he was responsible for the series, wrote the scripts, and acted as director and (in the beginning) cameraman.

Richard William Reinhardt Lund (1877–1963) was born in Viborg. He later went to Skive, where he worked as a post apprentice. Eventually he went to Copenhagen. He continued to work for the Postal Service, but at the same time he studied law and theology and served as an officer in the reserve. It was as an officer that Lund befriended Kay van der A. A. Kühle.

Lund was also very interested in politics. He belonged to the political left, and he actually beat Thorvald Stauning (later to become prime minister) at an election in the 11th constituency. This did not please the Danish Social Democrats Party, and he was relocated to a provincial town in Jutland — Holstebro — in 1905, where he continued his work in the Postal Service and remained active politically within the context of the local community. Around 1913 he worked at the political magazine *Social-Demokraten* as a local editor, and it was also around this time that he developed an interest in professional film production. Lund must have become associated with Filmfabriken Danmark in 1913; at least the feature *Zigeuneren Raphael* (*Raphael, the Gypsy*) premiered in 1914 — the manuscript of which was written by Lund. This was, as far as I know, Lund's first piece of film work.

The Film Work

Footage for the nature films that Filmfabriken Danmark produced between 1919 and 1923 was shot at locations all over the country, including Limfjord, Saltholmen, and Dyrehaven; while a significant portion was filmed in the studios of Filmfabrikken Danmark — large premises situated on Almevej in Hellerup (a suburb of Copenhagen). Over the years, Filmfabriken Danmark amassed a number of tame animals, and this eventually became a regular zoological garden, with reptiles, amphibians, insects and foxes. It was handy to have these "actors" on standby during filming in the studio. Working in the studio also meant the availability of special equipment: water, glass, projectors, etc.[17]

Not all of the company's staged animal scenes were successful, but they were easier to make than authentic shots, and so naturally the film crew preferred the former. Nonetheless, they tried to hide from the audience the lack of genuine locations on the screen. For one particular film, the crew created a small forest fragment with a lake in it. Four fox cubs and a gull had been placed in the scene. Inevitably, one of the cubs sneaked up on the gull and was ready to attack, when the gull, debonair and unimpressed by the approaching attacker, lashed out with its wing and sent the unfortunate predator into the lake. The crew adored the scene but were afraid to use it. The audience might become suspicious and think that the

Director of nature films Richard Lund (The Danish Film Institute, Stills Archive).

whole film was a mere creative "construction." The scene is from the film *Foxes* (1923), about the life cycle of the fox.[18]

Shooting scenes in "real" nature demanded a lot of patience. When filming the hatching of a merganser's egg, the crew spent an entire day hovering around the nest. Four hours alone were spent in burning sunlight when the actual hatching took place. This scene probably belongs to *From Birdlife* (1923), which depicted how birds are fed by their mother while the father keeps watch. When a young bird falls out of the nest, it is brought back and gently taken care of. The film also offers a fight between a blackbird, a starling and a thrush, and a duck teaching her young to dive.[19]

Considering the problems such scenes inevitably posed, it is obvious that the crew had an easier time shooting scenes in a studio among controllable surroundings. An example is *Forest Brook* (1922), which depicts the brook during spring and summer. We follow its course through steep slopes covered with beech trees. Some of the film was shot in Dyrehaven (a deer park north of Copenhagen), but one scene that was supposed to illustrate some rapids with spawning trout swimming against the current was shot in a studio. The crew had created a 10 to 13 foot zinc basin that held an artificial dam, while 5 garden hoses created a strong current, natural looking movement and splashes.[20]

Fate of the Films

Although Filmselskabet Danmark produced nature films from 1919, these were not released until 1921. By January 1921, Filmselskabet had produced 17 films, but, to the bitter disappointment of Richard Lund, the company had not yet been allowed to distribute them to schools. At one point Richard Lund stated, "Denmark is lacking behind almost everybody when it comes to an understanding of the educational value of the film medium. But this is changing." Lund then mentions that a mayor, Ernst Christian Kaper, is working towards using film in the classroom.

The Film law of 1922 changed this, however, making it possible for the schools to plan for some of their lessons to be in the form of visits to the cinema. Here they could see some of the nature films of Filmfabriken Danmark.

In time, the nature films of Richard Lund were to receive a lot of positive attention, and on the premiere of Carl Th. Dreyer's *Der Var Engang* (*Once Upon a Time*) in 1922, one of them was shown as a short. In cinemas all over the country this nature film accompanied Dreyer's, and was even said to have received better reviews than his.

Richard Lund's films have all disappeared. For this reason the written sources that deal with the films are very important. The picture that has been described in most detail is *Dyreliv I Vore Moser* (*Animal Lite in Our Bog*), which premiered in World Cinema on 28 November 1921. On March 14, 1920, a reviewer from *Kinobladet* had attended a sneak-preview, and the magazine later stated: "The intrigue — the unending battle fought by nature — and what has been captured on this film is breathtaking." According to this review, as well as a later review in *Dansk Arbejde* from 1 April 1921, the film includes scenes with water beetle larvae crawling up a rush. It depicts how the water beetles act as the vultures of the marshes and finish what is left of a dead fish. We follow the life of insects under water (e.g., how a water spider constructs his diving bell and chases a rival away). Drama is added here and there. For instance, the audience becomes aware of the stork that surveys everything from the roof of the farm; and when the stork approaches, the little creepy things flee in horror. But the stork manages to find food eventually. According to the reviewer, the film shows how the stork catches insects, frogs and fish. There is a crosscut to the nest where the young birds chatter, impatiently awaiting their food.[21]

Only a few of the 28 films premiered in Denmark, but, as mentioned earlier, those that did received enthusiastic reviews in the press. On 1 April 1921, *Dansk Arbejde* wrote that the new series was impressive and explained that the series places the animals, their lives and activities, in the context of their surroundings in such a way that there is an inherent continuity in the series that is both dramatic and amusing. *Kinobladet* was also very positive. An article in this magazine called "Nye Veje for Dansk Film" (*New Ways for Danish Film*)[22] indicates that the films were of a very high standard, even compared to their international competitors, and may have been copied by later nature films.

The Films

Until now we have not had access to these films, which, according to a number of sources, are supposed to have been sent to America or England. According to Jan Nielsen's book about the company, the director of Filmfabriken Danmark, Johan Christensen, believes they were sold to a publishing house in England.[23] According to Richard Lund, the negatives were sold to America, where they were supposedly distributed as American until the middle of the 1930s. An unpublished source indicates the sale took place in 1928.[24] As the alert reader may have noticed, I wrote that *until now* these films have been lost. However, when researching for my Ph.D. project about Danish documentaries, I came across a couple of the above mentioned films. Maybe they had not been discovered earlier because they have different titles than previously thought. Moreover, no attempts had been made to find them because all sources claimed that they had been shipped abroad. The re-discovered films are 1922's *From the Sandy Bottom of the Fjord* (which until now was thought to bear the title *The Sandy Bottom of the Fjord*) and *The Frogs and Their Enemies* (1921), which was known as *The Lives of the Frogs*. A review of *From the Sandy Bottom of the Fjord* in *Politiken* (22 February 1922) stated that the film contained "very interesting pictures from the sandy bottom of the fjord."

I found these films at the archive of the Danish Film Institute. Unfortunately, only a fragment of *From the Sandy Bottom of the Fjord* exists. The beginning of this fragment depicts the surface of the sea. Then there is a cut to a red iris opening, through which the bottom of the sea becomes evident. Through this cross cutting between the bottom and the surface of the sea, we gradually see jellyfish, eels and crayfish on the bottom, and mergansers near the surface. The focus moves closer and closer to the "actors," and then we see mergansers diving through the bottom vegetation. The end of the film still exists; it depicts a coastline. The waves come rolling in and an iris ends the show. The fragment only lasts 3 minutes (20 percent of the original length). What is left of the film still captures some of the original ingenuity, both when it comes to the tension-building crosscutting and the diving birds, but there is something artificial about the shots. Missing are some establishing scenes to indicate that what we are watching is indeed nature and not an aquarium or water tank. The fragment also lacks variation. There are no close-ups, for instance. The fragment is far from perfect and in no way indicates that Denmark was at the forefront of nature cinematography.

How about the second film? *The Frogs and Their Enemies* exists in its original form

Frame shot from *The Frogs and Their Enemies* (The Danish Film Institute, Film Archive).

and length. It opens with an establishing shot of a bog hole surrounded by reeds and irises. An intertitle explains what is shown on the screen, after which the camera approaches the water. Another intertitle states: "The frogs have been spending their hibernation on the bottom of the marsh or in holes on the dry land. Here is one — just woken up and beginning to move upwards." And so proceeds the film — everything is explained and illustrated. Sometimes there are some good shots — for instance, a frog spawning her eggs, after which we follow the development of the eggs in brief sequences. But the many intertitles make it all a bit tedious. This is a common problem with nature films of those days; from an educational point of view, they were very useful, but many of them lacked excitement. When shifting attention from the frog to its enemies, the film becomes much more dramatic: we see caddis worms, swans and ducks. The best sequence of the film is one that gradually builds a sense of tension. The first shot is pure idyll: we see frogs swimming between water flowers, but then swans and ducks appear on the scene and ruin the peace. We then see the frogs diving into the water, and subsequently how they are surrounded by diving ducks.

After a while, the following intertitle appears: "But when the stork arrives on the scene, things get ugly. For storks eat everything that comes their way." Then the stork appears. With the help of intertitles, it is explained that the following pictures depict the storks catching frogs, which they bring home to their hungry young nestlings. At the end of the

Scene from *The Frogs and Their Enemies*, filmed outside a huge aquarium (The Danish Film Institute, Film Archive).

film, the transition from day to night is indicated by the opening and closing of an iris. An intertitle explains: "At night the frogs do not have to fear the stork, for he is at home, but at night comes the horned owl." We see the horned owl in a close up, and afterwards — from the owl's point of view — we see the buffet table of frogs.

When the film crew needed shots of a stork they originally intended to find a tame one, but this was not possible. Instead, they obtained shots from Brønshøj (a suburb of Copenhagen) where a stork had settled down at the top of a factory chimney. They were lucky. A few yards away was another chimney — somewhat taller than the one the stork was in — and from here it was possible to get a good view — and good shots — of the nest: the comings and goings of the stork, the nest building, hatching and the growth of the nest-lings.

This film definitely has qualities that could have given it international appeal; it has a good story, there is variation in the focuses, and it is very informative. In countries where film had become a teaching device, *The Frogs and Their Enemies* must have been an obvious sales target. It may not stand next to the very best of the genre from this period, but it is one of the better films of the time.

Lund After the Nature Films

Sadly, the finances of Filmfabriken Danmark were not sound, and eventually Lund had to give up the production of nature films. When Filmfabriken Danmark finally closed in 1923, Richard Lund began working at Palladium, where he wrote manuscripts and directed non-fiction films (among them, *Danmarksfilmen* from 1925). Political propaganda took up much of his time, and he made quite a few socialist propaganda films. At Palladium, Lund and Ingvald Lieberkind worked together again on the production of nature films. What films they produced and whether or not their collaboration was fruitful remains unclear, but according to Jan Nielsen the planning process was underway in 1927,[25] given the correspondence between Richard Lund and Ingvald Lieberkind. In a letter to Lund written by Lieberkind, it appears that some nature films had already been made, which Lieberkind had wanted to see. However, we cannot say for certain whether these new nature films were in the planning stages or had been produced at the time. It *is* certain, however, that Ingvald Lieberkind was lecturing at Dansk Skolefilm in the years 1927 and 1928.

In 1930, Lund sought challenges outside the sphere of Palladium; he helped set up a number of small companies, and in 1931 he produced the documentary *Blandt Nomader i Lapplands Polarsommer* (*Among the Nomads in Lapland During the Polar Summer*), a film which we know little about. For the rest of his life, Lund continued to promote the educational film. For a while he worked for the Danish Union for Office Workers, and in 1940 he started Dansk Folkefilm, which distributed films to schools and various organizations. He gradually stopped writing manuscripts, but continued to write for *Social-Demokraten* until the very end. He died in 1963 in Copenhagen.

Norway and Sweden — Oscar Olsson

In Norway and Sweden there were three important people when it comes to expedition and wildlife filmmaking from this period: Carl Lumholtz, David Sjölander and Oscar Olsson. Lumholtz had an ethnographic focus, Sjölander an interest in birds, and Olsson in African wildlife.

In 1915 the Norwegian Carl Lumholtz went on an expedition to Borneo, journeying far into head-hunter territory. Here Lumholtz spent two years, and he brought a camera with him. The result of this venture was to be *In Borneo — The Land of the Headhunters* (1919–1920). But Lumholtz was to become more famous for his still shots of native people than his capabilities with a film camera.

Bengt Berg, Sweden's number one bird cinematographer, was not the first Swede to make films about birds. Around the end of the 1910s, David Sjölander, an eminent taxidermist, made short films for the film company Skandia about the birdlife of Lapland, at Stora Karlsö and around Tåkern. Unfortunately, little is known about his life, and there remain no traces of the films he made. According to Leif Furhammer, Sjölander's bird films are supposed to have been terrific for their time.[26]

The adventure-globetrotter expedition of the Swedish company Svenska Biografteater to British East Africa (1919–1921) began with cinematographer Oscar Olsson (1880–1936) going to Africa early in 1919 with instructions to "film nature, animals and negroes" (Heland

1966, 113). With him he had two film cameras and a wooden tripod. A year after he arrived in Africa, Olsson sent the first film reels back to Stockholm. The material was used in a couple of short films about African wildlife. According to the African farm manager Erik von Heland, English officers and farmers in Africa considered Oscar Olsson to be the best and most daring animal cinematographer of his day.

Shortly afterwards, this African expedition got into difficulties — mostly due to the fact that the guide, Gunnar Sandberg, had left the expedition. Svensk Film decided to call off the project, but it was saved when it received support from a number of Scandinavians in East Africa. Thus, Oscar Olsson was able to continue his film work. Olsson set up his working quarters at Karen Blixen's farm (Isak Dinesen), which was situated outside of Nairobi. This had come about because the Swedish Erik von Heland worked as manager on the farm. A dark room was established, as well as a photo laboratory, and it was here that Olsson exposed and edited the films. He used the farm as his base, and made both short and long trips into the African wilderness to film.

Oscar Olsson's three years in East Africa led to the making of 20 short films and a long film called *Bland vildar och vilda djur* (*Among Wild People and Wild Animals*). The latter premiered in Stockholm at the end of 1921. Film historian Leif Furhammer writes the following about the picture: "Oscar Olsson's Africa films do not merely depict hunting scenes. They also include lengthy pastoral scenes of great beauty — e.g., the undisturbed wildlife of the savannahs, lakes with birds and the mountains" (Furhammer 1982, 14). Furhammer's comment represents a present-day interpretation of the film. If we look at the advertising material released for the Danish premiere of the film, it does mention the undisturbed wildlife, but it also underlines the rareness of the shots. "Before long the last lion will have died," and "in few years, the major animals that are still living in Africa will probably have disappeared; only this film will be left to show our children and grandchildren what they looked like." When one considers the extent of the slaughter of wild animals that took place at the time, the fear of the annihilation of the African wildlife was not that exaggerated.[27]

According to Heland, the most beautiful animal shots that Olsson ever produced were taken during the shooting at a waterfall.[28] I have seen a 1 minute 34 second extract of the film that shows baboons, marabous, and two scenes of waterbucks. An intertitle informs us: "Of all birds, the most awful ones are the vultures." This is followed by three shots — one of vultures sitting in a dead tree, one of a dead zebra lying in an otherwise empty savannah, and finally a large group of vultures hovering over the zebra, which is almost hidden from view by the many birds. The last shot lasts for 36 seconds. The photographic quality of the individual shots is very high when it comes to sharpness, contrast, composition and density. The use of a large telephoto lens makes sure that we come close to the animals that are depicted either in full or in close-ups. None of the shots are out of focus or shaky. There is no doubt that Olsson was one of the best wildlife cinematographers of those days.

According to Olsson himself, his greatest personal experience was when he filmed a leopard eating a zebra carcass. It is certainly a privilege to film such an elusive nocturnal animal, and naturally Olsson was proud to have succeeded in filming such a scene. Olsson also filmed around the Tana River, where he obtained shots of crocodiles, hippopotamuses, buffaloes, and rhinoceroses. Here he filmed the animals from a distance of some 160 feet.

Sweden also had notables who, like Roosevelt, went on hunting "expeditions." One of them was Prince Wilhelm, who was accompanied by Oscar Olsson on his expedition to

Carl Lumholtz (Museum of Cultural History, University of Oslo).

Right: Prince Wilhelm of Sweden (by hof atelier Jaeger).

Central Africa in 1921. Out of this journey came the 1922 film *Med Prins Wilhelm på Afrikanske Jaktstigarr* (*With Prince Wilhelm on African Hunting Grounds*). The prince and Olsson began their expedition, which lasted for about nine months, just north of the island of Zanzibar. During their trip they killed some 1000 mammals and 1700 birds, and collected around 10,000 insects that were brought to Rigsmuseet (the National Museum) in Stockholm. The trip consisted of a 1,864-mile trek through Uganda, the Sudan and the Congo. In the course of the film the viewer meets the Batwaers, looks at the 14,700-foot tall Birunga volcanoes, and accompanies the hunters in their hunt for gorillas, elephants and lions on the Ruindi plains. On one occasion, when Olsson was hunting with Prince Wilhelm, they shot 15 lions within 24 hours.

A number of other African animals were captured under more peaceful conditions. Moreover, there are many shots depicting the lives of indigenous peoples, including a tribal battle, which in the film is called a "gladiator-fight." During the expedition, Prince Wilhelm caught malaria, but after an emergency stopover the expedition continued. Back in Sweden, Prince Wilhelm stated:

> He whose blood has been infected with the wilderness, who has lived its life, fought its battles, enjoyed its pleasures, he is beyond redemption, for he will continue to long for the wilderness. Nothing can pinion such a longing; indeed, the strength of it will grow the greater the distance is between himself and the landscape he left.[29]

USA — *Irene and William L. Finley*

The Road to Nature Film

William Lovell Finley (1876–1953) grew up in Santa Clara, California. From early on he had a passion for collecting birds' eggs, but gradually his interest in birds developed into an interest in photography. This occurred after his family had moved to Portland, Oregon, where William became friends with the neighbors' boy, Herman Bohlman. The two of them were to become active in establishing an ornithological society for egg collectors in 1898, but three years later the public resistance to such collections became so fierce that Finley — who was now the director — wrote the following: "If there is anything there should be avoided it is collecting of eggs for collecting's sake, collecting simply to increase a collection. This tendency is carried entirely too far" (Mathewson 1986, 2).

Bohlman and Finley turned their attention towards bird photography instead, and they worked together in this field from 1899 to 1908. The fruits of their collaboration are recognized for their high quality even today, and Finley's photographs have been published in many bird magazines and books — for instance, *Birds of Oregon* (1940) and *Birds of America* (?).

In 1906, William Finley married Nellie Irene Barntart, whom he had met at the University of California where they had both graduated in 1903. Irene and William came to work very closely together; among other things, they wrote articles about their wildlife and wilderness experiences. The articles were accompanied by William's photographs and were published in family and nature magazines such as *Country Life in America*, *National Geographic*, *Nature* and *Bird Lore*. In the early 1910s, Finley's interest in visuals set him on the path to filmmaking. In 1905, Finley had met the famous photographer Edward S. Curtis at the Lewis and Clark expo in Portland. Finley's interest in motion pictures might well have arisen during a conversation with Curtis about camera equipment and techniques.

It has not been possible to find sources describing their early motion picture productions, but Irene and William Finley filmed Indians in Arizona in 1910 (this was probably their first film). According to the biographer Worth Mathewson, the couple were deeply involved in their filmmaking by 1912; and they are said to have made a film as early as 1915 about antelopes, and two years later a film about the mating rituals of a grouse species.

Opposite: **A whole family of gorillas hunted down by Prince Wilhelm (Swedish Filminstitute, Stills Archive).**

**William Finley (middle) and Herman Bohlman (right) with an unidentified third man research-
ing for photographs.**

According to Mathewson, these motion pictures became classics within the nature film
genre, but I have not been able to verify this.[30]

The Career Takes Shape

In 1918 a series of nature films were released under the main title *Finley's Nature Studies*.
The film *A Ramble with a Naturalist* (1918) was number seven in this series. Through the
use of continuity editing, the film shows the beginning of life from various perspectives.
The copy I saw lasts about 5 minutes, and begins with some children collecting animal eggs
by a lake. Afterwards we see the children bringing the eggs (of a toad) to school, where they
look at the eggs. First we see the egg, then we see the tadpoles, and finally we see different stages
of the toad's legs. Later in the film we see newts, sandpipers and pheasants. In the depiction
of the individual bird species, we see the bird's nest, the hatching and the young birds.

In the middle of the 1920s, Finley, in collaboration with the American Nature Association, produced a series of 16 films about the nature and wildlife of North America. Each
picture had a length of 14 minutes. The archive of the American Museum of Natural History
in New York has a copy of the series which they have filed under the title *Nature Magazine
Collection*. Assessing their films according to their scientific value, the Museum comments
on the series: "The quality of content of the films ranges from great scientific value to light
entertainment" (Root 1987, 259).

The series was made between 1924 and 1927, and the subject matter was filmed by
William and Irene Finley, but Arthur N. Pack and his wife Eleanor also contributed. Pack
was the president of the American Nature Association. Finley worked for the Association
as field zoologist and as leader of the preservation department.

A hummingbird by its nest (William L. Finley).

Working with Nature Films

The majority of the material for the films in the *Nature Magazine Collection* was shot during three adventure-globetrotter expeditions sponsored by the American Nature Association: Finley's expedition to the Tucson Mountains in Arizona, the Church-Finley expedition to Northland, and the Pack-Finley expeditions to Oregon and Wyoming. During the Church-Finley expedition, they used Campbell Church's yacht for transport on the waterways. They reached British Columbia, the Bering Strait, the Kenai peninsula, the Isle of Umiak and the Gletcher Fjord in Alaska.

Some of the animal scenes in the series are of a very high quality — for instance, the ones of bighorns and wapiti deer in *When Mountains Call* (1927). Watching the compositions of the wapiti deer and the mythological atmosphere of the scenes, I was reminded of Walt Disney's *Bambi* (1942) and Arne Sucksdorff's nature films from the end of the 1940s. *When Mountains Call* may have functioned as a source of inspiration for these later films.

Another standout quality of some of these films is the use of the continuity editing technique, which constructs small stories that created a natural, progressive narration. One of the better examples is to be found in the humorous *Queer Creatures of Cactus County* (1925). The camera pans across the desert landscape, and suddenly one of the cacti starts to move. There is a cut to a desert hare observing the cactus and looking somewhat surprised. The following shot shows the cactus walking, and the next depicts the hare hopping away. The edits work really well. Visually, the film explains how the cactus was actually a hiding place from which the cinematographer has filmed his close-ups of the various desert animals. It should be mentioned, however, that not all of the films in the *Nature Magazine Collection* have employed such advanced narrative techniques. For instance, the films *Big Game Parade* (1926) and *Nature's Side Show* (1925) both appear to be a random selection of film footage edited together, with the only thing the shots seem to have in common being the fact that they depict big game.

In several of Finley's films there are one or more sequences in which young animals are employed to evoke sympathy in the viewer. This is particularly evident in *Babes in the Woods* (1926), which is full of young animals. In other films, Finley uses bear cubs as the cuddly elements that would raise a smile. Scenes like these appealed to the romantic disposition of the Americans. In films where the appearance of the bears would seem inappropriate — e.g., in a desert in Arizona — Finley instead included small humorous scenes; but it was not always important whether or not the appearance of the cubs (Cuffy and Tuffy) was authentic in the milieu the film depicted. Finley used them on the isles of Pribilof where the crew was filming the breeding grounds of fur seals — a disastrous decision, for Tuffy disappeared and Cuffy burned his paws on the hot, lava-strewn ground.

Finley resorted to other sugary tricks to catch the attention of the audience. Thus, in their early nature films, William and Irene often included their dog Pete, who, over a twelve-year period, became a recurrent character, as did William and Irene's two children, Phoebe and William Jr.

The Films

Queer Creatures of Cactus County (1925) was shot during Finley's expedition to Arizona in 1925. The beginning of this film shows many of the plants that grow in this desert landscape (e.g., the Saguaro and Cholla cactuses). The film shows that the Cholla cactus is an important source of water. We also see how Finley builds the aforementioned cactus hiding place from where he films a desert hare, a kangaroo rat, a greater roadrunner, a gila-woodpecker, a big horned owl and a red-tailed hawk. Shots of a greater roadrunner shows how it catches lizards and brings them to its nest in a cactus. The film ends rather unusually: Finley (played by Finley's brother in disguise) is shown sleeping under a cactus. He wakes up because the cactus kicks him and subsequently chases him around the desert. In the final shot we learn that this was all a dream.

Getting Our Goat (1927) contains one of the techniques that Finley often used to get close to wild animals. In fact, the majority of the film details how the expedition team succeeded in obtaining shots of mountain goats. It appears from the film that this was no easy undertaking. In the beginning they get some footage of the goats from a great distance, but then Finley has an idea. He pulls a goat's skin over himself and, using this disguise, manages to get close to the goats. This is portrayed humorously by cross-cutting between Finley and a "real" goat; while they both advance up the steep rocks, one of the goats is somewhat more agile than the other "goat."

Finley's Mission — Nature Preservation

According to the writer Greg Mitman, Finley's conscious appeal to the romantic disposition of Americans was a good approach for the preservation work of the American Nature Association:

The film lectures of William Finley did more to promote wildlife conservation through images of wildlife as cute, adorable human companions than did the works of sentimental nature writers or the practice of feeding bears in the national parks [Mitman 1999, 96].

Sweetness and romance notions of nature were not the only instruments Finley used when he wanted to gain the support of the nation — which is the purpose of all nature and wildlife preservation. Finley simply tried to turn the attention of the Americans towards the inherent qualities that nature had to offer mankind. One example is *Renting Houses for Songs* (192?), a film that advocates the building and setting up of nest boxes — because the mere presence of the birds will bring joy to all who listen to their songs, and because the birds will help keep down the number of insects (and thus the amount of pesticide needed). We see the fun children have making the boxes and setting them up, and later we see the children's delight when the boxes are inhabited by birds and nestlings.

The Forest (1926) is a good example of how Finley drew attention to contemporary nature problems. The film tells us about the usefulness of the forest — not only because it is a home to many animals, but also because the roots of trees prevent erosion. The film opens with a beautiful shot of a morning in a steaming forest — after which, as stark contrast, we see trees being cut down, the forest burnt down, and the inevitable erosion.

The film also lends a helping hand to the beaver, which at this point in time was on the brink of extinction. At first we see a beaver in a lake. This is followed by an intertitle: "When men kill beavers streams go dry." Somewhat later, the film advocates re-establishing the balance of nature in economic terms: "Taxpayers spend millions for one dam, while the beaver build a million dams for nothing." With this explanation as to why the beaver should be protected, the film continues to illustrate how it is possible to release beavers into those areas from which the beaver population has disappeared.

Irene and William Finley toured all over America with the photos and films that had come out of their extensive relationship with nature. In addition to 50,000 photographs, they had 55½ hours of film of birds, mammals, Indians, flowers and North American wildlife. Like their films, the lectures of the Finleys were a mixture of teaching and entertainment. The number of natural history film lectures decreased drastically during the Depression, and all but ended by 1935. But the films lived on, and the rights were sold to major film companies like Paramount, Warners and Universal.[31]

Those of Finley's films that I have seen were viewed at the American Museum of Natural History in New York. The Museum only stores a minor portion of Finley's productions, and it is difficult for us today to judge the qualities of the early Finley films. Until 1980, most of the couple's films had been completely forgotten by the outside world and were stored in an archive of a major university. When the archive burned down that year, about 90 percent of Finley's films disappeared for good.*

Americans loved the films of Irene and William Finley. They laughed, learned and gaped at the experiences offered by nature. In the 1920s and '30s, Finley's name had become synonymous with North American nature romance and nature preservation.

---

*Unfortunately the source does not state what university stored Finley's films (Mathewson 1986, p. 17).

Knowledge-Imparting Films of the Period

In my compiled list, the number of motion pictures that may be grouped under the heading "knowledge-imparting films" is rather big in the period 1911 to 1921: In all, 51 films fall into this category, but they cover a wide field. I will mention a few of them here to indicate how diverse the films in this category really are: *The Life of Ants* (1912), *How Wild Animals Live* (1913), *Bird Life in Scotland* (1915), *The American Fish Hawk* (190?), *Tides and the Moon* (1919). These are films that may have been shot in studios, zoos or in the wild.

The knowledge-imparting films without hunting scenes or other sensation-seeking elements went through an enormous development during this period. Among other things, a film festival for this type of picture had been established. At an international exhibition in Torino around 1911, prizes of 45,000 francs were awarded to the films that best communicated their topic. Five thousand francs were awarded to the best popular science film, 5,000 francs for the best educational film, etc. *The Life of the Butterfly* and *The Bee*, from the Ambrosio Company, won the prizes for best popular science films. Talbot praised the former film in the following manner: "This is one of the best natural history films that has been seen yet" (Talbot 1912, 325).

The United States of America

During a stay in America around 1922, Bengt Berg from Sweden, who was an internationally known writer, nature enthusiast and cinematographer, commented that the USA was the country in the world that was most advanced when it came to using film for educational purposes. The other leading countries were Sweden, France and England.[32] Several things suggest that the USA had consciously considered both the production and use of knowledge-imparting films. Among other things, in 1913 Thomas Edison proclaimed that his film company would produce films communicating all sorts of elementary facts. In addition, the article "Edison's Revolutionary Education" states that the educational motion pictures were tested on focus groups consisting of students, and that the films were not released until one was certain that all the information in the films had been properly presented (i.e., readily understood by the audience).[33] Moreover, around 1920 American teaching colleges instructed their students on how they could utilize films in the classroom. Nonetheless, only about 15 percent of the schools used film in their teaching—which is evident from a survey conducted in elementary and high schools around the country. Of the 10,000 schools that responded to the survey, 1,513 stated that they used film in their classroom teaching.[34]

In 1912 Thomas A. Edison took out a patent on *The House Fly*, a small film about the various stages of development of the house fly—from the eggs that are laid in a pile of horse dung, through the larval stage and the pupal condition, to the young fly cleaning its wings. All this is shown in 2 minutes 42 seconds, and the topic is made understandable through informative intertitles. Matter-of-factly and in an easily comprehensible language, 10 shots and 7 intertitles explain what goes on onscreen. The flies appear rather small on the screen, and sometimes it is difficult to see what is happening; here the intertitles are very helpful, often providing additional information, like, "Maggots are full grown five to seven days after hatching."[35]

During this period a new man entered the field of educational films in America; his name was Raymond Lee Ditmars (1876–1942). His speciality was reptiles, and he was the director of the reptile section of the New York Zoological Garden. The first long film that Ditmars produced was shot at the Reptile House in the Bronx. The film, *The Book of Nature* (1914), shows, among other things, close-ups of spiders, lizards and frogs. Ditmars had thought a lot about the content of this film:

> We ought not to be satisfied with merely showing a specimen of the animal. We must show the habits, the structure, and all distinguishing characteristics of the creature which is to be shown on the screen and to be understood by the beholders. That is why I have sought to inject an element of humor into these pictures, humor which has its source in the animal itself [Bush 1914b, 1096].

Ditmars' intentions were good. He wanted to avoid a simple depiction of animals and instead focus on characteristics, structures and behavioral patterns of the individual species. His tool was humor. At the end of *The Book of Nature*, Ditmars included an epilogue that he called "Jungle Circus Company." Here a number of animals perform various tricks and display an unnatural, anthropomorphic behavior (for instance, frogs climb a rope in front of an "audience" of toads).

When Ditmars started making films, he made them for scientific purposes. He needed financial support to buy equipment, and therefore he presented his material to a commercial film company. The company was not unsympathetic towards the project, but advised him to add a continuous storyline, or at least some humorous intertitles. Ditmars was disheartened by this; he was afraid that he would lose standing within the scientific community if he used such narrative techniques. His assistant, Andy, tried to cheer him up and suggested how the two of them could edit the material they already had — with intertitles they could make a *Jungle Circus Series*. According to Ditmars, he was convinced when Andy made a plea with a scientific twist: "Tell 'em you made the reels to get the kids interested in animals" (Ditmars 1934/1970, 103). The result was to create a circus performance in which it looked as if the audience was composed of animals. In order to do this, they had to freeze a number of toads. Only this way would they sit still in their chairs for the 15 minutes it took to film the sequence. A chameleon was also in the "audience." Ditmars and Andy made it look as if this animal got much more out of the performance than all the other animals because it could look in several directions simultaneously. The circus animals themselves were set to do all sorts of strange tasks. There was a trial of strength between two flies, and the film contained cross-cutting scenes showing a monkey, a grasshopper and a millipede seemingly engaged in an eating match.[36] Needless to say, the scene displaying an experiment involving bubblegum and a fly's wings was hardly more scientific than the rest of the scenes in the *Jungle Circus Series*. Nonetheless, the circus performance was received with enthusiasm by the human audiences, and, more importantly to Ditmars, it made it possible for him to buy new equipment.

In 1916 G. E. Stone filmed and produced a film about the creation of organic life on earth. *How Life Begins* makes use of micro-cinematography, time-lapse sequences, graphics and semi-scientific intertitles (like this one, which appears at the thirtieth minute: "One hundred hours old: A network of blood vessels has extended further over the yolk and carries nourishment to the embryo").[37] Despite the fact that the information is complex, the film manages to present its topic in a clear and well-arranged manner. Thus, the film begins with the development and reproduction of the plant kingdom (flowers, leguminous plants and fruit trees), after which it presents the animal kingdom (arthropods, amphibian, birds and finally mammals). The mammals are introduced by means of a white rat, a cat, a cow and a human being. During the presentation of the mammals, the intertitles inform us that all mammals reproduce and develop similarly to the rat. Such a claim must have caused great commotion at the time, but the next two shots may have been intended to make up for the previous scenes. First we see two figures that resemble classical representations of the Virgin Mary and little Jesus on her lap. Afterwards we see a family and a symbolically rising sun in the background. The mother kneels at the left of the frame, while on the right the father holds their baby over his head at arm's length. Thus the child forms the center of the picture and becomes the central portion of a biblical symbol stretching towards the sky. This may be seen as a retreat from the scientific explanation of the creation of life and recognition of a divine creator.

France

In the beginning of the 1920s, Bengt Berg claimed that America was way ahead of other nations when it came to the production and use of educational films, but Berg also mentioned France as being far advanced in this respect. My own research confirms this.

The French company Éclair produced a popular scientific series called *Scientia*. Although the series consists of knowledge-imparting films, it cannot be said to be pedagogical, scientifically objective or in any way matter-of-fact. Despite the scientific purpose of the series, it remains an entertainment product, which is clear from the intertitles of the individual films in the series — intertitles that clearly consider the world of natural history in anthropomorphic terms. Examples are *Le Dytique* (1912), *A Spider That Lives in a Diving-Bell: The Argyronetta* (1913), and *Two Snail-Eaters: The Glandida and Ophisaurus* (1913). The film *Two Snail-Eaters: The Glandida and Ophisaurus* shows two snakes eating. One of the intertitles comments, "The snake ingests the 'tasty contents' of the shell, takes ... a moment's rest before the final course ... a quick wash before his siesta" (Lefebvre 1997, 93–4). The intertitles clearly use anthropomorphic means to awaken the curiosity of the audience, as well as make them laugh. The texts make the audience identify with the animals. To the technical director of the *Scientia* series, Georges Maurice, there was no doubt as to the correctness of this method:

> The term "popularization," already so familiar in this context, is very appropriate. Fulfilling the twin aims of "profit and education" involves two things: 1. That the subject should be accessible, if not to everyone, then at least to the average viewer, 2. That the presentation should be simple and entertaining. Any subject, however dry it seems, can be made interesting: this is the aim not only of modern education, but also of cinema [Maurice 1913, 13].

I have seen a Pathé Frères film about ants that was released in this period — *Das Leben der Ameise* (1912). Displaying a kind of circus performance, the film attempts to illustrate the strength and daring of an ant. We see how the ant fights a human finger, and later we see how it lifts a piece of plant that is much larger than itself. Hanging from a pair of tweezers, the ant holds on to the plant for dear life. Finally, we see how it (still hanging from the tweezers) tries to hold onto a coin. This is clearly difficult, but the ant finally succeeds.

Britain

The aforementioned British production companies that made popular scientific nature films continued to be active during this period. The Charles Urban Trading Company still made natural history series, for instance. In 1912, *Urban Science Series* launched *Australian Kangaroos*, while *The Animal World Series No. 1* was launched in 1915. None of these films added anything new to the genre. The Williamson Company's *The History of a Butterfly: A Romance of Insect Life* (1910–11) *did*, however. I have seen a German version of this film called *Die Lebensgeschichte eines Schemetterlings*. The film, which lasts for 5 minutes 55 seconds, includes many fine examples of early micro-cinematography. The first scene shows a man with a net running after a butterfly. The man trips and falls. In the next two scenes we see some eggs on a cabbage leaf. An intertitle informs us that these are butterfly eggs, and in close-up we see how they hatch. The next several sequences show various caterpillars. The individual shots are only divided by means of intertitles that provide the name of the species. Towards the end we see the pupation and later the miraculous transformation into a butterfly. Despite the fact that the print was worn, its superior quality shined through. The informative qualities and the narrative technique of *Die Lebensgeschichte eines Schmetterlings* make it interesting to watch even today.

The New Nature Film Production Companies

Apart from the outfits producing nature and wildlife films that I have already mentioned, several more companies specializing in this genre were established during this period. I cannot say precisely when they began producing nature films; I only know that they were established during this period of time. Examples include Midgar Features, Savoia Films and UFA.

Midgar Features produced *How Wild Animals Live* (1913), a five-reel film describing all sorts of creatures from the animal kingdom (from dingoes in Australia to bears in North America). According to one reviewer, W. Stephen Bush, all the climatic zones of the world were represented in this film.

Unfortunately, I have been unable to find this film, but Bush calls it unique because it points to new directions and possibilities within the genre.[38]

Savoia Films produced *Habits and Customs of Swallows* (1915), of which I have seen an incomplete copy. It lasted 3 minutes 48 seconds and lacked parts of both the opening and ending. However, judging from the intertitles, as well as the various shots from the film, the original version must have been very informative. A narrator in a white coat and a woman wearing a beautiful Victorian outfit appear. The copy I saw contained 12 shots, and included scenes of swallow nests as well as swallows at various stages of development. The man in the white coat explains various things about the nests and hatchlings. Sometimes he is shown in a close-up holding a nest or a young bird in his hands. At other times there are establishing shots in which he is seen explaining things to a woman. As far as narration goes, the film is well made; but when it comes to camerawork or the presentation of its topic, *Habits and Customs of Swallows* is nothing special. This does not mean, however, that the information of the film was imparted in a simplistic or ineffectual manner to the original audience. From the then-contemporary point of view, the variation of shots, as well as the informative intertitles, were quite advanced.

The German film company Universum Film Aktien-Gesellschaft (UFA) was established in 1917 and in time produced many films, among them several nature films. However, I have been unable to find any of those films made before 1924, the year when *Salmon Fishing* premiered. But I do know that Lola Kreutzberg made animal films for UFA before that time, primarily shot at the Berlin Zoo. *Salmon Fishing* (1924) from UFA shows various methods of catching salmon (e.g., using a steel basket or a net from a rowboat). It also depicts a bear cub catching salmon with his paws.[39]

In 1926, UFA sent cinematographer August Bruckner on an expedition to the Amazon jungle, resulting in the film *Primeval World of the Forests*. It shows the wildlife of the Amazon delta and the jungle. According to Guggisberg, the film included a sloth, an anteater, a tapir, a hummingbird, and leaf-cutting ants. In one scene we see piranha skeletonize a carcass within minutes.[40]

Underwater Nature Films

After the series Denizen of the Deep (1905), the first film dealing with life in sea or fresh water that I have been able to find is *Giants and Pygmies of the Deep* from 1909. Until 1917, underwater films appeared intermittently, after which the production of this special genre ceases until 1922. I have registered only eight underwater films between 1909 and 1921.

Aquarium

The first films of marine wildlife were shot in aquariums. The producers of these films had carefully considered how they could obtain authentic depictions of the behavior patterns of fish. 1. The fish were not to be aware of the presence of any human beings, as this would create disturbance in the aquarium. 2. The light had to come from above, as this seemed to have a calming effect on the fish and thus guaranteed that they behaved "naturally" during filming. 3. The aquarium had to look like the natural habitat of the species in question.[41]

In the early 1910s the Eclair studios made a number of special nature films that were intended for enlightenment and teaching of students. Examples are *Life at the Bottom of the Sea* (1910), *Among the Fishes* (1912) and *The Stickleback* (1912). (I use the English titles because I have no knowledge of the original French titles.)[42] The latter was reviewed in a new column in *The Moving Picture World* called "Moving Picture Editor": "The usual Eclair success attends this production; ... The details are of marvellous distinctness ... lessons of special importance to the classes in natural history" (Nov. 15, 1913, 724).

I have seen the film *Die Geheimnisse Der Meerestiefe* (1910–11) at the British Film Institute. This (incomplete) version lasts for 3 minutes 7 seconds. It consists of 9 intertitles and 17 shots. The texts are longer than they were in the early days of nature films, and they are not merely informative but express an opinion. For instance, the ninth text suggests, "The most beautiful fish species is the amazing Japanese sailfish." The film shows many different animals: crayfish, lobster, fighting fish, turtles and lumpsuckers. The texts provide the audience with the names of the animals appearing on the screen but are not particularly informative when it comes to behavior patterns. The film manages to convey a sense of the animals that live on the bottom of the sea and how the animals move. Considering that it was made in 1910, it is quite an impressive film technically, and the composition of some of the shots is of a high standard.

One part of the film begins with an establishing shot, after which we move closer to the fish. In another scene the camera pans across the bottom of the sea — or, rather, the bottom of the aquarium, for films were not yet shot in authentic lakes or oceans. The review from *The Moving Picture World* shows that he was well aware of this: "from a very good aquarium" (Nov. 18, 1911, 552). Whether the audience in general were as enlightened as the reviewer is hard to say. The shots of the lumpsucker are particularly beautiful. In the first two scenes we see the fish in "semi" close-ups. For the first shot the lumpsucker moves, and in the second it lies still. In the final shot the lumpsucker fills the whole frame. This gives the fish an impressive size, while we see it from the front. Considering that well-respected film historians like Bordwell and Thompson suggest that establishing shots and close-ups of details did not become mainstream techniques until the mid–1910s, this nature film is quite innovative.[43] So, all in all, while the technical standard of this film is high, the way it conveys information is fairly ordinary.

Underwater Chamber

Around 1911 or 1912, Dr. Francis Ward from Ipswich attempted to film fish in their natural environment. Ward constructed a little underground chamber that adjoined a pond or brook. Between the water and the camera he inserted a wall of mirrored glass through which it was possible to film. The camera chamber had a cover so that no light appeared from above, and thus the fish could not look into the chamber but merely saw themselves in the reflection of the glass. The underground chambers were constructed for ordinary photography, and were not geared to filming. A cameraman sitting in the underground chamber could barely move and so could not stay for much longer than an hour. Nonetheless, interesting motion pictures were made in this way. Percy Smith made a film about an angler's choice of bait and the correct handling of this. Later, a film was made called *The Otter* (1915) that included scenes shot in such an underwater chamber.

A recurrent problem with these chambers was condensation. On hot days the glass steamed up so fast that it was impossible to do any filming. This happened because the earth in the chamber warmed up quicker than the water in the brook or pond.[44]

Underwater Films

A young photographer from Norfolk, Virginia, whose father had invented the diving bell, was the first man to photograph and film in the actual ocean. His name was John Ernest Williamson; his brother was his assistant. The diving bell could be lowered to a depth of 500 feet, and on 18 June, 1913, Williamson took the first ever photograph from inside the bell; shortly afterwards he filmed from it.[45] Getting into the actual diving bell was made possible by a tube connected to a boat. This tube had a plastic coating that bent according to the movements in the water and within the tube itself.

Since there is not much light in the depths of the ocean, an electric device was invented that made it possible to shed light on the underwater subject — a construction that consisted of steel and lamps that was driven by a battery onboard the ship. Most likely, the brothers made short films at the bottom of the ocean from around 1914, but I have not been able to find these early motion pictures or even learn their titles. It is certain, however, that Universal Pictures commissioned the Williamson brothers to film authentic underwater scenes for the feature film *Twenty Thousand Leagues Under the Sea* (1914).

According to the writer Homer Croy, the Williamson brothers are supposed to have made a five-reel non-fiction film that, in my estimation, premiered between 1914 and 1919.

John Ernest Williamson going down in the bell with a still camera (Library of Congress, LC-DIG-ggbain-13789).

It was about life on the bottom of the sea and included shots of coral reefs, and various species of fish and underwater plants. It also depicted young native boys diving for coins that people onboard a ship threw into the water.[46] The only non-fiction film of John Williamson that I have confirmed is *The Wonders of the Sea* (1922).

According to author Ernest Dench, the Englishman Z. H. Pritchard is supposed to have tried to film while wearing a diving dress before 1919. He was lowered down to the bottom of the ocean in a primitive diving dress, and was supplied with oxygen through a hand pump installed on a boat.[47]

In the period 1911–1921, cameras, lenses and tripod equipment went through an incredible development, and the knowledge-imparting film made increasing use of narrative structure, descriptions of behavior and composition variety, thus increasing the attractiveness and digestibility of their "informative" content. A new development was the appearance of films shot partly in underwater chambers.

Top professionals like Oscar Olsson, William L. Finley and Herbert Ponting began making films. The new cinematographers contributed to people's knowledge about wildlife and nature. They had an incredible talent for composition and, when necessary, they "staged" nature in order to capture the scenes they wanted. They made sure, however, that the result appeared "natural."

The nature preservation tendency of the period was evident in the "pure" animal scenes — ones that did not entail hunting or otherwise stressed the animals. This tendency was even evident in the hunting films themselves — directors began to abstain from using vivid slaughter scenes, and eventually the subgenre disappeared.

1922–1928
Higher Quality and Different Conventions

From around 1921, most nature films contained fairly complex narratives, enhancing both their educational and entertainment value. The English nature film series *Secrets of Nature* was launched in 1922. It was very popular throughout the western world and paved the way for creative new directions within the genre. A number of dramatic animal films were produced during this period, as well as wildlife films making use of the cine-technical improvements of the period: lighter cameras, bigger telephoto lenses and panchromatic film.

The Development of the Period

Cine-Cameras

In 1918, Carl Louis Gregory Akeley (1864–1926) put the finishing touches on his invention, the "Akeley camera," but it was probably not used until the beginning of the 1920s. He had spent several years developing and improving the camera, and at the end he nearly lost his financial sponsors, who were becoming impatient with him. Sources disagree, however; I have read that Akeley patented the camera in 1915, and that all the cameras he made were sold to war cinematographers during the First World War. Eventually, Akeley obtained a museum assistantship at the American Museum of Natural History; and within this field his invention had major advantages. The body of the camera was shaped like a drum and was especially built for the use of telephoto lenses. A built-in optical system provided for an even position of both eyepiece and lens, no matter the position of the camera. A gyroscopic head improved the ability to pan and tilt smoothly. For this reason the camera was especially well-suited for filming animals in motion. The camera itself weighed 5 pounds, and when ready for shooting it weighed around 10 pounds. The impetus behind the construction of the Akeley camera was the installation of a big telephoto lens.[1]

Two identical lenses were installed onto the camera. One of these was a focus lens — the one you looked through when looking into the eyepiece. When you adjusted the sharpness with this lens, the real lens was automatically distance-adjusted to match its "twin-lens." This was useful for those occasions when you could not determine the outcome of the scene — e.g., nature or wildlife shots. In addition, it was possible to change the reel without special precautions. Neither dark room nor particular caution was necessary, as both used and new film reels were protected in coupled reels. It is said to have taken about 10 seconds to change a reel.[2] A contemporary review comments: "The Akeley is unique in its field, and for that reason it has met with approval of certain cinematographers who specialize in the recording of sports, wild life, military events, races and so on" (Coe 1981, 83).

Moreover, author Bodry-Sanders claims that the Akeley camera had an aperture diaphragm that allowed 30 percent more light onto the film than other contemporary cameras.[3] I doubt that this ability of the aperture is true, however, as it is primarily a question of lenses. It was also said that the weight of the camera was half that of contemporary cameras, which is certainly *not* true.

The first Akeley model had a hand crank, but a later model featured an electric agent. Akeley received an award for his camera design in 1926: the John Price Weathermill medal from the Franklin Institute of Philadelphia.[4]

In 1922, Newman & Sinclair started the production of Kine Camera Model 3. This camera was run by an electrically-driven motor. The battery of the motor had to be connected externally, which made it more mobile than was the case with other mechanic or hand cranked camera types. This meant that the cameraman could use both hands when working the camera. For instance, the cinematographer could pan and change the focus simultaneously. Moreover, the camera made it possible to look directly through the applied lens. This became possible through the use of a special 45 degree prism, which is what we today would call a "reflex camera."

Martin Johnson is standing with an Akeley camera fitted with long binocular lenses. Osa is standing with a Universal camera (Martin and Osa Johnson Safari Museum).

Nonetheless, many shots of animals were still taken with hand cranked cameras. Throughout the 1920s, most cameras and tripods were very heavy. In 1924, an expert in the filming of African wildlife complained about the heavy equipment. He claimed that camera and tripod together weighed 50 pounds, which made fast movements impossible. This problem was to be resolved soon, however.[5]

Eyemo was a special Bell & Howell camera that had been intended for amateur use when it appeared on the market in 1926.

Bell & Howell's Eyemo tag (Danmarks Fotomuseum, Palle Bøgelund Petterson).

An Eyemo film camera held a fairly small film reel (100 feet) but had the advantage that the reels could be changed in broad daylight; this made it possible to use the entire reel. The special reels were produced by Eastman Kodak and minimized the waste of film. Moreover, the camera only weighed just over 6 pounds and was useful as a handheld camera in "spontaneous" situations. The DeVry camera, which was also launched in 1926, had similar advantages and almost the same specifications, but it weighed a little more—almost 8 pounds.[6]

Lenses

In 1920 the standard lens had a diaphragm of $f2$. It was produced by the recognized English company Taylor, Taylor & Dobson. On the longer focal lengths, the diaphragm was at $f3.5$, at best. All in all, the improved apertures of the diaphragm made creative control of the light conditions much easier. At the turn of the 1920s, the Akeley and Debrie cameras used telephoto lenses of some 580mm (20 inches). Taylor, Taylor & Dobson helped develop the big lenses, but it must be remembered that lenses of this size were unusually big and not widely used.[7]

The Screen

Magnascope is a system that can dramatize individual sequences in otherwise conventionally shot films. Behind the ordinary screen you placed a much bigger screen. This larger screen was concealed, and behind it were a number of operators who revealed the bigger screen by removing the curtain that hid it. With the use of a special Simplex projector, a chosen film sequence was now shown on the big screen, which was about four times bigger than the ordinary one. The effect was used to dramatize individual moments or climax situations, but only major theaters offered this experience. The Magnascope technique was used to show the stampede of a group of elephants in the film *Chang* (1927) at the Rivoli theater in New York.[8]

Exhibition Venues

At the end of 1920, American cinemas were filled to the brim with people who had made money on America being the granary of the world. During the First World War, America had exported food and consumer goods to countries all over the world, and in turn a lot of money circulated in the American society. This created the foundation for many new cinemas, and the film media reached even thinly populated areas, where small towns wanted their own cinema.

In the early 1920s, America had about 15,000 cinemas, and was the largest film market in the world. The number of film theaters with flamboyant interiors also increased during the 1920s, but the Depression put an end to this extravagance.[9]

Editing Techniques

When dealing with the development of non-fiction films in the silent film period, it is impossible to avoid the name of Robert Flaherty (1884–1951). Flaherty applied his knowledge of narration within the film media to his first motion picture, or rather to his second. For in 1913, Flaherty brought a camera with him on an expedition that searched for precious metals. The expedition went to Northern Canada, and filming was a secondary assignment on the journey. The chosen camera proved to be unfit for the polar climate; there were constant problems with the individual parts of the camera because the oil inside the camera froze. In 1916, Flaherty returned from the expedition; he had — despite the technical difficulties — managed to shoot many hours of film, but the material was lost due to an accident. Flaherty was packing the films to be sent away, and was smoking at the time. Some ashes from the cigarette fell onto the film, and in seconds the material had vanished. Before this accident, Flaherty had shown a test film in various museums to special audiences. After having seen the picture, the director of the Ontario Museum of Archaeology wrote to Flaherty: "I cannot too strongly congratulate you on the moving picture you exhibited in convocation Hall. They are much the best I have ever seen.... I have never known anything received with greater enthusiasm" (Barnouw 1983, 35).

Flaherty himself believed the burnt material to have been pretty worthless. He considered the film a simple travelogue and the praise mere politeness. Through hard work, Flaherty managed to find a rich sponsor for a regular film expedition to Northern Canada, and this time he chose a more handy and mechanical camera — an Akeley. On this expedition Flaherty was much more focused on the film work, and he had an idea of what he wanted the film to contain. This time, filming was his primary function. He brought two Akeley cameras, 75,000 feet of raw film stock, exposing equipment and a Haulberg electric lamp.

He spent 16 months in inhuman conditions; and in the course of only 6 months, Flaherty edited the material into the justly acclaimed film *Nanook of the North* (1922). The picture cost $53,000 to produce, but it made $251,000 globally.[10] *Nanook of the North* displays the special balance between wilderness and man, a balance which necessarily brings man to his knees because life must be lived according to the rules and temperament of nature. Flaherty also revisited this theme in the later productions of *Moana* (1926) and *Man of Aran* (1934).

Nanook of the North represents the knowledge and technique that had accumulated since the early days of the non-fiction film. It showed scenes from several different points

Promotion still from *Nanook of the North*: Nanook listening to a gramophone recording for the first time (The Danish Film Institute, Stills and Poster Archive).

of view in order to make the material more interesting. Moreover, the film displays an incredible variation in its use of the camera, the scenes and the editing. This way, Flaherty made the audience identify with the Inuit Nanook, and the tension-building editing style created expectations in the audience about what would happen next. In some ways, Flaherty used the narrative techniques of the fiction genre: character casting, reconstruction of events, showing the life of earlier times, and directing the scenes. He used a creative manipulation of reality — an adaptation and personalization of reality into a filmic, tension-filled story.

Bengt Berg and Nature Preservation

The Road to Nature Film

In elementary school, Bengt Berg (1885–1967) managed to flunk Swedish, math and natural history. This did not mean that he was a lazy student, however; he simply did not study the curriculum required by the school. Instead, he read everything he could lay his hands on about animals and foreign countries. The math teacher advised Bengt's mother to send her son to become a shoemaker's apprentice. Berg did become an apprentice, but he never earned his certificate. Around 1909, one of Berg's longstanding hobbies changed the course of his life: he was a keen bird taxidermist. On one occasion he sent some of his stuffed birds to a museum, attaching a letter on how he felt a biological bird collection must be arranged in order to make it seem natural and timeless. His basic idea was to make a very lifelike museum diorama of the lives of rare bird species by means of drawings and photographs, and to place the birds in their right biotopes and in characteristic situations.

This letter reached a university professor in Bonn. The professor, Alexander Koenig, was a Russian ornithologist who had a fantastic private collection of zoological items. Koenig planned to create a zoological museum displaying (among other things) the birdlife of Europe. Koenig asked Berg to conduct research on those of the museum's dioramas that dealt with northern bird life. Throughout an entire season, Bengt collected material in Lapland and the Finmark. Berg painted color samples of all the plants he came across in the biotope, and photographed trees, herbs, moss, stones and birds of various biotopes. It was here that his interest in photography commenced.*

I have not been able to verify how Berg came to make nature films, but his authorship has been an important source for his early production method, as well as his preparations and research. From his writings one can glean how fanatical and pedantic he was during the preparations of his films on African and Swedish wildlife.[11]

The Career Takes Shape

The bird films that Bengt Berg made before 1920 have been mentioned sporadically in various sources, mostly in flattering tones. Contemporary reviewers were enthusiastic about his films, and designated him a "poet" and a "genius." The sources only give us a limited insight into his pictures made before 1922 and may not in any way be considered a sound basis from which to build an understanding or evaluation of his early work.

---

*On page 12, it appears that the offer was made 15 years before the book was written; for this reason, it is with some caution that I write around 1909 (Berg, *De Sidste Ørne*, 1927, pp. 7–8, 12).

Bengt Berg's first films were brief studies of Swedish birdlife; storks, herons, wild geese, and eiders were some of the ornithological subjects he included in his films. Berg is said to have filmed crane colonies in Sweden in 1917, with some of the shots depicting them nesting. Afterwards, Berg followed the cranes to their African winter abode by the Nile. Berg sailed down the Nile from Khartoum, and during this trip he filmed huge groups of cranes and other migrating birds, but also marabous, crocodiles and a group of vultures hovering over a hippopotamus carcass.[12]

Bengt Berg in a happy moment: sharing a pipe with his goose (Iens Illum Berg).

From this point on, Bengt Berg started filming for Svenska Filmbyrå, making films that lasted as long as regular features. The first picture to be released was 1922's *Som flyttfågel i Afrika* (*Migratory Birds of Africa*), a film about Swedish migratory birds' winter stay in Africa. A year later, *Sagan om De Sista Örnarna* (*The Story of the Last Eagles*) was released, which dealt with the impending extinction of the Swedish golden eagle, as well as its behavior and life conditions.

Bengt Berg had noticed a drastic decrease in the number of golden eagles in Sweden. This decrease was partly due to the fact that they were disturbed during their nesting, and partly due to the interest in collecting bird's eggs at the beginning of the 20th century. Interest in ornithology had exploded, and museums, universities, and amateur ornithologists collected eggs with a passion — which led many great birds of prey to the brink of extinction. Berg wanted to make a film about the white-tailed eagle, which would inform the Swedish public as to the seriousness of the situation and make them want to help save the reduced population of eagles in Sweden.[13]

The Work with Nature Film

Sagan om De Sista Örnarna illustrates that Berg was unusually innovative and ahead of his time. He had many ideas of how he wanted his film to look. He wanted scenes of an eagle's nest, and he wanted to do this by placing himself and the camera above the nest so that he could film directly into it. Finding the right nest took a long time. The most unusual — and, in the end, successful — solution was to build a nest in a suitable tree and hope that a pair of eagles would find it attractive enough for their purpose. Berg then built a shelter of pine branches for himself and the camera in a neighboring tree. Hidden behind the branches, he could work without disturbing the eagles. The distance was some 165 feet, and Berg was far from satisfied, but he got the scenes he wanted.

Another of Berg's innovative ideas was to film the eagles from the air in a propeller-driven floatplane. The gyroscope that connected the camera to the hull of the aircraft did not work very well, and due to the enormous power of the air pressure, it was not possible to move the camera horizontally, which again made it difficult to keep the camera steady. The difficulties were aggravated by the fact that the camera was worked by means of a handle, so that filming from the air was hard work indeed. On his first flight, Berg managed to film the landscape, the sea and the land from the eagle's perspective, and later he captured scenes in which the eagles soar on the wind. These scenes of soaring eagles were an early example of using an animal's point of view.

Sagan om De Sista Örnarna premiered in Röda Kvarn on 27 November 1923. A review in *Aftonbladet* describes the film thus: "We look down upon the hunting ground, we see the eider, we see the crow with her young in wild flight towards the rocky beach. We gain an insight into what happens when the king of the air inspects his reign" (Nov. 27, 1923). The film follows the development in the nest until the day when the young birds are old enough to fly and explore the world.

The Films

I have studied a copy of the documentary program *Filmen I Virkeligheten* (*The Film in Reality*), which contains a 1 minute 58 second extract from *Sagan om De Sista Örnarna*. Even from such brief footage it is clear that Bengt Berg was far ahead of his time. The quality of both the camerawork and editing is very high, and the film builds tension and informs the viewer at the same time. The sequence encourages the viewer to identify and involve himself emotionally with the animals on the screen. This effect is enhanced because Berg has edited the film so that the audience experiences the scenes from the eagles' point of view. The following shot-by-shot description reveals the extent to which Berg mastered the art of building tension, using cross-cutting to depict a golden eagle attacking an eider family.

> Intertitle: "From the outpost his sharp eyes watch the entire skerries."
> Shot 1. Two eagles sit in a tree — we only see the very top of the tree (long-shot).
> Shot 2: A panning camera shows the skerries.
> Intertitle: "Out there on the beach."
> Shot 3. The camera, placed in a boat, moves towards an eider family (long-shot).
> Intertitle: "Then she sees the eagle approach."
> Shot 4. The eagle floats in the air (long-shot).
> Shot 5. The landscape is seen from onboard a plane.
> Shot 6. The eagle in the sky.
> Shot 7. Shot of the skerries taken from the aircraft.
> Intertitle: "She rushed through the breaking of the waves."
> Shot 8. The eider female is obviously distressed and tries to flee with her young.
> Intertitle: "Would it help if the young eiders could dive?"
> Shot 9. The eider family swims away from the camera (full-shot).
> Intertitle: "The eagle killed them easily and bought them to his young."
> Shot 10. In the nest, young eagles fight for an eider young (full-shot).

Berg was aware that the effect of such a sequence could work against his original intention — to create sympathy for the eagle. In order to get his message across, Berg therefore includes thoughtful scenes like this one: After depicting an eagle arriving at its nest with a small perch (which is swallowed whole by one of the young birds), Berg cuts to a fisherman with his net full of wriggling fish. The message is difficult to miss — the eagle is not a competitor to the fishermen, and a place should be reserved for this animal in the Swedish fauna.[14]

Berg's next film, *Abu Markub och de Hundrede Elefanter* (*Abu Markub and the 100 Elephants*) (1925), was for him a return to the African fauna. Abu Markub is a shoebill. Together with the Scottish big game hunter Major Ross, Berg hired a paddle steamer on which they sailed on the Nile delta and later to Bahr-el-Ghazal. When they arrived at the enormous marshland at Sudd, Berg filmed amazing sequences of shoebills and got some nice shots of huge elephant groups.

The film never reached a broad public audience and was only shown a few times at functions where Berg himself participated as lecturer. It appears from a contemporary review written by Robin Hood that *Abu Markub och de Hundrade Elefanter* made use of very untraditional methods. Among other things, Berg is said to have mixed the ordinary scenes with colored still photos. But this is not a part of the existing material on the film.

After the production of *Abu*, Berg left Sweden due to a disappointing and humiliating experience with the Swedish government. Berg had offered the state the rights to *Sagan om de Sista Örnarna*, but they declined,

A shoebill stork, alias Abu Markub (photograph by su neko, Wikimedia Commons).

although the amount Berg asked for is supposed to have been more than fair. Berg had contacts in the German film industry, and after this incident he turned his back on Sweden and left for Germany, with the intention to produce films.[15] However, this dream of his did not materialize. The only film he did participate in, *Der Sehnsucht nach Afrika*, had its German premiere in 1938. It was directed by Georg Zoch, and Berg was cinematographer, together with Günther L. Arko. It is a children's film in which we see six young people visit Bengt Berg in Sweden.

Instead Bengt Berg continued his career as a writer. By his death in 1967, he had published around 24 books. The last one, *Örnar*, was released in 1960. He made only three feature-length films.

Nature Protection

In 1922–3, Englishman J.C. Faunthorpe traveled around Nepal, Burma and India as part of the Faunthorpe-Vernay expedition, the purpose of which was to collect material for the Asian collection of the American Museum of Natural History (a diorama and a skeleton collection). They also wanted pictures and films of the wildlife of India, to be used in their lectures, and brought the cinematographer G.M. Dyott with them to do the filming. Dyott had worked as a photographer in South America, and during the First World War he worked as an air photographer for the Naval Flying Corps. On this expedition Dyott filmed with an Akeley camera and managed to obtain very good shots of tigers. Faunthorpe later commented that these scenes were "probably unique in the history of cinematography" (Faunthorpe 1923, 188). Dyott also took fine footage of boars and deer at a watering hole. About Dyott, Faunthorpe commented, "He spen[t] about three days and the results are, I think, the most beautiful cinematographic pictures I have ever seen" (Ibid, 193). All in all, some 26,000 feet of film were shot and entered into the archive of the American Museum of Natural History.

Faunthorpe became infuriated upon discovering the state of the wildlife. The world had only just discovered the rapidity with which the wildlife of Europe, North America and Africa was disappearing. Now Faunthorpe realized that the future looked bleak in Asia too: "The almost complete disappearance of game animals in the United States is, of course, notorious, but the same thing is going on practically all over the world" (Ibid, 175). He blamed the hunters, but also civilization itself: "The work of destruction entered upon by civilized man goes on with terrible swiftness.... Today there is still time in the case of many species. In a few years it will be too late" (Ibid, 176). But the expedition succeeded in filming elephants from a short distance, as well as Indian rhinoceroses, tigers, crocodiles, gharials, chital, and antelopes. Despite Faunthorpe's misgivings and worries on behalf of the global wildlife, his comments on the expedition's killings are dealt with fairly casually. For instance, in Nepal he commented indifferently, "Vernay bagged a couple of tigers" (Ibid, 179). One minute Faunthorpe laments how the Indian rhinoceros is threatened with extinction; the next he complains how difficult it is to find and shoot two rhinoceroses. Four hundred and fifty animals were killed during this expedition; 129 of these were mammals!

In 1921, Pathé Frerès released *What's Left of the Bison Herds*, a film whose title alone connotes a concern for nature. The picture addresses its message anthropomorphically and humorously. The mixture of intertitles and visual scenes effects a great variation, so that one minute the audience receives factual information, while the next minute the decrease in the number of bison is presented with much regret. And this is followed by an anthropomorphic intertitle providing a "solution" to the problems presented, thus maintaining the attention of the audience. In one particular scene we see the half cast-off fur of two bison oxen. The intertitle reads: "The tailors' war 'down strand' doesn't bother the American bison — he just 'drops' his coat when the heat arrives and during summer slowly grows a new one for the winter." Here the informative and the anthropomorphic content is mixed so as to make the informative part easier for the audience to digest.

Scandinavian Polar Expeditions

Knud Rasmussen, H.F. Rimmen and Leo Hansen

The beginning and the end of the fifth Thule expedition of Knud Rasmussen (1879–1933) was documented on film. Out of this came *Den Store Grønlandsfilm* (*The Big Film on Greenland*) (1922) and *Med Hundeslæde gennem Alaska* (*Travelling Through Alaska on a Dog-Sledge*) (1927). *Den Store Grønlandsfilm* was filmed by H. F. Rimmen in 1921 during the early part of the expedition, and was directed by Edvard Schnedler-Sørensen. For my present purpose, this is the more interesting of the two films.

Leo Hansen with a young musk ox (The Danish Film Institute, Stills and Poster Archive).

Leo Hansen was responsible for the filming of *Med Hundeslæde gennem Alaska*, and the camerawork in this film is far superior to that of *Den Store Grønlandsfilm*. This is especially evident in the camera movements. Composition-wise, the scenes shot by Leo Hansen are much finer, and his use of tilt and pans is much more even and smooth. It should be mentioned, though, that several of H.F. Rimmen's scenes were shot onboard the ship, and this may account for the shaky camera movements. *Med Hundeslæde gennem Alaska* does contain nature-related scenes, but first and foremost it remains a document of the final phase of the expedition; as such, it represents ethnographically irreplaceable research material on the idiosyncrasy of native Inuit culture.

Like all other copies, the version of *Den Store Grønlandsfilm* I have seen has its own story. It is a black and white copy which was found at the Netherlands Film Museum (NFM) in Amsterdam. It had Dutch intertitles, but during a restoration English intertitles were added. These were translated from Dutch by the Danish film historian Marguerite Engberg in collaboration with the staff at NFM. The film evenly documents 1. the expedition, its members, the preparations and tasks; 2. ethnographic recordings of the look, costumes and rituals of the Inuit people; and 3. the nature of Greenland and the arctic wildlife.

Den Store Grønlandsfilm contains many "pure" landscape scenes of wild and untouched nature: ice masses in the fjords, travelling shots of the rocks surrounding the fjords, etc. In one scene the camera tilts and so captures the source of a waterfall, following the water as it cascades down into a lake. The expedition ship gets very close to a glacier, and from this position we see a number of huge ice blocks in the water.

Apart from the regular landscape scenes, there are also many scenes of wild animals: Greenland seal, humpback whale, walrus and polar bear. The two latter animals are filmed while they are being hunted. The hunt for the polar bear is conducted from a kayak, and these scenes comprise a very good passage that could almost be called a "zoom." The effect is created because we, in the first scene, see the bear swimming away from the camera. Behind the bear we see two Inuit kayaks equipped with harpoon spears. The sequence has been filmed from aboard a rowboat sailing fast towards the bear until we get really close to him. After this zoom the film cuts to a shot of the hunters in the kayak and afterwards to a close-up of the bear, who is clearly distressed. The bear is then shot with a rifle and taken aboard the expedition ship.

Another impressive animal scene takes place at the mountain of Upernivik. Here we first see an intertitle that reads: "The mighty rocks at Upernivik offer shelter to millions of sea birds. A shot causes hundreds to take wing." Afterwards we see flocks of birds fleeing from the rocks. While the birds were sitting on the rock wall they were almost invisible, but when they take wing it becomes obvious that an enormous number of birds were hidden in the crevice. Most likely the birds are puffins and alcidaes. Compared to contemporary nature films, the technical refinement of *Den Store Grønlandsfilm* is not worth mentioning. Nonetheless, the scenes do represent an inherent authenticity, which is impressive considering the film's technical clumsiness.

The films of Knud Rasmussen may not have influenced the development of the wildlife and wilderness film genre, but on at least one occasion (the polar bear sequence) they did display a good sequence structure that created a sense of tension and excitement. They also show that people had a growing interest in wildlife and nature.

Roald Amundsen and Paul Berge

As mentioned earlier, Roald Amundsen beat the Scott expedition to the South Pole in 1911. An early film documenting an Amundsen expedition is *Med Mænd over Polarhavet* (*With Men Across the Arctic Ocean*), which focuses mainly on the journey and experiences of the members of the expedition. When the ship *Maude* arrived at Deering, Alaska, the cinematographer and Amundsen made a small circular tour in a single-motor aircraft. The air scenes depict ice masses, the ocean and beautiful mountains. The film contains few other nature-related scenes, but there are some shots of Inuits hunting for polar bears and walruses.[16]

Later, Amundsen went with another polar explorer, Lincoln Ellsworth, on an expedition, documented by the cinematographer Paul Berge. The resulting film, *Roald Amundsen og Ellsworth's Nordpolsekspedition* (*Roald Amundsen and Ellsworth's North Pole Expedition*) (1925) was advertised with the following words: "Excellent pictures from arctic landscapes and wildlife taken by photographer Paul Berge" (Braaten 1995, 89). I have no further knowledge of this film.

Other Expeditions

In 1922, the Citroën company sponsored an expedition through the Sahara. With a Citroën as the means of transportation, the expedition only lasted for 20 days — from mid–

Arctic explorer Knud Rasmussen center (The Danish Film Institute, Stills and Poster Archive).

December to January 7, 1923. The team consisted of the scientists G. M. Haardt and L. Audouin-Dubreuil, who were both from France. After a film lecture in Copenhagen called *Traversée du Sahara en Auto-Chinelle* (*Driving Through the Sahara in an Automobile*) (1923), the Danish newspaper *Kristeligt Dagblad* described the film as excellent.[17] It is not the wildlife of Sahara that the film depicts, however, but the people whom the expedition members meet and the harsh conditions they surmount during the tour. The film received much international praise and helped further develop a new tendency that had already been introduced with Knud Rasmussen's film on Greenland: major accomplishments achieved by people both in front of and behind the camera. This tendency is also evident in the next example — a film about the British expedition to Mount Everest called *Climbing Mt. Everest* (1922).

    The film work by Captain John Noel is an extraordinary achievement — as incredible as the hardships the leaders of the expedition (Mallory, Norton, Somervell, Finch and Irvine) went through. It is not about the ill-fated attempt by George Mallory and Andrew Irvine in 1924. *Climbing Mt. Everest* is about Mallory's unsuccessful attempt in 1922, where his team reached 26,985 feet (8,225 m.), and George Finch's team reached 27,300 feet (8,321 m.). Finch's team climbed with bottled oxygen.

Climbing Mt. Everest includes shots of the primeval forests of the Teesta valley, as well as scenes in the Rongbuk monastery; but otherwise the film follows the expedition team from camp to camp — past glaciers, steep rocks, and tremendous drops below rope bridges. Two thousand feet from the summit, the photographer stayed behind to film, while the other members of the expedition attempted a final push forward. However, the expedition teams had to give up before they reached the summit.

Captain Noel toured the world with this film, and wherever he went the picture was received enthusiastically. The film was a commemoration of human ability. The fact that it had been made on location meant that it became relevant and authentic to the people who watched it. One reviewer wrote:

> We were breathless at first, but then the entire cinema exploded in uncontrolled applause.... Nothing less than a photographic masterpiece. The landscape scenes with the clouds drifting past the highest summit of the earth were spectacular [*Politiken*, November 4, 1923].

Antarctic explorer Roald Amundsen (Library of Congress, LC-US262-12515).

The motion pictures mentioned in this section were not cinematic masterpieces in an artistic sense, nor even in a filmic sense, but the photographers behind the cameras helped show the potential inherent in films depicting desolate wilderness areas. The first picture to capture the combination of expedition, wilderness, wildlife and human achievements in a way that may be termed magnificent was the film *Grass* (1925), which tells an interesting story — artistically, as well as from a filmic point of view. This film did not need an accompanying lecture — it did the work on its own — which was not really the case with the other films mentioned in this section. In a way, they were more like lecture films. Nonetheless, they hold enormous significance for the development of non-fiction motion pictures because they placed a new focus on films depicting reality.

Secrets of Nature

British Instructional Films only made educational films of the popular-science kind. One of their most popular series, *Secrets of Nature*, began in 1922. The series was distributed

Program cover for Noel's *Climbing Mt. Everest* (author's collection).

to countries all over the world, and in 1934 the series changed its title to *Secrets of Life*. *Secrets of Nature* has had a tremendous significance for the development of the nature film genre. Sadly, it is difficult to actually study the films in the series, for although the British Film Institute stores many of the pictures, these have not been transmitted to "viewing copies"—in other words, they are not available to the public. A mere glance at the compiled list of films, however, should indicate the importance of the series in the years 1922 to 1928. At least 63 *Secrets of Nature* films from this period have been registered, films that encompass an incredible variety of topics and species. Broadly speaking, the series focused on British flora and fauna, and did not really deal with "exotic" topics like big predators or foreign countries. Sixteen of the films made between 1922 and 1928 are about birds, while 19 films deal with insects; neither group of films were tempted to include birds of prey or carnivorous insects. The descriptions of the individual films indicate the broad spectrum of species that the series encompassed; we also get a sense that the people behind the series were very serious when it came to conveying their message. This "seriousness" in the presentation of nature is evident in the collaboration between the film crews and professionals within the particular field of nature studies that the individual film covered. On those occasions when the factual information of the program had to be verified, the series used specialists from various scientific fields. Indeed, the series employed experts in each field. J. Valentine Durden was the professional biologist. He had attended the Royal College of Science, and was thus able to provide factual evidence in support of his analyses. For many years he worked as an editor and director at Educational Films, and as a freelance director and cameraman on various nature film productions. Mary Field was part of the series almost from the beginning, in 1922. She began working at British Instructional Films because they needed her expertise for a film about the 18th century fishing traditions in the western part of the Atlantic Ocean. She was then offered a regular position with the company, which she accepted. Over the years, Field came to work as a script writer, editor, and continuity presenter. She also worked as a director, especially within the framework of *Secrets of Nature*. Other specialists were Charles D. Head (expert in insect cinematography), Oliver G. Pike (expert in bird cinematography) and F. Percy Smith (expert in plant and micro-cinematography).[18]

The episodes of *Secrets of Nature* usually lasted between 8 and 14 minutes. The majority of the entries were filmed under controlled conditions, either in film studios or big aquariums. In some cases, tame or entrapped animals were used, just as some scenes were filmed in zoological gardens. Often an authentic-looking set piece was shot to hide the fact that filming took place under "controlled conditions"; however, many of the scenes were actually filmed in natural surroundings. In fact, in my opinion the manipulation of reality — which the controlled conditions represented — does not make the films less interesting or less valuable. This method often added narrative creativity, which, at that point in time, would have been difficult to achieve "naturally." Moreover, even today it is not uncommon for nature films to feature "staged" situations.

Battle of the Ants

Battle of the Ants (1922) is a good example. Here follows a summary of the plot. Two ant hills are separated by a hollow in the ground. As a wooden plank is placed across this hollow, a war commences between the two ant colonies. The most aggressive colony attacks mercilessly, and long and bloody battles ensue. The battlefield is soon strewn with war casualties, but the aggressor is not satisfied until the conquered hill is destroyed completely. Not only do they carry off building material to their own hill, they also abduct the opponents' queen! Naturally, this is a fairly dramatic description, but this, it seems, was the intention behind the film. But how is it possible, in 1922, to make such a dramatic film about ants without the use of sound and computer animation?

First of all, the intertitles take up a lot of the film. There are an equal number of scenes and intertitles: 24. The individual intertitles are quite comprehensive and take up 40 percent of the total screen time.* Often the pictures cannot live up to the dramatic action described in the intertitle. Intertitle number 7 is a good example: "The colony on the left were not aware they were being invaded, so the scouts had no opposition." The following scene shows the plank across the hollow from above, and we only see a few tiny dots (i.e., ants). The next intertitle reads: "But they soon awoke to the fact that strangers were in their midst, and rushed to the bridgehead which became a struggling mass of ants." The film then cuts to the plank scene from before, in which it is impossible to see any change whatsoever. Such sequences clearly demand a certain imaginative power on behalf of the viewer. I believe, however, that the film works well — although in a literary rather than visual sense.

There *are* scenes in which the visual impression and written text go hand in hand. This is evident when an ant guard is stationed on the "bridge" between the colonies. The ant must inspect the passing ants. Here the visual side works well, for it really looks as if an inspection takes place.

---

*The running time of the film is 8:44 and that of the texts is 3:41.

Battle of the Ants clearly experiments in its attempt to make its story about the ants dramatically interesting. Today, however, the dramatic and very anthropomorphic texts appear unintentionally humorous. This is one of the funniest: "The Antennae which are fitted with organs of smell enable the challenger to detect a stranger. He is at once taken below ground, and put to death as a spy: if too strong he is held until assistance is forth-coming."*

Together with the Danish series produced by Filmfabriken Danmark, *Secrets of Nature* must be praised for its broad range of subjects, which makes the majority of the then con-temporary nature films look terribly narrow. The makers of the series were innovative indi-viduals who pushed the boundaries for what topics were relevant and for how the stories inherent in nature films were told.

Hunting Films vs. Nature Preservation

The number of adventure-globetrotter expeditions to Africa peaked in the period between 1922 and 1928. I have noted 13 such films in my compiled list. However, it does look as if the tendency had changed in favor of making films about the African wilderness and wildlife; and more often than not, films from Africa produced in this period encouraged nature preservation rather than hunting. In many of the motion pictures about Africa that will be mentioned here, hunting was still present but not a particularly important part.

Snow and Son

From 1919 to 1922, H.A. Snow and his son Sidney traveled and hunted in South Africa. Here Sidney shot 33,000 feet of film, and this material was edited into the picture *Hunting Big Game in Africa with Gun and Camera*. The film, which premiered 18 January 1923, was a commercial success; it ran at the Lyric Theatre in New York for three months. Later the two of them also produced successful films about Arctic regions, like *The Great White Arctic North* (1928).[19] A reviewer, Robert Littell, from *The New Republic* wrote the following about the film: "The penguins are apart from the rest of the film, which records animals surprised, chased, overtaken or killed in the long trek" (Littell 1923, 251).

It appears from this quote that *The Great White Arctic North* is a hunting film, and that the reviewer disagrees with the underlying method (which obviously stressed the ani-mals). The review also indicates that the Africa films were under pressure, because people were no longer keen on watching terrified animals being hunted; rather, they were interested in seeing the animals' natural behavior. This change of attitude is also evident elsewhere. The adventurer F. Radcliffe Holmes comments on how a tribe, which he calls the Wa-Sanya tribe, wonders why he does not kill any wild animals:

> Why we should sit for a whole day in a hide-up and allow animals to approach within a few yards without killing a single one, and afterwards walk many miles to get meat was quite beyond them, for they had never seen or even heard of such things as pictures [Holmes 1929, 124].

---

*This copy was sold to America under the title *Bray Nature Pictures*, but the film was produced by British Instruc-tional Films. The copy must have been shortened, for in comparison, the English version lasts for 14 minutes while the American lasts for 8 minutes 44 seconds.

Buchanan, Treatt and Glover

In 1922, an experienced cinematographer, T.A. Glover, accompanied Angus Buchanan on the latter's expedition across the desert of the Sahara. The expedition was undertaken in camel caravans, and the purpose was mainly to collect data and specimens of animal species for natural history museums. The film was made in order to show how difficult this work was. In 1924, Glover went on a globetrotter journey with C. Court Treatt and his wife Stella. The film *Stampede* (1929) shows their car trip from Cape Horn to Cairo, and is full of scenes of animals filmed in southern Tanganyika (present-day Tanzania).[20]

Carl Ethan Akeley

Carl Akeley (1864–1926) created a camera that was to become the preferred choice for many wilderness and wildlife cinematographers. His motivation for making the camera stemmed from his frustrating experiences with an Urban film camera he had used during an expedition to Africa in 1909–11. He found the camera utterly hopeless — it was too complicated to work with, clumsy and difficult to manoeuvre in tense situations. Akeley considered the film camera to be a tool for his scientific work — similar to field notes, surveys and other methods of documentation. Akeley did make one commercial film himself, *Meandering in Africa* (1922), that he shot with an Akeley camera. The film was shot during the AMNH's Akeley African Expedition to Belgian Congo (Zaire) in 1921–22.

In *Meandering in Africa* we first see some of the preparations for the expedition; later

After a lion hunt with Lumbwa warriors. White men from left: Carl E. Akeley, Martin E. Johnson, and big game hunters Pat Ayre and Philip Percival (Martin and Osa Johnson Safari Museum).

there are shots of Victoria Falls. Akeley films these with beautiful compositions that include three depth-creating levels. The film also includes a number of animals in their natural environment engaged in their "natural" activities: weaver birds, shoebills, topi, ostriches, elephants and baboons. During the expedition, Akeley also took the first ever shots of wild gorillas, but these were filmed from a great distance and are of interest mainly for historical reasons.[21]

Upon taking a closer look at Carl Akeley, we see a person that in many ways is typical of his time. Nature lovers in those days where drawn to nature in the same way we are today, but nearly all of them would forget any kind of preservation if they had the chance to shoot a rare animal. Let's have a look at some of the things Akeley has written:

> That led us to base our plans on gorillas alone, and it was a gorilla expedition, although Miss Miller killed an elephant the first time she shot at anything in Africa and both she and Mrs. Bradley killed lions. To me the gorilla made a much more interesting quarry than lions, elephants, or any of the other African game, for the gorilla is still comparatively little known. Not many people have shot gorillas and almost none have studied them in their native habitat. The gorilla is one of the most remarkable and least known large animals in the world, and when is added to that the fact that he is nearest to man of any other member of the animal kingdom, a gorilla expedition acquires a tremendous fascination [Akeley 1921, 190].

But overall, given his actions, movements and written words, it becomes apparent that Akeley was one of the greatest nature lovers and preservation activists of his time. Just read this:

> I look upon it with more disapproval than I can well state, for I think that many of the titles on the pictures are misleading and that some of the pictures fall into the same category. All naturalists welcome the spread of animal lore by motion pictures so that a knowledge of true natural history may become more general, and there is no better way to disseminate such information. But if in order to make a film a more hair-raising and popular picture, the moving picture producer puts misleading titles on the pictures and resorts to "fake" photography, the harm they can do is just as great as the good they would otherwise effect [Akeley 1921, 157].

Akeley was also a great daredevil, and he didn't gloss over his close encounters with the animal world. Here follows a description of a very dangerous meeting he had with an elephant:

> He drove his tusks into the ground on either side of me, his curled up trunk against my chest. I had a realization that I was being crushed, and as I looked into one wicked little eye above me I knew I could expect no mercy from it. This thought was perfectly clear and definite in my mind. I heard a wheezy grunt as he plunged down and then — oblivion.
>
> The thing that dazed me was a blow from the elephant's trunk as he swung it down to curl it back out of harm's way. It broke my nose and tore my cheek open to the teeth. Had it been an intentional blow it would have killed me instantly. The part of the trunk that scraped off most of my face was the heavy bristles on the knuckle-like corrugations of the skin of the under side.
>
> When he surged down on me, his big tusks evidently struck something in the ground that stopped them. Of course my body offered practically no resistance to his weight, and I should have been crushed as thin as a wafer if his tusks hadn't met that resistance — stone, root, or something — underground. He seems to have thought me dead for he left me — by some good fortune not stepping on me [Akeley 1921, 48–49].

Whether this recounting is the truth down to the bone is impossible to say, but it is an amazing description.

Meandering in Africa clearly indicates that Akeley lacked skills both as storyteller and cinematographer — he had no eye for drama and paid little attention to light. Unfortunately, he was unable to transmit his creativity to the world of film, but he did understand the strength of the medium in capturing the attention of a broad audience, and he was able to use his experiences with the film medium to make people aware of the endangered wildlife of Africa.[22]

William N. Selig

The Selig Studios did not merely focus on making exciting nature films. In 1923, William N. Selig presented *Beast of the Veldt*, a motion picture which I believe to be a "pure" wildlife film. I have seen 1½ minutes of the film, and there are no people present — or, indeed, anything created by humans. There are eight different scenes depicting a group of cow-antelopes, which is very much in keeping with the then contemporary nature preservation films shot on the African savannah.

Other Parts of the World — Wavrin

Few films from "other" parts of the world came out of the silent film period, but French researcher Marquis de Wavrin spent 12 years in South America. From May 1926 until June 1930 he went on an expedition from

A leopard Carl Akeley killed with his own hands.

which his film assistants, Alberto Cavalcanti and Paul Raibaud, brought 6,600 feet of film. They travelled close to the impenetrable forests around the hinterland of the Amazon and in the countries of Ecuador, Peru, Colombia and Brazil. The film is a unique documentation of costumes and life among native tribes, like the Boro, Jivaro and Napos. The wildlife of the Islands of the Galapagos appear in such numbers that it will make any animal lover swoon. When the finished film, *Au Pays du Scalp*, was launched, a sound track by Maurice Jaubert was added.*

Arthur Radclyffe Dugmore

The Road to Nature Film

Arthur Radclyffe Dugmore (1870–1955) was the son of an English marine officer. His father abandoned his career and spent the family fortune on acquiring a yacht. The family

---

*In Scandinavia the film was launched under the title of *I Skalpens Land*. (*In the Land of the Scalp*) Press material from the Danish Film Institute.

Arthur Radclyffe Dugmore with a still camera.

sailed the Mediterranean and the Atlantic Ocean for years, and all this time Arthur Dugmore did not receive any education. When the family finally settled down, they did so in Florida, but by then Arthur had become tired of his father's unsettled ways. He left his family and moved to Tarpon Springs, where he got a job as a photographer. During his time there some friends of his introduced him to W.E.D. Scott, who was a famous ornithologist. Over a two-year period, Arthur Dugmore assisted Scott with collecting and conserving bird species, and this inflamed a passion for wildlife and wilderness photography. Dugmore gradually became a recognized animal photographer who not only photographed birds and the fauna of North America, but also filmed wild animals in and around Nairobi in 1909. By the early 1910s, Dugmore had a family of his own; they moved to England, where he began experimenting with film and later became an artist specializing in wildlife paintings.

The Films

I have little knowledge of what Dugmore's life was like until 1922, but it obviously led to the Dugmore-Harris expedition in Africa. It began one February day in Nairobi in 1922, and ended five months later. The purpose of the expedition was to film those African animals that, even then, were becoming rare. Their film, *The Wonderland of Big Game* (1923), was intended to leave behind "live pictures" of species that were becoming extinct, so that future scientists would have an understanding of the animals' behavior in their natural environment.[23]

A copy of *The Wonderland of Big Game* exists at the British Film Institute. The copy is complete and lasts for 18 minutes 16 seconds. From a filmic point of view, the compositions are average and the camerawork unsteady, but the film reflects the new tendency: concern for nature and its preservation.

In the introduction to *The Wonderland of Big Game*, it is pointed out that no animal was shot or harmed during the making of the film, and that species appear which are threatened with extinction. These species might well have been, for example, the white rhinoceros and the oryx.[24] Dugmore filmed animal flocks in Ngorongoro, he filmed rhinoceroses, giraffes and zebras by a watering hole in the Northern part of Kenya, and he filmed elephants on the plains of Marsapit.

In 1923, Dugmore filmed in Africa again. This time the purpose was a bit different, but then the British government had partly financed the expedition. Dugmore writes about the experience: "My purpose was not merely to see the country, but to make a cinematographic record of its people, its animals and, above all, of the development that has taken place under our administration" (Dugmore 1924, 50).

Among other places, Dugmore filmed in the Sudan, and an experience here nearly cost him his life. An elephant with a cub felt threatened by his presence, and while Dugmore was filming, the furious elephant suddenly charged in his direction, trumpeting. The attack proved to be merely a warning, however, and the elephant changed direction at the last second. Dugmore comments: "It seemed as though the whole world was coming and I was almost paralysed with fear. All that I can remember was that I turned the handle of the camera and trusted that it was pointed straight" (Dugmore 1924, 144–5). He watched the elephant approaching through the eye piece of the camera but, quite impressively, remained still. Dugmore was not satisfied with the animal scenes shot in the Sudan, however, because the film remained nothing but a travelogue and a snapshot of the Sudan. Dugmore made the following observation on the wildlife of the Nile: "It was not a good year. Animal life was abnormally scarce near the river, and doing much with the camera was a matter of luck" (Dugmore 1924, 238). Dugmore shot with a camera—he rarely used a gun. At one point he came as close as 35 yards to a group of some 400 elephants. What to do? Shoot or film? Dugmore continues: "I wanted photographs more than ivory, and anyhow I don't think I could bring myself to shoot these great creatures except in self-defence, they are so much more interesting alive than dead" (Dugmore 1924, 146–7).

Dugmore did shoot animals, but it was never for the fun of it—he was one of the few genuine nature preservationists of his time. During his stay in the Sudan, Dugmore praised the beauty of the Nile, but he clearly despised the sports hunters sitting comfortably in their boats on the Nile, reading books, drinking sherry and making ready to shoot an animal every time a scout announced the presence of prey. The "sportsman" would then get up, shoot the animal—which he would often neglect to collect—and return to his book. Dugmore writes: "Birds were killed or wounded and left where they fell, and the same was true of animals.... It was all delightfully simple and so very safe. Thank goodness that has been stopped" (Dugmore 1924, 72 and 75).

Apparently this form of hunting had become illegal by the time Dugmore wrote this passage in 1924, but he had other reasons for being indignant. He became especially angry when witnessing natives and sports hunters shooting giraffes:

> There is certainly no sport in shooting them and they furnish no trophy, and no one could possibly claim that they are dangerous. Alive they are perhaps the most beautiful and interesting of all rare animals.... I have seen thousands, but still they fascinate me [Dugmore 1924, 279].

In 1928, Dugmore filmed in areas of the Canadian Rocky Mountains that he had visited previously. Here he managed to film bighorns, mule deer and wapiti deer. Although Dugmore was born in England, he moved to the U.S. around 1900 and lived in New York for many years. He died in 1955.

Drama-Documentary and Wilderness

Both Robert Flaherty's films, *Nanook of the North* (1922) and *Moana—A Romance of the Golden Age* (1926), depict the struggle of native peoples for survival in the wilderness. Throughout the 1920s similar motion pictures appeared, and some of these were much more influenced by fiction films than had been the case with Flaherty's pictures. Flaherty presented native peoples as heroes, and in the following section I will provide examples of films that turned wild animals into anti-heroes.

Cooper and Schoedsack

Merian Caldwell Cooper (1893–1973) was born in Florida. He served as a pilot in several battles during the First World War, and his plane was shot down twice. He survived both crashes only to be taken prisoner by the enemy—first by the Germans and then by the Russians. He managed to escape both times, and his heroic achievements made him a regular war hero at a very young age. As a civilian, Cooper sought the exciting life as an explorer with Captain Salisbury at the beginning of the 1920s.

From left: Merian C. Cooper, Marguerite Harrison, and Ernest B. Schoedsack in Angora (courtesy Milestone Film & Video).

Ernest Beaumont Schoedsack (1893–1979) was also familiar with war situations, but this had been as a film correspondent.

Cooper and Schoedsack met by chance on a railway platform in Vienna, and when Captain Salisbury needed a film man, Cooper recommended Schoedsack. Schoedsack, then onboard the ship *Wisdom II*, received a telegram from Salisbury and rushed to Djibhouti, where the expedition ship was anchored. *Wisdom II* was later to capsize, and the crew nearly lost their lives.

Through their conversations, the thought of a film had gradually taken shape in the minds of Schoedsack and Cooper. Schoedsack obtained a Debrie camera, and, having bought additional equipment, they left for Iran, where they came across the story that was to become *Grass* (1925). Cinematically and historically speaking, it is a pearl. Swedish researcher and explorer Sven Hedin called *Grass* the best film he had ever seen.[25]

The story of *Grass* is told magnificently, and seeing it today is still a breathtaking experience. We feel the reality behind the thing, and the moment seems real, relevant and meaningful, although we never get very close to the characters. The Bakhtyari people portrayed in the film are seen as a collective group and not as individuals. They are nomads, and the film depicts them while they travel to their summer pastures. They must overcome major hindrances like rivers and snow masses, but the biggest obstacle is the mountain pass Zardeh Kuh. Like Robert Flaherty's *Nanook of the North*, *Grass* portrays people who must struggle to survive in a nature which gives and takes. It is not so much a nature or expedition film as it is a depiction of the conditions of the wilderness; as such, it may have been an inspiration for many later wildlife, travel and expedition films.

Chang: A Drama of the Wilderness

Cooper and Schoedsack's next film, *Chang: A Drama of the Wilderness* (1927), was founded on a vague draft, and the actual story was not created until the directors went to Siam, Northern Thailand, where the Nan District was chosen due to the local stories of man-eating tigers. In their attempts to make an exciting film, they went about their business in a more "active" manner than previously. Their goal was to construct a carefully crafted dramatic structure. Basically, the film accompanies a family who lives in the jungle, and who meets various dangers and experiences associated with a life in the jungle. The opening scenes of *Chang* are pure family idyll. The family fells trees and grinds seeds into flour. They have a pet, a langur, who adds a lot of humor to the film, but who also expresses the inner fear or joy experienced by the family in the various situations.

The family cannot fight the dangers from the jungle single-handedly, and they seek assistance from the nearest hamlet. They join forces against the wild animals of the jungle, and during the film they come across a constrictor, a Himalayan bear, a leopard, an elephant stampede and a tiger.

If we take a closer look at the animals in the film, there is no doubt that they are

Cooper and Schoedsack with the langur while recording *Chang* (1927) (courtesy Milestone Film & Video).

Chang—a staged drama of the wilderness (courtesy Milestone Film & Video and The Danish Film Institute, Stills Archive).

"wild"—in fact, they seem a bit too "wild." Most of the animals behave in a manner that is not representative of their species. They seem alarmed—maybe because they hear disturbing sounds.

Cooper and Schoedsack never revealed how they managed to get their material. On the one hand, they cannot have known exactly how the animals would behave; on the other, they must have had some sort of control over the actions. The animals appear incredibly aggressive, confused and ready to attack. The most likely explanation for this behavior is that they were exposed to some kind of pressure or abnormal situation that would stress them; they might have been exposed to unnatural sounds, like the ones made during a battue, or maybe they were locked up. I do not know, and the above speculations are pure guess work. Nonetheless, I believe they are close to the truth. My best guess is that the animals had been captured but were kept in such a manner that they could move about relatively freely. Anyway, the scenes in which wild animals appear must have been difficult and unpredictable to film—which is also indicated by the fact that the filming took 14 months.[26]

Chang contains a scene in which an elephant calf is tied to one of the native huts; the mother is also tied up—within full view of her calf. Quite predictably, the wish to protect her young awakens the wild beast in the mother elephant, and a violent scene ensues in which she smashes the hut to which her offspring is tied. Other scenes from the film were probably staged in a similar manner.

We cannot consider *Chang* to be a wildlife documentary in the traditional sense; the meeting between animal and man is quite simply too staged and over-dramatized. Kevin Brownlow reached a similar conclusion: "The exception to every rule, *Chang* (1927) was no more a documentary than *King Kong*" (Brownlow 1978, 529). What Brownlow refers to here are the conditions under which the film was made. The family — the focus of the film — was not a family at all. It was put together by local people in the Nan District; the father, mother and the two children belonged to four different families.

The events of the film were made up too, and many of the animal scenes were mere film tricks, including the climax of the film in which a group of 300 elephants destroy an entire village. The herd was put together with help from a number of local people, and the scene itself was shot at a different locality than the rest of the film. Moreover, a scene depicting a monkey throwing a coconut at one of the elephants was never filmed in Thailand, but in Central Park, after the film crew had returned to America. I consider *Chang* to be fiction, a drama-documentary depiction, rather than a factual account. *Chang* was nominated for an Oscar in 1927, and for Paramount it was one of their five best-selling films that year. In the following months, the picture made $500,000.[27] The contemporary press loved the film, including Gilbert Selves from *The New Republic*, who described it as "one of the best moving pictures ever made, regardless of classification" (Selves 1927, 333).

Cooper and Schoedsack's most famous film is *King Kong* (1933).

Is There Any Wildlife in *The Silent Enemy*?

H. P. Carver's *The Silent Enemy* premiered 19 May 1930, at Broadway's Criterion Theatre; technically, it falls beyond the scope of this book, but since it is a silent film I have decided to make an exception and include it.

The film centers on the life of an Indian tribe in a glorious, fabled past. Nonetheless, the picture contains three animal scenes. In the first one, a puma fights a bear; in the second one, a Canadian moose is attacked by a pack of wolves; and the third animal scene shows the migration of a caribou herd. The animal sequences received an authenticity "seal of approval" from Madison Grant, who was a significant naturalist and nature preservationist. He did suspect that certain scenes had been staged (he believed, for instance, that the wolf pack mentioned above was really a group of huskies). But he was convinced of their genuineness after a conversation with the film's producers, William C. Chanler and W. Douglas Burden.[28]

Grant, however, was fooled. The "authenticity" he ascribed the animal scenes was in many ways staged, including the fight between the puma and the bear. The animals had been starved for some days, after which they had been let into an enclosure — in the middle of which lay a carcass. The fight ensued because the two animals had to compete for the carcass. When the bear was released it immediately went for the puma, which fled up a tree. In its hunger and frustration, the bear followed. Both animals ended up at the end of a tree branch and fell down, after which the fight continued.

In *The Silent Enemy* there were also problems with the authenticity in the scene depicting the migration of the caribou. Filming this event was a strenuous task; Ilia Tolstoy, whom Burden had entrusted with the assignment, had paddled an enormous distance to get to the Barrenlands, only to discover that she had arrived too late. The caribou had already begun their summer migration. Instead, another cinematographer succeeded in filming the caribou migration. These scenes, included in the film, were shot by Earl Welsh during an expedition to Alaska. In the finished film, shots of tame caribou filmed on a farm were added — a breach in authenticity, which Burden later regretted. In private letters that were later published he apologized and explained that the only way he had been able to film interesting wildlife scenes was by using artificial or constructed situations.[29]

The Drama-Documentary OO-tang

Similarly, *OO-tang* (1928?) is a fictional film that attempts to imitate the structure of the wilderness and wildlife film genre in hopes of attaining a sense of authenticity. The result, in my opinion, is a disaster. The film depicts three white people travelling through the jungle of Sumatra. One moment the film provides long intertitles explaining the difference between the African and the Asian elephant; the next moment it portrays the orangutan as a "killer-animal" — an Asian King Kong. The shots of the orangutan in the individual scenes have been taken either from a worm's-eye view or by the use of close-ups, so that the audience is forced to believe that the crew was indeed in danger, as indicated by the intertitle: "Now all around us were hairy, terrible monsters."

Chang, The Silent Enemy and *OO-tang* probably made animal films more appealing to the public, but the films were drama-documentary pictures that probably did more harm than good when it came to understanding the animal kingdom.

Jean Painlevé

The Road to Nature Film

Jean Painlevé (1902–1989) was born in Paris on November 2, 1902. His father was a famous mathematician and politician, Paul Painlevé. One of the senior Painlevé's achievements as a politician was to set up a commission that was to examine the possibilities of using film in teaching. This occurred in 1915 under the auspices of the Ministre de l'Instruction Publique et des Inventions. Paul Painlevé no doubt had some sort of influence on his son.

Paul Painlevé married Marguerite Petit de Villeneuve shortly before the birth of Jean in 1902; it was to be a brief marriage, for Marguerite died shortly after her son was born. Paul Painlevé's sister, Marie, who was a widow, helped her brother with housekeeping and taking care of her nephew. This was necessary, for Paul was often away from home due to his work, and during these periods Jean had to make do with paternal letters. He usually spent his summers at his grandmother's house on the coast of Brittany, close to Ker Ster. Here Jean spent many hours by the sea collecting seashells and catching small water animals. He brought these back to Paris, where they found a new home in the family bathtub.

When Jean was 8 years old he began taking pictures with a 4x4 cm box camera. Later he received a Kodak Brownie No. 0. Jean took pictures of everything that he found interesting, including nature.

Early in his education, Jean followed in the footsteps of his father. He studied mathematics at the prestigious Lycée Luis le Grand, but he found the courses tedious. Rather than following the lessons, he would go to the local animal park, Jardin des Plantes, where he helped the animal keeper feed the animals. Jean Painlevé did graduate from Lycée, but he gave up mathematics and began studying medicine at the Sorbonne in 1921. After having studied for two years, he had an argument with a professor and subsequently changed his subject of study to physics and biology. Here he met Geneviève Hamon, who was to become his lifelong companion. Jean Painlevé graduated in physics and biology when he was 21.

In the 1920s, Painlevé's interest in the underground avant-garde movement in Paris commenced. He had several friends in these circles, and in 1924 he wrote for the magazine *Surréalisme*, which only appeared in one edition. In keeping with the spirit of avant-garde, Jean was fascinated with everything that was new, experimental and dynamic. For instance, he loved to drive race cars.

The Career Takes Shape

The 1920s was also the decade when Jean Painlevé began attending the small ciné clubs that had sprung up all over Paris. They were venues that showed non-commercial films, like Fernard Léger's *Ballet mécanique* and Luis Bünuel's *Un Chien andalou*. Thus Painlevé became interested in the film business. He first worked as an actor and later as a director. During his time as an actor he became fascinated with the time-lapse technique of the cinematographer André Raymond. This technique gave Painlevé the inspiration for his first scientific film, *L'oeuf d'épinoche: De la fecundation à l'éclosion* (1927). Painlevé described his film in these words:

> I filmed stickleback embryos at different stages of development for over a week. You could actually see a spermatozoid enter an egg, which was totally new, and how this fertilized egg formed its first cells and how these divisions changed over time. You saw the little cells that would later form the digestive tract, and the heart as it expanded over the vitelline membrane [Hazéra and Leglu 1986, 173].

André Raymond worked as an advisor, cameraman and technician on the film. *L'oeuf d'épinoche* was shown at the Académie des Sciences in 1928, where it was greeted with massive skepticism and a certain amount of contempt. Science still considered film to be merely entertainment for the less intellectually gifted. This, however, did not discourage Painlevé, who continued his work. Similar to his father, Jean hoped to make the film media a recognized tool of science.

Painlevé then made a series of popular-science films. With these silent shorts he returned to the beloved sea creatures of his childhood. These films, *La Pieuvre, La Daphnia, Le Bernard l'ermite* and *L' Oursin*, were all made in 1928, and were shown in major cinemas before the actual feature film. *L'Oursin* was about octopuses, with which Painlevé had been fascinated ever since his summer vacations at his grandmother's house in 1911. By means of cinematographic tricks, Painlevé shows the octopus as the mythological monster Man has often believed it to be. After this dramatic introduction, the actual octopus is shown. This is done with the help of close-ups and micro-cinematography — the same techniques with which *La Pieuvre* and *La Daphnia* were made. Already in these early films, Painlevé's interest in structures and patterns is evident, but they do not really indicate his fascination with avant-garde ideas. The reaction to these "underwater" films, which had been shot in bog aquariums, was mixed. Some were irritated with his films, others were mesmerized by the exotic world that the films depicted.[30]

Painlevé would later become famous for combining lyricism with informative content. While depicting the behavior of an animal, his films were structured in an avant-garde

Jean Painlevé ready to go under the surface (Iconothèque de la Cinémathèque Française).

manner: a jazz-like sound track was added, and ultra close-ups gave the films (and, by implication, the creatures of the sea) an abstract expression. In a review from 1937, Patricia Hutchins describes the work of Painlevé in this manner: "Characteristic of his work is an almost ruthless elimination of the superfluous, a dry sense of humor, and above all, the perception and imagination of an artist" (Hutchins 1937, 101).

Painlevé's interest in structures and abstract, avant-garde art forms is most evident in the film *Crevettes* (1930). I saw a copy of the film at the BFI. It lasts about 9 minutes. It is a sound film, and has music composed by Maurice Jaubert. Since it actually lies beyond the period in question, I will only describe it briefly here. The film offers many close-ups of crabs and the individual parts of prawns (e.g., an ultra-close-up of a part of a prawn's tail). As is typical, Painlevé often begins with an establishing shot and then moves closer and closer to his subject. Sometimes abstract forms and patterns are blurred in the beginning but then gradually become distinct.

Painlevé in an awkward position to get the right shot (Iconothèque de la Cinémathèque Française).

Martin and Osa Johnson

The Road to Nature Film

The early years in the lives of the Johnsons have been described in the first period under the section on travelogues and lecturers. The married couple's first film journey, which began in 1917, lasted nine months; during this trip they shot 40 reels of film. The New Hebrides and the Solomon Islands alone took up 20,000 feet of film. The result, *Cannibals of the South Seas* (1918), lasts three reels.* The film contains humor as well as racist undertones; however, the main draw was the meeting between supposed cannibals and young innocence, represented by Osa. The notion of a white woman among wild natives was a surefire blockbuster. The film was distributed by Robertson-Cole and premiered at the Rivoli Theatre in 1918.[31]

After this success, there were plenty of investors interested in financing the next journey of the Johnsons, and at the beginning of 1919 the couple returned to the Pacific. On November 9, 1919, they arrived from Sydney to the New Hebrides after having shot some 25,000 feet of film. In Sydney they received a telegram from their film distributor, Robertson-Cole, which read: "The public is tired of savages. Get some animal pictures" (Brownlow 1978, 468). This message was to change the direction of their lives.† The shots from Melanesia were discarded and not released before 1922 (under the title *Head Hunters of the South Seas*). But the animal film that they began working on as soon as they received the telegram premiered in 1921. The film material from the two expeditions to the islands of the Pacific were not intended to show the wildlife of the area, but focused on the culture and lifestyle there — not to mention the daring and wondrous experiences of the Johnsons. The Johnsons were some of the first Caucasians to visit the area, and among anthropologists the films from these trips are famous for their ethnographic value.[32]

The Career Takes Shape

The making of *Jungle Adventures* (1921), the first animal film of the Johnsons, proved to be much more difficult than Johnson had ever imagined. The jungle of Borneo was damp, it rained a lot, and the light rarely shined through the dense, leafy canopy — not ideal conditions for the light-sensitive raw film and lenses of those days. When the Johnsons visited the island, no roads had yet been built. To get close to the animals, the couple sailed 417 miles in canoes and houseboats up the river Kinabatangan towards the center of the island and the impenetrable jungle. They were escorted by interpreters, police and native scouts, but the river navigation did not lead them to what they had come for — wild animals. According to Osa, they obtained shots of water buffalo, elephants and crocodiles all in their natural environment. They never succeeded in securing footage of orangutans, however. Martin Johnson spent hours trying to get close enough to film them, but the dense foliage made it a fruitless venture. He was on the verge of giving up completely: "He realized how little experience he actually had in photographing wild animals. The jungle and the lighting problems fooled and confused him. He was terribly tired" (Johnson 1947, 144).

---

*The mentioned title was published in July 1918. Another version of the film material, *Among the Cannibals Isles of the South Pacific*, was released in Dec., 1918.

†The Kabel message is also described in Imperato 1992, p. 83. Osa Johnson describes the incident as a conversation with Robertson-Cole (Johnson 1947, p. 130).

Still shot taken on their Melanesian trip, 1919 (Martin and Osa Johnson Safari Museum).

Nonetheless, Martin came up with a plan, and on the way back, sailing against the counter current, he worked to accomplish it. Martin passed around a "price list" among the natives, a list that indicated how much they could earn if they brought him a live specimen of this or that animal on the list. Martin then (according to Imperato, against his better judgment) filmed a number of staged scenes with these animals (for example, a honey bear and a muntjac).

Despite the impossible odds, the Johnsons tried to obtain authentic scenes during a 16-mile hike into the jungle, where they had their first, dangerous confrontation with wild animals.

Their camera lenses only had short focal lengths, and for this reason the couple had to get very close to the animals. Generally speaking, trying to get close to wild animals is not the best of ideas — and this was demonstrated when the pair came upon a herd of elephants. Martin was just setting up the camera when the male leader of the group attacked them. The situation could have cost them both their lives, had it not been for a gunshot from a Malayan guard. Over the years, life-threatening situations like this one were to become regular features in their lives. Often they went looking for trouble — tense situations that they knew would add drama to the film. When necessary, they provoked these tense and dangerous situations because they looked good on the screen. One thing they learned from the elephant experience, however, was always to bring a professional rifleman.

Martin and Osa Johnson in Borneo in 1937 (Martin and Osa Johnson Safari Museum).

In November 1920, Osa and Martin returned to America after 20 months on the road. Osa especially enjoyed being close to the family, just as she appreciated the shopping sprees and the entertainment venues offered by city life.[33] The film that came out of the Borneo trip, *Jungle Adventures*, drew crowded houses.

The Films

Jungle Adventures illustrates the couple's journey up the Kinabatangan River, as well as the people and wildlife they met on their way. The film begins with a prologue in which we see the Johnsons talking to some guests about their trip. Then we see pictures of the street life of Sandakan, the point of departure. The boat trip itself includes some authentic animal shots that Martin *did* manage to film, as well as additional scenes of captured animals. The film ends with the trip back to Sandakan. The feature originally consisted of five reels and lasted for about an hour.

Not only was the audience impressed, the reviewers received *Jungle Adventures* with open arms. The reviewer of *The New York Times* said the following: "Some of the pictures are amazing, considering the difficulties under which they must have been made. And all of them are entertaining" (Sept. 12, 1921, 16).

The success of the film no doubt lay in Martin's fine sense of camerawork and editing. Similarly, Arthur Hoerl should be mentioned. He was an experienced scriptwriter, and composed the intertitles for the film — texts that, rather than over-dramatizing and distorting the visual side, adds depth to the film. Apart from *Jungle Adventures*, Martin made over 20 single-reel films out of the material they brought home with them from Borneo. These pictures were distributed under the umbrella title *Martin Johnson's Voyages* and were sold as educational films.

Nineteen twenty-one was the year Martin Johnson first met nature historian and sculptor Carl Akeley at the Explorers Club in New York. The two soon became close friends, and Akeley taught Johnson to show much greater respect for animals. Many years after this initial meeting they met again in Africa. Osa, Martin and Carl had an incredible, peaceful experience where they observed lions at close range. This proved a supposedly favorite theory of Akeley's — namely, that lions do not attack people unless they feel threatened. Akeley impressed Johnson immensely, and Johnson spoke highly of Akeley on several occasions.[34]

At their first meeting Akeley had encouraged Martin to go on an adventure/globetrotter expedition to Africa, a continent that Akeley had visited four times, and on whose fauna he was an expert. The purpose of Akeley's expedition was similar to that of *Jungle Adventures*— to film authentic scenes of wild animals, with an emphasis on the word "authentic." In the end, 100,000 feet of film came out of the expedition. This was boiled down into a 7-reel film called *Trailing African Wild Animals* (1923), which lasted for an hour. Martin Johnson and author Terry Ramsaye were responsible for the editing and the intertitles. The film was edited to show Martin and Osa on a search for a "forgotten lake." During their search they encounter many wild animals and go through many dangerous experiences. The film's PR campaign claimed that animals had been killed during the expedition only when absolutely necessary. This was good publicity, considering that many people by now were disgusted with the concept of the hunting film. Allegedly, many of the animals were shot because they attacked the expedition members, but what the PR material neglected to mention was that these animals had actually been provoked on purpose.[35]

Seventy-five percent of the film was financed by the Johnsons and Martin's father, John. They found additional economic support from diverse sources: the Coca-Cola Company, Maxwell House Coffee and the American Museum of Natural History. *Trailing African Wild Animals* premiered on May 20, 1923.[36]

The Johnsons experienced considerable problems with the animal scenes, for they had little experience with African wildlife, but they learned a lot during the journey. Imperato noted the couple's development:

> A year and a half of intense experiences in the African bush had successfully transformed Martin and Osa into first-rate wildlife photographers.... They had produced films that were truly unique and spectacular for their times [Imperato 1992, 109].

This first savannah production taught them a lot, and they managed to obtain fairly good animal scenes. Their biggest lens was specially constructed and had a focal length of 425mm (16.7 inches). Still, the press material accompanying the picture exaggerated when it claimed that the filmmakers used "lenses that pulled animals 330 ft. away so close to you that you could almost count the individual hair in their fur."[37]

Working with Nature Films

Johnson was well aware that the road to making a good animal film lay in the quality of the equipment. This is evident when he made an Africa film for which he not only

Hunting? No. Defense against the fierce creatures of the wild (Martin and Osa Johnson Safari Museum)!

acquired the best lenses from Dallmeyer and Bausch & Lomb, but also brought 21 cameras, 10 of which were film cameras. Half of these were Akeley cameras. Uniquely, two of them were joined in such a way that one of them filmed at ordinary speed while the other filmed at a high speed.[38]

Another device Johnson utilized was a film camera installed at the end of a long iron pole which could then be used for filming animals running beside a car.[39] Johnson thought a great deal about his work and his role, and should be recognized as a major animal cinematographer. Kevin Brownlow praises Johnson, commenting, "Johnson was probably the best cameraman of all the African explorers.... To capture such pictures required dedication of an almost religious intensity" (Brownlow 1978, 469–70).

Johnson was a fine cinematographer, but his talent was most remarkable when it came to technique. Over the years, Martin and Osa gradually developed advanced systems and methods for filming. When they went on extensive film expeditions, they usually brought a considerable group of natives to carry the rifles and boxes with equipment. When Martin needed some special equipment, he simply called out a number, and the servant who carried the box with this number would step forward. Johnson also used a native assistant in his rolling dark room. I use the word "rolling" deliberately because it was set up inside a Willys-Knight truck. Here Martin kept the necessary chemicals, and he would develop the films as they were finished. After he had developed them, he would go through the filmed material very carefully, and he would pack it in a tin container and give it a number. Finally, he would seal the box with paraffin, which protected the films against the damp climate.[40]

Circumventing authenticity became a trademark of the film productions of the Johnsons. When a scene needed a little action, Johnson might well stage an artificial set piece and subsequently film some close-ups of tame animals. Martin also admits that he sometimes approached the wild animals in order to provoke a dramatic situation: "This time Osa took the crank while I went forward as 'movie director' to start action among the animals" (Johnson 1928, 125).

The meeting with Carl Akeley mentioned earlier eventually changed Johnson's views on such methods. Akeley was a scientist rather than an entertainer, and he helped push Martin towards securing authentic shots, and made him understand that the African wildlife were threatened with extinction.[41] Martin, however, was first and foremost a businessman, and he knew what the paying audience wanted: excitement. Therefore, he continued to dramatize events, and would exaggerate and stage the dangers he and Osa encountered.

A mere glance at the literary works of both Osa and Martin suggests that the couple were ambivalent when it came to shooting and killing animals. They usually have a couple of good explanations as to why this or that animal was shot (for instance, that the pair felt threatened or the crew needed food). But at times their treatment of animals was anything but respectful or admirable.

During the filming of *Simba*, the Johnsons made a series of questionable experiments or "games." On one occasion Martin put cayenne pepper into a zebra carcass. The zebra had been killed for the purpose of serving as bait for lions. Osa and Martin thought it terribly amusing when a female lion came upon the pepper, pulled a wry face and sneezed.[42]

On another occasion, Osa and Martin wanted to create a scene for a deliberately funny film about the wildlife of Africa. The sequence was to be called "African Golf" and included a lion being hit by a flying golf ball. When they came upon a male lion who was taking a nap, Osa threw the ball at him while Martin filmed the incident.[43]

The couple's ambivalence regarding the killing of animals was also evident in their films. Some animals, they seemed to believe, simply deserved to die; others must be provoked to be killed; and still others one cannot avoid killing: "I could set the group in motion and solve our meat problem simultaneously.... 'Aah, if only I hadn't killed it.' I sobbed, pressing my head against Martin's chest. 'It is so peaceful ... and so beautiful!'" (Johnson 1947, 176).

The African servants expected two things of their Bwana. 1. That he does not run away in fear of the wild animals; and 2. That he is a good marksman. During Osa and Martin's first film expedition, they could not live up to these expectations. The couple ran away the first time they encountered a group of buffalos — which lost them the respect of both carriers and servants. One of them, Jerramani, especially felt humiliated by their lack of courage and abilities. Osa's intuitive reaction was to scream loudly — her shriek is said to have saved them twice from attacking buffalos; while her strange, but natural, behavior is said to have won her at least *some* respect among the natives.[44]

Over the years, Osa became quite a good marksman. For this reason her filmic role was often to keep watch while Martin photographed or filmed. This talent of hers did not come naturally. To begin with, she behaved quite clumsily. On one occasion she dropped her rifle, which then went off. Indeed, for the better part of three years the couple had

The natives liked "Little Woman" (Martin and Osa Johnson Safari Museum).

difficulties hitting anything at all, which meant that the expedition team on the first trip to Africa starved for long stretches of time. The pair began their training in Borneo, where Osa tried to shoot crocodiles, and continued it in Africa. This training was intensified when they became particularly tired of their own lack of skills, and then practiced rigorously for weeks.[45]

Due to her pleasant personality and her ear for language, Osa was the more liked and respected of the two. She spoke Malaysian and Swahili, and was able to communicate with the natives. In Africa she was known as "Memsahib Kidogo"—"Little Woman." Martin was considered the amazing camera enthusiast who was always very keen on getting the pictures he wanted; when necessary, he took on the role of leader and told people off. The natives in Africa called him "Bwana Piccer"—"Image-Maker."[46]

The values of home life, children and cooking were important to Osa, but they were not allowed to play a significant role in her marriage. In this light, the title of her autobiography, *I Married Adventure*, takes on a significant meaning. Already after the making of *Head Hunters of the South Seas*, Osa suggested that they should buy a house. Her need for practical chores and a safe haven was only allowed to flourish in the camps they lived in on the road. Here, Osa tried to create homely coziness and, when possible, cooked traditional American dishes. This was especially the case during the four-year stay in Africa, where their guests dined royally at Osa's table. Her joy of shopping was legendary. In London, when they received a check for $10,000 for *Head Hunters of the South Seas*, Osa immediately spent $1000 on clothes. When they left New York to go to Africa for four years, they had a major argument about the life they led; Osa broke down in tears, and Martin had to bring forth his most appeasing and gentle qualities. Furthermore, the couple discussed the possibility of adopting children shortly before Martin's tragic death.[47]

Simba

On December 1, 1923, Martin and Osa left New York to go on a new adventure-globetrotter expedition to Africa. They were not to return until four years later. Their goal was to make a film about primeval and untouched nature, but they wanted to do this in a manner that had never been done before. Filming had originally been planned to last for five years. The raw material was intended to form the backbone of three films: *Wanderings of Elephants*; *Songa, the Tale Bearer*; and *African Babies*; but due to unknown circumstances, this never happened.

Shooting took place in the Northern part of Kenya, by the Paradise Lake and the Tanganyika plains, and their hope was that the footage would show future generations an "embalmed" image of nature: a documentary about wilderness and wildlife as it must have looked thousands of years ago.[48]

The costs reached somewhere around $250,000, but the footage from the film expedition was not originally intended to be used for commercial purposes. The film material was to be used in lectures and at museums. The reason for this was that the American Museum of Natural History (AMNH) was responsible for the financing of the expedition, and in the beginning they had no commercial motives. This attitude changed, however, when the museum found that they were short on money for a new Africa section.*

For this reason, AMNH gave the footage to a businessman called Wilson (no Christian name was found in the literature) who immediately understood the commercial value of the film reels. He saw to it that the 200 reels were edited into a commercial version of 6 reels, which were distributed under the title *Simba*. The film premiered in New York in January 1928 with the incredibly high entrance fee of $1.65. Internationally, the film made $2 million.[49] The success made Wilson realize the lucrative market for non-fiction film, and he established Talking Picture Epics, Inc., which distributed this type of film. Many of the scenes in *Simba* were shot at the Paradise Lake or by watering holes near the lake, but some of the wildlife scenes were shot on the Athi plain, in the Marsapit National Park, at the Southern Game Reserve and at the Itching highland.

The scenes depicting African wildlife are of a high quality in the sense that the animals seem at peace and unaware of the presence of the camera. This is no doubt due to the big telephoto lenses that Martin used.

The film was edited in such a way that it offers good drama. On one occasion a caravan is crossing a river. Here cross-cutting between the crocodiles on the river bank and the people who are about to cross the water generates tension. As the caravan begins the crossing, the film cuts to the crocodiles gliding into the water and disappearing below the surface.

---

*The financing of the film material handled by AMNH was mainly due to the work of Carl Akeley but also naturally Osa and Martin Johnson themselves. The financial support came mainly from the vice president of Bankers Trust Company's managing director Daniel Pomeroy and the founder of Kodak-Eastman, George Eastman. (Imperato 1992, pp. 116–118).

Another dramatic scene, created by inventiveness behind the camera and in the editing room, depicts a group of elephants who at first seem frightened by the presence of various camera people. Their fright appears to increase when an inserted scene shows a steppe fire. The situation goes out of control as the fire spreads. As the flames approach the elephants, the herd scatters and takes flight. In the turmoil, Osa and Martin are nearly run down by an elephant, and are "forced" to shoot it. It *is* possible to detect that the situation was created in the editing room, but the scene is still nerve-racking.

The staging of the events in the film and the creative use of the material are done intelligently to create tension and exciting sequences; but, sadly, they also ridicule the animals and the natives. In *Simba*, the infamous Johnson humor appears when two natives — obviously for the first time in their lives — open a beer with a bottle opener, or when native women put on some of Osa's make-up. A hippopotamus is also called "just a marine pig," and a group of lions are described "as gentle as a load of dynamite."

Nonetheless, at the time, *Simba* was the culmination of Martin Johnson's technical skills. He had become much better at filming the ordinary behavior and the natural environment of the animals. He had become better at finding watering holes with many animals nearby, and had also increased his skills when it came to building hiding places, so that the animals were not disturbed by his presence. He also used animals and fresh blood as bait,

Martin Johnson, together with natives during the recording of *Simba* (Martin and Osa Johnson Safari Museum).

Recording of sound for *Congorilla* in 1932 (Martin and Osa Johnson Safari Museum).

which he knew the predators could not resist. In this manner he was fairly certain of getting good close-ups of African animals.

One of the reasons for the fine finish of *Simba* may be the fact that Lillian Seebach helped edit *Simba*.[50] Her work is not even credited on the film; only Terry Ramsaye and Martin Johnson are mentioned.* Ramsaye and Seebach probably created the continuity flow in *Simba*, but this flow was greatly enhanced by the intertitles of the film, which create ideal transitions between otherwise incoherent events.

Simba contains material filmed by others (e.g., Alfred J. Klein's *Equatorial Africa: Roosevelt's Hunting Grounds*, the rights of which are said to have cost $30,000). Moreover, the lion spear hunt from *Simba* is said to contain film material of both Carl Akeley and A. Klein. They have been credited in the silent film version.

Simba was made in both a silent and a sound version. The producers wanted to accommodate the audience who wanted to go to the cinema just to experience the new phenomenon — sound film. *Simba* had been filmed without sound equipment, but the producers added a sound track with Martin's voice-over, as well as a musical soundtrack.

Both film versions of *Simba* premiered on 28 January 1928, but the sound version was the more successful of the two. This was a clear indication that the days of the silent film

*Seebach came to work on the Johnson films until the death of Martin Johnson in 1937.

were numbered. In the future, Martin and Osa would bring sound recording equipment with them on their adventure-globetrotter expeditions.

Africa continued to be a playground for the people who made wildlife and wilderness films. This continent was visited by many such children — not least of them Martin Johnson. The film business continued to move away from hunting films towards the direction of nature preservation/protection films — which may have been instrumental in changing people's attitudes as to how they wanted to see animals and wildlife depicted on the screen. An antithesis to this claim lay in the drama-documentary nature films that depict predators as killing machines, films that in no way paved the way for nature preservation. *Secrets of Nature* followed in the footsteps of the nature series made by Filmfabriken Danmark and set new standards for how knowledge-imparting films were to be made. And Bengt Berg — the most creative and innovative cinematographer of the period — did the same.

As it has been shown several times, many of the people behind wildlife and wilderness films had an ambivalent attitude toward wildlife preservation. One minute they would speak solemnly of the terrible reduction in the number of wild animals; the next they would speak denigratingly of a particular species, encourage its extinction and shoot large numbers of wildlife.

CONCLUSION

In this book I have compiled the information I have been able to collect on non-fiction films containing wildlife and wilderness aspects from the period 1895 to 1928. On the basis of my first research experiences in 1997, I knew that my endeavor would be a strenuous one. Still, over the years I have managed to gather much more material than I had ever dreamed of. Few people, least of all myself, could have imagined how much the nature and wildlife film genre developed in the years between 1895 and 1928.

As I mentioned earlier, I have deliberately included a considerable number of factors, and in this conclusion I will summarize those which I believe to have been the most important elements in the development of the genre. The conclusion will be structured along the lines of the rest of the book (i.e., according to historical periods). This will create a fairly complex conclusion, indicating that many aspects of the development of the genre may well have influenced one another. It is not possible to draw definite conclusions from a historical perspective when so many unknown factors are present. Nonetheless, working on *Cameras into the Wild* has led me to believe that there is a pattern in the development of the genre; this pattern I will attempt to elucidate in the following pages.

In the period between 1500 and 1850, man withdrew from nature to such an extent that an increasing number of people looked at nature from the outside rather than from within (or as part of nature). In other words, man was separated from nature, and because of this he looked at nature with different eyes, a fact which helped lay the foundation for natural science and nature tourism. Nature only became a topic of interest among the general population from around 1870, when "ordinary" people began to look at nature not as a mere resource but as an interesting concept in itself. Man started to concern himself with the structure and life of nature. First of all, an increasing interest in the organization of nature appeared. Second, the inclusion of natural history and science in school curricula started. And third, the boon of a decreasing work load helped make the general population aware of the beauties of nature. This all meant that in 1895 there was a big enough potential audience to support the appearance of the nature film.

1895–1902: 62 Films Registered

In this period film was part of the amusement offered at fairs. Films were screened at variety theaters and by touring lecturers. From the very beginning, the programs included films containing scenes of nature and wild animals. The first of these was a zoo film, *Lion, London Zoological Garden*, that had been shot by Louis Lumière in 1895. In 1896 a number of landscape nature films followed, and two very popular special genres appeared: the wave film, which had its days of glory before 1900; and the waterfall film. The latter special genre appeared in large numbers until 1916. Water had the advantage of embodying the characteristics of the new media: movement. Only a few wildlife films, such as Frederick Blechynden's *Wild Bear in Yellowstone Park* (1897), appeared during this period, and they remained rarities until 1907.

The Technical Conditions Until 1910

1. Like many other cinematographers after him, George Méliès, who made wave films in 1896, has described how hard it was to film in nature in the early days of the medium. His lamentations were quite understandable when we consider that the weight of a camera and tripod easily reached 100 pounds. Such heavy loads no doubt kept a lot of people from making nature films.

2. The ones that did take on the genre faced more challenges than the mere presence of wild animals. In the early part of this period, the lens was permanently attached to the camera, but innovative cinematographers made sockets in order to replace the ordinary 50mm (2 inch) lens with a 150mm (6 inch) lens. This occurred around 1905, and three years later, in 1908, it became possible to use a 230mm (9 inch) lens.

3. The apertures of the diaphragm were very small, and so the subject required a significant amount of light. So did the film, and clear weather was necessary for good results. The first type of raw film was atmosphere-weak and had to be developed fast (or else the pictures would simply disappear). At the same time, the raw film was not very sensitive to green nuances, which was obviously the dominant color in many landscapes.

4. From around 1904, Williamson's box camera made it possible to frame and focus on one's subject; and although this was difficult to do, it was an improvement in comparison to earlier cameras.

1903–1906: 74 Films Registered

In this period real cinemas were established in major cities, and with such permanent exhibition venues came the need for frequent changes in the film programs. The moving pictures were no longer news, and the audience needed more persuasion to go to the cinema. Film production became much more organized, and thus many non-fiction films lost ground to the fiction genre. This did not affect the wildlife film genre much, for it simply sought new directions. From 1903, hunting films started to appear — the first one being *Une Chasse à l'ours blanc*. But not until 1905 did hunting films appear in great numbers, and they continued to be popular until 1915. The hunting film had the advantage that its topic was dramatic in itself and had an inherent, natural chronology. The films depicted wildlife and nature scenes, but did so from a rifle's perspective. The camera mostly captured prey, and a lot of the wildlife that appeared had already been shot dead. Nineteen-hundred-and-three to 1906 was a pioneer period for the knowledge-imparting film, which created "newness" within the film media and helped lure the audience to the cinemas. Knowledge-imparting films often featured micro-cinematography and aquarium scenes. Charles Urban and F. Martin-Duncan launched the nature film series *The Unseen World*, which contained *Cheese Mites* (1903), a small film coordinating time and place — a picture that was clearly ahead of its time.

1907–1910: 91 Films Registered

In the western world there was a great increase in the number of cinemas during this time period, which may have helped induce an administrative organization and standard-ization of the film industry in general. Several of the major film companies saw the value inherent in the nature and wildlife film genre, and hired cinematographers with experience in this field. Three of the major cinematographers were to leave their mark on the entire period: Oliver G. Pike, Cherry Kearton and F. Percy Smith. They helped popularize bird films, time-lapse sequences and animal films. As regards the time-lapse technique, it is remarkable that *Mother Love Among the Animals* (1908) is the first nature film I know of that includes a time-lapse scene. The knowledge-imparting films became regular merchan-dized goods, and film companies increasingly hired specialists and set up special departments for the production of such pictures. A few films copied the narrative technique of the fiction film, such as continuity editing, P.O.V., establishment scenes, close-ups, and variety in scenes and compositions. In this regard, *Nature's Hidden Beauties — Pond Life* from 1908 is one of the most interesting examples. In this period, the standard of both cinematographers and equipment improved. Thanks to experience and technical developments, cinematog-raphers began to master camera movements, despite the cumbersome tripod. Thus, *Die Geheimnisse Der Meeres Tiefe* (1910) includes some stunning pans.

The Technical Advances After 1910 and Before 1920

After 1910, dramatic technical improvements occurred, making life a lot easier for the cinematographer. These improvements:

1. Brought him closer to wild animals. From 1914 a 430mm (17 inch) telephoto lens appeared, and from 1911 camera noise was reduced considerably.

2. Created much more beautiful results, depicting landscapes by means of gliding camera movements that enhanced the films' ability to capture animals in motion. This became possible because the tripods improved; they became more stable and easier to handle. This development peaked in 1918, when the first gyroscopic tripod head appeared.

3. Made it possible to act faster because the cinematographer became less dependent on the light conditions. A lens carousel was invented in 1914, and an aperture of the diaphragm of up to $f3.5$ was on the market from around 1916.

4. Created more detailed images and a varied range of grey nuances — this due to the launching of the orthochromatic raw film in 1914.

1911–1921: 242 Films Registered

At the beginning of this period cinemas were growing bigger and bigger. Some of them were lavishly decorated and accommodated over 1000 people. Such houses encouraged films that appealed to a large audience. Once again, wilderness and wildlife film rose to the occasion. John Hemment's film *Paul J. Rainey's African Hunt* from 1912 was one of these; it had more wildlife scenes (without hunting) than any other previous hunting film. It had become important for a considerable segment of the audience to see the wildlife depicted in their natural environment without being hunted down and killed, or even stressed by the presence of the film crew.

In time, natural behavior came to be seen as a sign of quality, and the hunting and killing of animals for fun came to be considered bad taste. Already from 1911, the number of traditional hunting films that included the shooting of animals decreased. They were succeeded by bloodless hunting films like *Lassoing Wild Animals in Africa* (1911) — motion pictures that embodied natural excitement and tension. This tendency may have been expedited by the film magazine *The Moving Picture World* when, in 1909, it printed a couple of articles encouraging and praising authentic wilderness and wildlife films. Herbert Ponting's expedition film, which was recorded under extreme conditions during Scott's expedition of 1911–13, included fascinating scenes of the natural behavior of wild animals. Two important nature film cinematographers appeared on the scene during this period: William L. Finley and Raymond L. Ditmars. They both used humor in their nature films, a narrative "trick" that became common during the 1910s. Finley and Ditmars discovered that the optimal situation was to mix information, drama, explanations and feelings; and several films from this period attempt to evoke feelings. The most common method was to include anthropomorphic intertitles, and show anthropomorphic activities of cuddly animals. There are many examples of such films. The first ones appear around 1911 — for instance, *The Strength and Agility of Insects*, in which the animals are associated with various human traits. But there were many other films that were very matter-of-fact — for instance, *Insect Pond Life* (190?).

The underwater film also went through changes and improvements. The first attempts to film from underwater chambers were probably made around 1911; a diving bell was used from 1912; and the first attempt to film while using a diving suit probably occurred around 1917–18.

The knowledge-imparting film had now become such a well-established genre that companies had been set up which specialized in films that could be used as teaching material. Gradually, more and more schools accepted the film as an educational tool.

The wilderness and wildlife film also learned from the authenticity inherent in the expedition and adventure-globetrotter films, and from the topic of man vs. nature. The tension that arises when man enters unfamiliar territory, and the unpredictability this entails, were well-suited to the film medium. From the very beginning, travel, hunting and expedition films thrived on this quality of the medium, but gradually hybrid genres appeared in which wildlife film and other subgenres used whatever elements that appealed to the audience. Thus, the boundaries between them became less marked. This was especially the case when the purpose was to reach a large audience; the unpredictability of the wilderness and wildlife film lay in the uncertainty of how the animals and nature itself would "behave" when confronted by the Caucasian heroes (confrontations that often ended in life-and-death struggles). If these situations did not occur naturally, they were staged in order to meet the demands of the audience. These hybrid forms became so popular that regular feature films also began using the best and most dramatic features of the wildlife, hunting, travel and expedition pictures.

Technical Improvements 1920–1928

Technical development had a huge impact on the nature and wildlife film genre.

1. The cinematographer was able to get much closer to the animals. From 1921, telephoto lenses of 530mm (21 inches) were on the market.

2. Experimentation became easier (and hence more frequent) with the use of battery-run cameras that appeared in 1922. Moreover, from around 1926, a camera weighed no more than 7 pounds, and the movements of the cinematographer became much freer and more natural.

3. Cinematographers began to make more beautiful compositions: an ocular appeared on the market showing exactly what was being filmed; and from about 1920, the use of panchromatic film improved the picture quality considerably.

Oliver Pike's *Nature's Gliders* (1922) was one of the first films to use panchromatic film. The film also featured slow-motion sequences, which at that point in time was quite new.

1922–1928: 262 Films Registered

Nature and wildlife films may be said to have been "staged" ever since 1905, when the film *The Spider and the Fly* placed predator and prey in the same scene together, thus encouraging a mortal combat. Staged scenes occurred from the very beginning in the history of nature and wildlife films, but never before was the use of this method as frequent as in the period in question. Intertitles dramatizing events are evident in *Battle of the Ants* from 1922; and Osa and Martin Johnson staged events to dramatize (and ridicule) the actions of both animals and natives. This tendency increasingly flew out of control, and over-dramatic films like *Chang* (1927) and *Oo-tang* (1928) used drama-documentary techniques to present wild animals in what were basically fictitious narratives.

In contrast, many of the cinematographers whose names have appeared in earlier periods and who still made films at this point in time maintained a sense of respect towards their subjects. Three notable Scandinavian filmmakers appeared in this period: Oscar Olsson, Richard Lund and Bengt Berg. Lund and Berg were among the most innovative filmmakers of their time, and their work was succeeded by the series *Secrets of Nature* (which included the amazing film *The Cuckoo's Secret*). Both Berg and the people behind *Secrets of Nature* were experimental pioneers. Berg's 1923 film *Sagan om De Sista Örnarna* (*The Story of the Last Eagles*) and Lund's *Frøerne og Deres Fjender* (*The Frogs and Their Enemies*) from 1921 featured a tension-building structure, eye-line matching and animal P.O.V. shots. In addition, these films were part of a new tendency within the nature film genre, in which the motion pictures did not merely seek to *preserve* but also to *protect* wilderness and wildlife. This was part of the contemporary *zeitgeist*, evident both among ordinary people and at a political level (cf. the section on nature protection and nature tourism). In the early 1920s, some films expressed concern over species that were threatened with extinction — e.g., *What's Left of the Bison Herds* (1921) and *The Forest* (1925).

Looking to the Future

Hopefully, this book will make it a little easier for those who wish to study the history of the nature and wildlife film genre — a topic which has been seriously neglected and which must be one of the darkest areas on the map of film history. It is an unknown territory, offering many exciting adventures to those who dare to enter. A word of warning, however: it is a hidden jungle where the lianas are not necessarily joined with the tree crowns above, and which therefore provides very little support.

It would be obvious to examine what happened after 1928, but the period 1895–1928 has far more to offer than I have been able to elucidate in this book; and many areas require serious research attention before any final concluding remarks on the early history of nature film can be made.

We know far too little about films that may have had a major impact on the early history of the genre. Examples would be *African Bird and Animal Life* (1912) and *Alaska Wonders in Motion* (1917). In addition, there are important cinematographers about whom we know very little — e.g., American Frederick Blechynden, Russian Ladislas Starewitch and Swedish David Sjölander. These are but a few examples, and there are many other nature and wildlife films and cinematographers that deserve to be studied further.

FILMOGRAPHY, 1895–1928
Non-Fiction Films with Nature, Animals, Wildlife or Wilderness

I have spent many hours compiling this list of nature films, which is the foundation of *Cameras into the Wild*. I consider it to be a valuable tool in the quantitative assessment of tendencies and developments within the genre. But first and foremost, the list gives a fine overview of the genre which would otherwise be difficult to establish, since such a copious and detailed list has never previously been published. Each entry will be listed as follows:

Title
Prod.: Producer / production company / production country
Dir.: Director
Cin.: Cinematographer
Distr.: Distribution
Place of production, description, part of a series.

(Note: Sources used to calculate the average running time for the different periods of time: Hampton 1931, 29–31; Allen 1980, 288, 297; Bordwell & Thompson 1994, 37; Engberg 1977 (1), 187 and (2), 377; and finally, Low & Manvell 1948, 45.)

1895–1902

Nature films made between 1895 and 1902 last between 32 and 185 seconds. The average duration for films made during this period of time is between 40 and 75 seconds, but this average includes all kinds of films.

1895

Feeding the Swans
Prod.: France
Cin.: Louis Lumiére

Lion, London Zoological Garden
Prod.: France
Cin.: Louis Lumiére

1896

Feeding the Doves
Prod.: Edison / USA

Gros temps en mer
Prod.: Lumiére / France
Distr.: Charles Urban Trading Company

Niagara Falls, Gorge
Prod.: James White / Edison / USA
Cin.: William Heise
And 4 other films of the falls.

Pélicans
Prod.: France / Lumière

Rough Sea at Dover
Prod.: Robert Paul / Great Britain
Cin.: Birt Acres

A Sea Cave Near Lisbon
Prod.: Paul Acres / Great Britain
Cin.: Harry (Henry) W. Short

1897

American Falls — From Above
Prod.: James White / Edison / USA
Cin: William Heise
A part of a series, consisting of 6 films of Niagara Falls.

Elephants at the Zoo
Prod.: British Mutoscope / Great Britain
London Zoo.

Niagara—Les chutes
Prod.: Lumiére / France
Distr.: Charles Urban Trading Company

The Sea Lions Home
Prod.: James White / Edison / USA
Cin.: Frederick Blechynden
Golden Gate Beach.

Surf of Monterey
Prod.: James White / Edison / USA
Cin.: Frederick Blechynden
California.

Svanerne i Sortedamssøen
Prod.: Denmark / Peter Elfelt
Cin.: Peter Elfelt
A.k.a. *Swans in the Danish Lake Sortedamssøen*
Copenhagen.

Wild Bear in Yellowstone Park
Old Faithfull Geyser
Riverside Geyser
Upper Falls of the Yellowstone
Lower Falls, Grand Canyon, Yellowstone
Prod.: James White? / Edison
Cin.: Frederick Blechynden?
A series of films from Yellowstone National Park

1898

Africa
Prod.: Great Britain
Dir.: Sir Philip Brocklehurst

Feeding the Seagulls
Prod.: Edison / USA
Close to San Francisco.

Ostriches Feeding
Prod.: Edison / USA

Ostriches Running
Prod.: Edison / USA

A Panorama of Indian Scenes
Prod.: India / Great Britain
Dir.: Professor Stephens

Pelicans at the Zoo
Prod.: British Mutoscope / Biograph Co. / Great
   Britain
London Zoo.

Sea Waves
Prod.: Edison / USA
The New Jersey coast.

View from an Engine Front
Prod.: Warwick Trading Company / England

1899

Elephants in a Circus Parade
Prod.: American Mutoscope and Biograph / USA
Brooklyn.

Feeding the Pigeons
Prod.: American Mutoscope and Biograph / USA
Cin.: Billy Bitzer
Boston.

Feeding the Tigers
Prod.: Warwick Trading Company / England
London Zoo.

*Moving Pictures of Natural Scenes and Religious
   Rituals*
Prod.: Pathé Company / France / India
Dir.: Hiralal Sen

Panoramic View from the White Pass Railroad
Prod.: Edison Mfg. Co. / USA
Cin.: Robert Bonine(?)

Pianka and Her Lions
Prod.: ?

Prof. Paul Boynton Feeding His Sea Lions
Prod.: American Mutoscope and Biograph / USA
Cin.: F.S. Armitage
Coney Island.

1900

Feeding Sea Lions
Prod.: Lubin
Cin.: F.S. Armitage

Fight Between a Tarantula and a Scorpion
Prod.: British Mutoscope and Biograph
South Africa.

Phantom Ride
Prod.: England / R.W. Paul?

Rough Sea Breaks Against a Sea Wall
Prod.: Bamforth and Company, Ltd. / France

The Spider and the Butterfly
Prod.: Great Britain / Pathé

Spiders on a Web
Prod.: Great Britain / G.A. Smith

Views from a Train on a Mountainside
Prod.: France

Waves Break a Rocky Shore
Prod.: France
Distr.: Gaumont Company

1901

Dyregruppe i Zoologisk Have
Prod.: Denmark
Cin.: Peter Elfelt
A.k.a. *Animal Scenario in Zoo*

Sea Gulls in Central Park
Prod.: American Mutoscope and Biograph / USA
Cin.: F.S. Armitage

1902

Bird Rock, Nordland, Norway
Prod.: Burton-Holmes / USA
Cin.: Depue

Brook Trout Fishing
Prod.: USA / American Mutoscope & Biograph
Dir.: F.S. Armitage / W.K.L. Dickson

Deer in Park
Prod.: USA / American Mutoscope & Biograph
New York.

Deer in Wild Park, Göteborg, Sweden
Prod.: Burton-Holmes / USA
Cin.: Depue

The Elephant's Bath
Prod.: Deutsche Mutoscope und Biog./ Germany
Berlin Zoo.

Feeding the Bears at the Menagerie
Prod.: USA / Edison

Going to the Hunt, Meadow Brook
Prod.: USA / Edison
Dir.: G.W. Bitzer

Panoramic View Between Palliser and Field
Prod.: Edison Mfg. Co. / USA

Sea Gulls Following Fishing Boats
Prod.: Edison / USA
San Francisco Bay.

Trout Poachers
Prod.: American Mutoscope & Biograph / USA
Dir.: F.S. Armitage / W.K.L. Dickson

1903–1906

Nature films made between 1903 and 1906 last between 36 seconds and 6.22 minutes. The average duration for films made during this period of time is between 1.4 and 4.1 minutes, but this average includes all kinds of films.

1903

Arctic — Far North
Prod.: National Geographic / USA
Dir.: Anthony Fiala

Une chasse a l'ours blanc
Prod.: Pathé Frères / France
Distr.: S. Lubin

Desperate Poaching Affray
Prod.: Haggar and Son / Great Britain
A chase film that includes scenes of nature (the police chasing hunters in the wild).

Electrocuting an Elephant
Prod.: Edison / USA
Cin.: Jacob Blair Smith and Edwin S. Porter
Coney Park, NY.

European Rest Cure
Prod.: Great Britain
Dir.: Edwin S. Porter

Feeding the Elephants
Prod.: USA
Distr.: Lubin

Feeding the Hippopotamus
Prod.: USA
Distr.: Lubin

Feeding the Russian Bear
Prod.: USA
Cin.: Billy Bitzer
Glen Island, NY.

Feeding the Swans
Prod.: USA
Distr.: S. Lubin

Fighting Rams
Prod.: Edison / USA
India.

Llamas at Play
Prod.: USA
Cin.: Billy Bitzer

The Monkeys of Borneo
A Skirmish in the Jungle
Passing a Mango Swamp
The Rapids of the Gorge
Through the Jungle and the Forest by Rail
Panorama of Pandas River
Prod.: Charles Urban Trading Company / Great Britain
Cin.: H.M. Lomas
Into the Wilds of Borneo: a series consisting of 32 motion pictures, of which the above 6 are of great importance.

North American Elk
Prod.: USA
Distr.: S. Lubin

North American Grey Wolves
Prod.: USA
Distr.: S. Lubin

Polar Bears
Prod.: USA
Distr.: S. Lubin
Filmed in the USA.

Romance of the Rail
Prod.: Great Britain
Dir.: Edwin S. Porter

Ruby and Mandy at Coney Island
Prod.: Great Britain
Dir.: Edwin S. Porter

Soft Snow on the Mönch-Joch
A Winter Fairyland
The Panorama from the Summit
Prod.: Charles Urban Trading Company / Great
   Britain
Expedition Leader: H.M. Lomas
A series of films of expeditions to the Jungfrau
   and Matterhorn.

Water Flea and Rotifers
Circulation of Blood in a Frog
Cheese Mites
The Amoebe— the Beginning of Life
Prod.: Charles Urban Trading Company / Great
   Britain
Dir.: F. Martin Duncan
Selections from the series *The Unseen World*.

1904

Elephants at Work
Prod.: Edison / USA

Eléphants au travail aux Indes
Prod.: Pathé Frerès
India.

Fox and Rabbits
Prod.: Pathé Frerès

Lion and Lioness
Prod.: Edison / USA

Polar Bears at Play with Cubs
Prod.: Edison / USA

The Waterfalls of Wales
Prod.: Hepworth Manufacturing Co. / Great
   Britain
Rhaiidur de Falls.

1905

The Boa Constrictor and the Rat
Elephant in Native Surrounding
Empire of the Ants
Feeding Pelicans
In the Den with the Striped Huenas
The Spider and the Fly
Prod.: Charles Urban Trading Company / Great
   Britain
Dir.: F. Martin Duncan
Cin.: H.M. Lomas / A.G. Avery / J. Rosenthal
Entries in the series of films called *Natural History*.

Educated Monkeys in Costume
Prod.: Charles Urban Trading Company / Great
   Britain

Feeding the Otters
Prod.: Charles Urban Trading Company/ Great
   Britain
Distr.: Kleine Optical Co.

The Octopus
The Pollack
Sea Bream
The Dog Fish
Conger Eel
The Cray-fish
The Lobster
Sand Hoppers and Shrimps
Shore Crabs
Prod.: Charles Urban Trading Company / Great
   Britain
Dir.: F. Martin Duncan
From a series of films called *Denizens of the Deep*.
   One of them, *Stalked Ship Barnacle*, is
   described as follows: "A number of these re-
   markable animals are shown attached to the
   bottom of a bottle."

Rescued by Dover
Prod.: Hepworth Manufacturing Co. / Great Brit-
   ain
Dir.: Lewin Fitzhamon

1906

Bjørnen er løs [*The Bear Is Loose*]
En Tur Igennem Norge
En Tur Igennem Sverige
Guldbrandsdal
Lerfossen
Mellem Aber og Bjørne
Prod.: Nordisk Film Kompagni / Denmark
Films made in Sweden and Norway.

The Canadian Rockies in Winter
Prod.: Charles Urban / Canada-France

A Caribou Hunt
Prod.: Biograph Co. / USA

Deer Stalking with a Camera
Prod.: American Mutoscope / W.K.L. Dickson
Cin.: Billy Bitzer
Pinehurst, North Carolina.

A Devonshire Badger Hunt
Prod.: Mr. Hatt? / Great Britain
Distr.: Warwick Trading Company

Lion Hunt
Prod.: Charles J. Jones

Moose Hunt in New Brunswick
Prod.: W.K.L. Dickson / USA
Cin.: Billy Bitzer

Salmon Fishing Nipissisquit
Prod.: American Mutoscope / W.K.L. Dickson
Cin.: Billy Bitzer

Scene in a Rat Pit
Prod.: USA
Cin.: Billy Bitzer
New York.

Stalking and Shooting Caribou, New Foundland
Prod.: F.A. Dobson / Canada

Sweet Flowers
Prod.: Urban Trading Co. / Great Britain
Recorded in Kinemacolor.

Terrier Versus Wildcat
Prod.: USA

A Trip Through the Yellowstone Park, USA
Prod.: T.A. Edison Inc. / USA

Trout Fishing the Rangeley Lakes
Prod.: American Mutoscope-USA / W.K.L. Dickson
Cin.: Billy Bitzer
Maine, USA.

Waves and Spray
Prod.: Urban Trading Co. / Great Britain
Recorded in Kinemacolor.

Wild Turkey Hunt
Prod.: Edison / W.K.L. Dickson / USA
Cin.: G.W. Bitzer

1907–1910

Nature films made between 1907 and 1910 last between 2.06 and 12 minutes. The average duration for films made during this period of time is between 11 and 16.5 minutes, but this average includes all kinds of films.

1907

The Balancing Blue-Bottle
Blue-Bottle Flies Feeding
Prod.: Urban / Great Britain
Dir.: Percy Smith

Carl Hagenback's Wild Animal Park
Prod.: Urban-Eclipse / France
An animal park film.

Chasse á l'hippopotame sur le Nil Bleu
Prod.: Urban Trading Company / Great Britain
Dir.: Félix Mesguich
The Nile, Egypt.

Elephants in India
Prod.: Pathé Frères / France

Glimpses of Erin
Prod.: Urban-Eclipse / Great Britain-France
Ireland: Emerald Isle, Giant Causeway, Achill Isle, Gap of Dunloe and Killarney district.

Guillemots
Prod.: Great Britain
Dir.: Oliver Pike / H. Armytage Sanders

Hunting Above the Clouds
Prod.: Italy
Dir.: Carlo Rossi

In Birdland
Prod.: Oliver G. Pike / Great Britain
Cin. and dir.: Oliver G. Pike

Isbjørnejagten
Prod.: Nordisk Film Co. / Denmark
Dir.: Viggo Larsen
Cin: Axel Sørensen
A.k.a. *The Polar Bear Hunt*
Pure fiction, but it turned out to be very popular. Therefore, it was followed by *The Lion Hunt* in 1907, and *Hunting Bears in Russia* in 1908. They were all filmed in Scandinavia.

The Scottish Highlands
Prod.: Charles Urban Trading Company / Great Britain
Ross and Cromarty county, Scotland.

Shooting the Rapids in Africa
Prod.: Pathé / France

Wapiti Deer
Prod.: USA
Dir.: Stephen Leek
Jackson Hole, USA.

Wild Animals
Distr.: Williams, Brown and Earle / USA

1908

Chasse á l'hippopotame sur le Nil Bleu
Prod.: Pathé Frerès / France
Dir.: Alfred Machin
Expedition Leader: Dr. Adam David, Switzerland
The Nile, East Africa (Cairo, Khartoum, Fachoda, Victoria lake).

Chasse au lion
Chasse au léopard
Chasse aux panthéres et aux buffles
Prod.: France or Austria

Grævlingejagt
Moderkærlighed Blandt Dyrene
Vandfaldene i Kriml
Prod.: Nordisk Film Co. / Denmark

The Lion's Bride
Prod.: USA
Distr.: Selig Polyscope Co.

Nature's Hidden Beauties — Pond Life
Prod.: Williamson Kinematograph Co. / Great Britain
From the series *Hidden Wonders of Nature*.

St. Kilda, Its People and Birds
Prod.: Williamson Kinematograph Co. / Great Britain
Cin.: Oliver Pike

Toads-Leaping Batrachians
Prod.: Charles Urban Trading Post / Great Britain
A.k.a. *Habits of the Green Tree Frog*

Wild Animals, Cricks and Martin
Prod.: Great Britain?

The Wolf Hunt
Prod.: Oklahoma National Mutoscene Co. / USA

1909

Bear Hunt in the Rockies
Prod.: USA
Distr.: Edison
Rocky Mountains' Big Muddy.

The Bees Eviction
Prod.: J.C. Bee-Mason / Great Britain

Bird of the Moorland
Prod.: Great Britain
Dir.: Oliver G. Pike
Curlew.

Chasing a Sealion in the Arctic
Prod.: Pathé Frères / France

Chasse à la panthère
Prod.: Pathé / France
Dir.: Alfred Machin
Expedition Leader: Dr. Adam David from Switzerland
A.k.a. *Hunting the Panther*
Dinder River in East Africa.

Fra Elefanternes Land
Højfjældstur i Norge
Menneskeaben Darwins Triumf
Norske Fjorde
Rhinfaldene
Trollhätten
Vilde Dyr i Fangenskab
Prod.: Nordisk Film Co. / Denmark
Danish nature film series, of which none have survived.

Futterung von Riesenschlangen
Prod.: Komet-film-Compagne / Germany
A.k.a. *Feeding Big Snakes*

Giants and Pygmies of the Deep
Prod.: Charles Urban Trading Company / Great Britain

Hunting Big Game in Africa
Prod.: Col. Selig
Dir.: Otis Turner
Cin.: Emmett Vincent O'Neil
A.k.a. *Big Game in Africa*

Hunting Crocodiles
Prod.: Pathé Frères / Great Britain
Java.

The Lion Tamer
Prod.: USA
Distr.: Selig Polyscope Co.

Panther Hunting in the Isle of Java
Prod.: Urban-Eclipse / Great Britain
Java.

Peeps into Nature's Realm
Prod.: Williamson Kinematograph / Great Britain
Curlews, bluetits and red-throated loon.

Tears of an Alligator
Prod.: A.B. Film, New York / USA
Featuring the animal trainer Delmont.

Theodore Roosevelt's Africa Expedition
Native Lion Hunt
African Animals
Prod.: England

Dir. and Cin: Cherry Kearton
A.k.a. *Roosevelt in Africa*

Ved Havet
Prod.: Nordisk Film Co. / Denmark
Cin.: Ole Olsen

Voyage en Afrique
Prod.: Pathé / France
Dir.: Alfred Machin

Wild Birds in Their Haunts
Prod.: Pathé Frères / Great Britain–France
Cin.: Oliver G. Pike

1910

Bamsemoér Opdrager Sønnen
Prod.: Nordisk Film / Denmark
A.k.a. *A Mother Bear Raising Her Cub*

Birds of Prey
Prod.: France
Beautifully colored by Pathé.

The Birth of a Flower
Prod. and Cin.: Percy Smith / Great Britain
Distr.: Charles Urban Trading Co.
Time-lapse recordings of a flower's growth.

Breaking Waves
Prod.: Hepworth Film Company / Great Britain

Capture d'oursons blancs dans les glaces de l'ocean
Prod.: Pathé / France
The Arctic.

The Cecropia Moth
Prod.: Edison Co. / USA

Les Chillouks — tribu de l'Afrique Centrale
Prod.: Pathé / France
Dir.: Alfred Machin
Cin.: Julien Doux
The Nile and the Dinder River.

Chrysanthemum
Prod.: Edison Co. / USA
Time-lapse recordings of flowers.

Dans l'Ouganda (Afrique Centrale): Chasse à la Giraffe
Prod.: Pathé / France
Dir.: Alfred Machin
Cin.: Julien Doux
Expedition Leader: Dr. Adam David, Switzerland
The Nile and Dinder River.

Descente en barque a travers les gorges de L'ardeche L'orne
Prod.: France / Gaumont

A series of films featuring different French rivers: the Ardeche, Orne and Are.

The Dytiscus and Its Larva
Prod.: Pathé Frères / France
Dir.: Jean Comandon
Pathé Frères scientific series.

The Egret Hunter
Prod.: Kalem / USA

En Egypte, élevage des autruches
Prod.: Pathé / France
Dir.: Alfred Machin
Cin.: Julien Doux
The Nile and Dinder rivers.

Feeding Seals at Catalina Isle
Prod.: Essaney

Die Geheimnisse Der Meeres Tiefe
Prod.: Eclair / France
A.k.a. *Secrets from the Bottom of the Sea*

Gigantic Waves
Prod.: Gaumont / France

Une grande chasse á l'hippotame sur le Haut Nil
Prod.: Pathé / France
Dir.: Alfred Machin
Cin.: Julien Doux
The Nile and Dinder rivers.

Grindefangst ved Færøerne
Højfjældstur i Norge
Fra Sø og Land
Færøerne, Øgruppe i Atlanterhavet
Prod.: Nordisk Film Co. / Denmark
Footage of Norway and the Faroe Islands.

The History of a Butterfly — A Romance of Insect Life
Prod.: Williamson Kinematograph Co. / Great Britain

Hunting Bats in Sumatra
Distr.: Pathé Frères

Hunting Hippopotamus on the Upper Nile
Prod.: Gaumont Fréres / France

Hunting Sea Lions in Tasmania
Distr.: Pathé Frères / France

Il lago di thun
Prod.: Ambrosio / Italy
Distr.: Filmeries Hire Service
Switzerland.

The Life of a Salmon
Prod.: Thomas A. Edison / USA
Capilano Valley.

Madagascar—Manners and Customs of Sakalavas
Prod.: Pathé Frères / France

Nature's Children in Their Native Haunts
Prod.: Warwick Trading Co. / Great Britain

Rovfugle
Prod.: Pathé Frères / France
A.k.a. *Birds of Prey*
Years of production: 1909–1915. Pathé Color—
   stencil-colored.

Seal and Walrus Hunting
Prod.: Raleigh and Roberts / France
Distr.: Film Import and Trading

A Study of Flowers
Prod.: Pathé Frères / France
Probably the first time-lapse film of flowers.

Wapiti Deer
Prod.: USA
Dir.: Stephen Leek
Leek films dying wapiti deer, and uses the footage
   to promote nature conservation.

Wild Birds in Their Haunts
Prod.: Pathé Frères / France
A.k.a. *Wild Bird Hunt*

Wild Duck Hunt on Reel Foot Lake
Distr.: Lubin FMG Co.

1911–1920

Nature films made between 1911 and 1920 last
between 0.5 and 77.24 minutes. Multi-track films
became more common around 1912, but did not
break through in the USA before 1915.

1911

Les Abeilles
Prod.: Pathé / France
A film about bees.

The Actual Travels of a Fly Caught by a Moving Picture Camera
Prod.: Curtis Publishing Co. / USA

Arctic Hunt
Prod.: Frank E. Kleinschmidt / USA

Bilbao, Spansk Natur
Den Svenske Skærgaard
Fra det Høje Nord
Højskotland
Mellem Norske Fjælde
Norsk Natur
Pojusfaldene
Prod.: Nordisk Film Kompagni / Denmark

Travelogues from Spain, Sweden, Norway and
   Scotland.

Chasse aux éléphants sur les bords du Nyanza
Chasse ax marabout en Abyssinie
Chasse á l'aigrette en Afrique
Prod.: Pathé / France
Dir.: Alfred Machin
Cin.: Julien Doux
Dr. Adam David from Switzerland on the Nile
   and Dinder rivers.

Chrysanthemums
Prod.: Gaumont / France

The Culture of the Dahlia
Prod.: Pathé / France

Grand Canyon
Prod.: Brd. Kolb / USA
Dir. and Cin.: Emery and Ellsworth Kolb

The Growth of a Pea Plant
Prod.: India
Dir.: Dadasaheb Phalke

Lassoing Wild Animals
Prod.: USA–France–Great Britain?
Cin.: Cherry Kearton, William David Gobbett
Distr.: Pathé Frères

Life at the Bottom of the Sea
Prod.: Éclair / France

The Life of the Bees
Prod.: Italy

Niagara Falls
Prod.: Pathé Frères / France
A series of films on Niagara Falls.

Rocks and Waves
Prod.: Gaumont / France
Shot in 68mm.

The Scarab Beetle
Prod.: Pathé Frères / France
Distr.: Visual Education

The Strength and Agility of Insects
Prod.: Kineto / Great Britain

The Ways of the Wood Ant
Prod.: Kineto / Great Britain

Wild Animals in Captivity
Prod.: Essaney / USA
Lincoln Park Zoo, Chicago.

Wild Geese
Prod.: USA
Cin.: J.C. Hemment

1912

Across Australia with Francis Birtles
Prod.: Australia
A bicycle trip from Sydney to Darwin.

African Bird and Animal Life
Prod.: USA
Cin.: Cherry Kearton
Distr.: Adolf Zukor

Alaska-Siberian Expedition
Prod.: Alaskan-Siberian Motion Pictures / USA
Dir.: Frank E. Kleinschmidt
An expedition in the Arctic region with expedition leader Kleinschmidt.

Les Amibes
Prod.: Pathé Consortium / France
Distr.: Film Society

Among the Clouds with a Camera
Prod.: W. B. Spencer / Australia

Atop the World in Motion
Prod. and cin.: Beverly B. Dobbs
The Siberian Arctic.

Aus dem leben des Meeres
Prod.: Berlin-Steglitz / Germany

Australian Kangaroos
Studies of Reptile Life
Birds of Prey
Familiar Reptiles
Prod.: Kineto–Charles Urban / Great Britain
Parts of the *Urban Science* series.

Autotocht door Bandoeng
Prod.: Kolonniaal Instituut / Pathé / Holland
Dir.: J.C. Lamster
A.k.a. *A Railtrip through Bandung*

L'auvergne pitteoresque
Prod.: Lux / France
A.k.a. *The Picturesque Auvergne*

A Car Ride in the Pyrenees
Prod.: Pathé / France

Les chasseurs d'ivoire
La chasse aux singes
Prod.: Pathé / France
Dir.: Alfred Machin
Cin.: Julien Doux
A second expedition with Dr. Adam Davids along the Nile and Dinder rivers.

Crabes de Mer
Prod.: Gaumont Company / France

The Defenders of Our Orchards—The Tomtit
Prod.: Pathé / France

Le dytique
A Spider That Lives in a Diving Bell: Thargyroneta
Two Snail Eaters: The Glandida and Ophisaurus
Prod.: Éclair / France
Dir.: Georges Maurice
Entries in the series of films called *Scientia*.

A Fight Between Wild Animals
Prod.: Kalem / USA

The House Fly
Prod.: Thomas A. Edison Inc. / USA

Jack London in the South Seas
Prod.: USA
Dir. and Cin.: Martin Johnson

The Life of Ants
Prod.: Pathé / France / Great Britain

Med Bjergbanen
Nordsøen i Storm og Stille
Kullen
Prod.: Nordisk Film Co. / Denmark
Danish nature films.

Nature's Fairest
Prod.: Gaumont / France

Paul J. Rainey's African Hunt
Prod.: P.J. Rainey / USA–Great Britain
Cin.: J.C. Hemment
Distr.: Laemmle
Includes an amazing number of different wild animal species.

Possum Hunting in Australia
Prod.: T. J. West / Australia

Scenes of African Animals
Prod.: USA — England
Dir.: Paul J. Rainey
Cin.: John C. Hemment

The Sedge Warbler and the Cuckoo
Prod.: Pathé / Great Britain
Cin.: Oliver Pike

Tra le pinete di rodi
Prod.: Savoia / Italy
Rhodos.

The Wasp
Prod.: Pathé / Great Britain

With Captain Scott, RN, to the South Pole
Prod.: Great Britain
Cin.: Herbert Ponting
Scott's polar expedition.

1913

African Sea Birds
Prod.: Edison Co. / USA

Among the Fishes
Prod.: Eclair / France

Aquatic Elephants
Prod.: Vitagraph Company of America / USA

Aus dem Leben der Seevögel
Prod.: Germany?
A.k.a. *The Life of the Sea Birds*

The Bee
Prod.: Gaumont Co. / France

The Beetle's Deception
Prod.: USA / Russia??
Dir.: Loyshki
A love story in which the main characters are insects.

Dans les Pyrenees
Prod.: Gaumont / France

Dansk Natur
Ensomme Egne
Snestormen 1913 (Norge)
Vandfaldene ved Sarpen
Prod.: Nordisk Film Co. / Denmark
Dir. and Cin.: V. Stæhr

How Wild Animals Live
Prod.: Midgar Features / USA?

Mit der Kamera im Ewigen Eis
Prod.: Germany
Dir. and Cin.: Sepp J. Allgeier
Filmed in 1912 and 1913.

Les Mouches
Prod.: Eclipse-Urbanora / France

Nashornjagd in Deutsch-Ostafrika
Prod.: Deutschen Jagd-Film GmbH / Germany
Dir.: Robert Schumann

The Otter Hunting
Prod.: Heron / Great Britain

The Raven
Prod.: Great Britain
Dir.: Oliver G. Pike
Filmed between 1909 and 1913 in Wales.

The Series of Tallulah Falls, Georgia
Prod.: Thomas A. Edison / USA

The Stickleback, the Fish That Builds a Nest
Prod.: Pathé / France

The Undying Story of Captain Scott
Prod.: Gaumont / France and Great Britain
Dir. and Cin.: Herbert Ponting

Unique Studies of Nature
Prod.: Kineto / Great Britain

Whale Hunting in Jervis Bay
Prod.: Fraser Films / Australia

1914

Blinkhorn Natural History Travels
Prod.: Hepworth American Film Corp. / USA
A.k.a. *The Capture of a Sea Elephant and Hunting Wild Game in the South Pacific*
Filmed in California and on Guadalupe.

Bøhmiske Vandfald. Wildeklamm
Donauslugten
Hardangerfjord — Norway (Norge)
Klippeformationer. Sachsisk Switzerland (Schweiz)
Norsk Højland
Vandfald i Tistedalen
Vandfald ved Laholm. Sweden (Sverige)
Ved Skovsøens Bred
Prod.: Nordisk Film Co. / Denmark
Primarily travelogues.

The Book of Nature
Prod.: Raymond L. Ditmars / USA
Dir. and Cin.: Raymond L. Ditmars
Distr.: George R. Meeker

Bottom of the World
Prod.: AMNH and Ludwig Kohl-Larsen
Distr.: Talking Pictures Epics
Narration: Robert Cushman Murphy
South Georgia in 1912–13.

Bud, Leaf and Flower
Prod.: General Film Co. / USA

Captain F. E. Kleinschmidt's Arctic Hunt
Prod.: Arctic Film Co. / USA
Alaska.

Common Beast of Africa
Prod.: P.J. Rainey / USA
Cin.: J. Hemment

Home Life of the Birds
Prod.: USA
Cin.: William L. Finley
Filmed in Northern California and Southern Oregon.

Home of the Blizzard
Prod.: Australia
Cin.: Frank Hurley

Sir Douglas Mawson's Australian-Arctic expedition.

In the Land of the Headhunters
Prod.: Curtis Film Corporation / USA
Dir.: Edward S. Curtis
A.k.a. *In the Land of the War Canoes*
Filmed in British Columbia.

The Intelligence of Apes
Dir.: Wolfgang Köhler

Miscellaneous Flowers
Prod.: Natural Colour Kinematograph Company/
 Great Britain

Picturesque Tasmania or Exploring Tasmania
Prod.: Australia

Rainey's African Hunt
Prod.: P.J. Rainey / USA
Cin.: J.C. Hemment

The Shores of Gotland
Prod.: Sveafilm / Sweden
Distr.: New Agency Film Co.

Snakes and Spiders
Prod.: USA
Distr.: Pathe Frérès
Dir. and Cin.: Raymond L. Ditmars

Terrors of the Deep
Prod.: Submarine Pictures Corp. / USA
Dir.: Williamson Brothers
Filmed in the Bahamas.

Thirty Leagues Under the Sea
Prod.: USA
Dir. and Cin: John and George Williamson
Distribution: Submarine Film Corporation
Filmed in the Bahamas.

Through the Brazilian Wilderness
Prod.: USA
Following Roosevelt on an expedition through the
 Brazilian wilderness.

The Timber Industry, British Columbia
Prod.: Kineto / Great Britain–Canada

A Wealth of Flowers
Prod.: Gaumont / France

Young Bird Life
Prod.: Pathé / France

1915

American Game Trails
Prod.: Educational Film Corp. / USA
Dir.: Frank M. Buckland and J. F. Cleary

Cin.: L. Calezio
New Brunswick in Canada.

The Animal World No. 1
The Animal World No. 5 (1916)
Prod.: Charles Urban Trading Company / Great
 Britain
Distr.: Kineto
Part of the series of films called *The Animal World*,
 featuring different kinds of animals.

The Ascent of Mont Blanc
Climbing the Jungfrau
Prod.: Burlingham Films / Great Britain
Cin.: Frederick Burlingham
Distr.: New Agency Film Company

Birdlife in Scotland
Prod.: USA
Distr.: Pathe
In color (technicolor).

Habits and Customs of Swallows
Prod.: Savoia Film / Italy
Distr.: New Agency Film Company

Hare Shooting in the Baltic Archipelago
Prod.: Sveafilms / Sweden

The Hermit Crab
Microscopic Pond
Prod.: Edison Company / USA
Entries in a series of films called *Conquest Pictures*.

In the Amazon Jungle with the
Captain Besley Expedition
Prod.: Captain Besley Motion Pictures / Great
 Britain
Dir.: Franklin B. Coates
Cin.: J. K. Holbrook.
Through the Andes Mountains from Puenta del
 Inca in Argentina to Juncal in Chile. Twelve
 reels.

Into Australia's Unknown
Cin.: Frank Hurley / Australia
Francis Birtles and Frank Hurley's bicycle trip in
 Australia.

Italy — Landscapes and Cities
Prod.: Pathe Frérès / France

Lady MacKenzie Big Game Pictures
Prod.: Grace MacKenzie / Great Britain
Cin.: Harold Sintzenich
A.k.a. *Lady MacKenzie in Africa*
Kenya.

Med svenska lappar på vårflyttning
Prod.: Sweden
Cin.: Osvar Olsson

Native Gamefish and Birds
Prod.: Edward A. Salisbury / USA
California. Twelve reels.

Niagara Falls
Prod.: T.A. Edison / USA

The Otter
Prod.: Charles Urban Trading Company / Great
    Britain
Distr.: Visual Education
This film offered early examples of editing for con-
    tinuity.

Scener fra Fuglelivet
Prod.: Nordisk Films Co. / Denmark
A.k.a. *Scenes from the Birdlife*
Partly in color.

The Spirit of Audubon
Prod.: Mutual Film Corp. / USA
Adviser: Herbert K. Job

A Strange Pet
Prod.: Kalem Company / USA
Sea lions in a zoo.

Swat That Fly!
Prod.: Will Day Films / Great Britain

Wild Life of America in Films
Prod.: Edward A. Salisbury / USA
Cin.: Salisbury

1916

Dorsey Expedition
Prod.: Dorsey, Cooper and Bradley / USA
Distr.: Sun Exclusives
India, Japan.

Frontiers of a Forbidden Land
Prod.: American Museum of Natural History /
    USA

How Life Begins
Prod.: George E. Stone / USA
Cin.: George E. Stone and J.A. Long
Distr.: Kathrine F. Carter
An educational film in 5 reels that was distributed
    to cinemas around 1918. Stone and Long were
    associated with the University of California.

Norsk Fjeldnatur. Midtvinter
Prod.: Nordisk Films Co. / Denmark
A.k.a. *The Norwegian Mountain Nature During
    Midwinter*

The Porcupine — A Prickly Subject
Prod.: Kineto / Great Britain
Saltvands og Ferskvandsfisk

Prod.: Nordisk Films Co. / Denmark
A.k.a. *Saltwater and Freshwater Fish*

Storks, Cranes
Prod.: Kineto / Great Britain

A Strange Industry
Distr.: Davisons film sales Agency / Great Britain
Butterflies.

Two of Nature's Wonders
Prod.: Pyramid Films / Great Britain
Distr.: Davisons Film Sales Agency
Yellowstone and Niagara Falls.

1917

Alaska Wonders in Motion
Prod.: Smith Films / USA
Cin: Al I. Smith
Scenes of Valdez, Kenai, Kodiak shot around 1916.

Banff National Park
Prod.: Dept. of Trade and Commerce, Exhibits
    & Publicity / Canada
This film showcases Takahaw waterfalls and Emer-
    ald Lake, among other natural beauties of the
    park.

The Bernese Bears
Prod.: Swiss Film Industry / Switzerland

Fra Polarhavet
Prod.: Denmark
A.k.a. *From the Polar Sea*
The capturing of polar bears for zoos.

In the Grip of the Polar Pack Ice
Prod.: Australia
Cin.: Frank Hurley
Sir Ernest Shackleton's Antarctic expedition.

A Joy Rider of the Ocean
New York.
Birds of a Far-Off Sea
Malaga.
Caring for Birds in Winter
Scouts caring for birds.
Nature's Perfect Tread Spinner
Silk worms.
Prod.: Edison Company / USA
Distr.: Thomas A. Edison
From the series of films called *Conquest Pictures*.

Lion Hunting in East Africa
Filmed during Sir. Thomas Dewars' hunting ex-
    pedition to British East Africa.

The Sea Horse
Prod.: Thomas A. Edison / USA
Filmed at the New York Aquarium.

Shackleton's South Pole Expedition
Prod.: ITA Film Syndikat / Great Britain
Dir.: Ernest Shackleton
Cin.: Frank Hurley

The Valley of the Ten Thousand Smokes
Prod.: USA
Dir.: Robert F. Griggs
Cin.: Bros. Kolb and D.B. Church
Alaska.

1918

Allotment Holders Enemies
Prod.: Charles Urban Trading Company / Great
   Britain

Among the Cannibal Isles of the South Pacific
Prod.: Martin Johnson / USA
Dir. and Cin.: Martin Johnson
A.k.a. *Cannibals of the South Seas*
New Hybrids and Solomon Islands.

Beaver at Work
Prod.: Great Britain

A Ramble with a Naturalist
Birds of Crag and Cavern
The Pelican Bird of Florida
Sea Birds and Animals
North Carolina.
*Wild Birds and Animals at Home**
Taming Wild Birds
Prod.: Universal Film Manufacturing Co. / USA
Distr.: TransAtlantic Film Co.
Dir. and Cin.: William L. Finley
A series of films by the name of Finley Nature Pic-
   tures.

Town of Mischief
Prod.: Kineto / Great Britain
Recordings of different animals.

A Waswanipae Weekend
Prod.: C.L. Chester / USA
Eds.: Kathrine Helliker
Natives from James Bay, Canada.

A World of Scenic Wonders
Prod.: Dept. for Trade and Commerce / Canada
Jasper National Park; Athabaska Valley; Maligne;
   Mount Robson.

1919

Die Alpen. Geographische Laufbilder zu Lehrzwec-
ken
Prod.: Ufa Kulturfilm / Germany
Dir.: Felix Lampe
How educational films were made popular.

Back to God's Country
Prod.: Canada
Dir.: Ernest Shipman
Based on Curwood's *Wapi the Walros.*

Beaver and Deer
Prod.: USA
Deer on a farm and beavers in the wild.

Den Duktiga Ejderhonan
Prod.: Svensk Filmindustris Skolfilmavdeling /
   Sweden
A very innovative wildlife film.

*Inland Sea Birds
Great Salt Lake in Utah.
*Pelican Birds of Florida
Prod.: Universal / USA
From the series of films named *Trans-Atlantic*
   Screen Magazine.

Snowflake Land
Prod.: Svenska Biograf / Sweden
Distr.: General Film Renting Company

South
Prod.: Australia
Dir. and Cin.: Frank Hurley
A restored version of Shackleton's expedition via
   the use of tinted glass plate photos.

The Stream
Prod.: Pathé Frerès / France–Great Britain
Cin: Oliver G. Pike
Birdlife along a stream.

Teneriffe
Prod.: Sweden
Distr.: Visual Education
Mt. Teide, Santa Cruz, etc.

Through Australian Wilds: Across the Track of Ross
   Smith
Prod.: Australia
One of Francis Birtles' bike trips in Australia.

Tides and the Moon
Trained Sea Lions, 1920
Hunting Wasp, 1920
Mysteries of Snow, 1921
Taos Indians, 1921
Prod.: Bray Studies / USA
Distr.: Visual Education
Dir.: Mainly Francis Lyle Goldman
Nature films from the series *Goldwyn-Bray Picto-*
   graph: The Magazine of the Screen.

191?

Alaska
The American Fish Hawk

Wild Animals and Their Young
Prod.: National Non-Theatrical Motion Pictures
  / USA?
Educational films.

Ants: Nature's Craftsmen
Prod.: Pathé Freres / France
Part of the series *Plant and Animal.*

Insect Pond Life
Prod.: George Kleine / USA
Footage of water striders, back swimmers, dobson
  flies, whirligig beetles, caddis-worms, and stone
  flies, among others.

1920

Afrika im Film
Prod.: Germany
Dir.: Hans Schomburgk
Filmed in Togo, Liberia and the Sudan.

The Anteater
Prod.: Grangers Exclusives / Great Britain
Distr.: Visual Education

Aus der Afrikanischer Wildnis
Prod.: Germany
Dir.: Robert Schumann
Footage of wildlife.

The Gift of Life
Prod.: American Social Hygiene Association /
  USA
Different kinds of natural reproduction.

In Borneo, the Land of the Head Hunters
Prod.: USA / Norway / Sweden
Dir. and cin.: Carl Lumholtz
The Norwegian Carl Lumholtz's expedition in
  1919.

Kamchatka Ekspedition
Prod.: Norway / Sweden
Dir.: Sten Bergmann

The Living World
Prod.: University of California, Berkeley / USA
Cin.: George E. Stone
This might be a re-titling of *How Life Begins.*

La nuit agitée
Prod.: Pathé Frérés / France
Dir.: Alfred Machin
Dir. and Cin.: Henry Wulschleger
Animals dressed like humans.

Polly All Alone
Two Little Orphans
In color.

We Are Seven
Dir.: Oliver G. Pike
Prod.: British Film Institute / Great Britain
Cin.: Oliver G. Pike
These films were made between 1919 and 1938.

Separate Trails
Prod.: Educational Films Corp. of America / USA
A man and his dog wander through different land-
  scapes.

Storkarna
Prod.: Sweden
Dir. and Cin.: Bengt Berg

Story of a Mountain Glacier
Prod.: Society for Visual Education / USA

Wunder des Meeresgrundes
Prod.: Komet-Films / Germany
Distr.: Harmonia Film
Three reels of film.

Das Zahme Tier
Krieg und Frieden im Feuchten Element
Verborgene Wunder Unserer Gewässer
Wanden und Werden im Insektenreich
Was Uns der Walt Erzählt
Prod.: Decla (Decla-Bioscop-Ufa) / Germany
Distr.: Ufa (Universum-Film A.-G.)
Entries in the film series *Natur im Film.*

1921–1928

Natural films made between 1921 and 1928 last
between 1.2 and 114 minutes. Longer films became
much more common during this time period.

1921

Allerhand Fischjäger
Die Hydra des Süsswassers
Die Wunderwelt des Mikroskops
Fisch und Muschel. Familien-Gründung auf Gegen-
  sietigkeit
Katzenbilder
Muttersorgen im Tierreich
Prod.: Decla (Decla-Bioscop — Ufa) / Germany
Distr.: Ufa (Universum-Film A.-G.)
Entries in the series *Natur im Film.*

*American Spider
Prod.: Charles Urban Trading Company / Great
  Britain
Distr.: Butchers Film Service
A part of the series *The Urban Chat.*

Bland Vildar och Vildar Djur
Prod.: Svenska Film / Sweden

Cin.: Oscar Olsson
A.k.a. *Auf Afrikanischen Jagdpfaden: Unter Wilden und Wilden Tieren*
From East Africa.

Blandt Syd-Amerikas Urskovsindianere
Prod.: Norway
Dir.: Ottar Gladtved
A.k.a. *Among the Virgin Forest Indians of South America*

A Child of Nature
Stone Marten.
The Kings
Lions and polar bears.
What's Left of the Bison Herds
Animal preservation.
Prod.: Pathé Frères Cinema / Great Britain
Entries in the series *Pathe Pictorial.*

Dyreliv i Vore Moser
Prod.: Filmfabriken Danmark / Denmark
Dir. and Cin.: Richard Lund / H.F. Rimmen
A.k.a. *Wildlife in Our Swamps / Marshlands*

Evolution of a Butterfly
Prod.: Ensign / USA

Four Seasons
Prod.: Urban Popular Classic / USA
Cin. and dir.: Raymond L. Ditmars
One reel for each season.

Frøerne og Deres Fjender
Prod.: Filmfabriken Danmark / Denmark
Dir.: Richard Lund
Cin.: H.F. Rimmen
A.k.a. *Frogs and Their Enemies*
Very inventive.

Im Kampf mit dem Berge
Prod.: Germany
Dir.: Arnold Fanck
Cin.: Fanck and Sepp Allgeier
Subtitle: Im sturm und eis.
Fanck's first mountain film features climbers climbing Lyskamm. It was filmed on Monte Rosa and the Matterhorn.

Jungle Adventure
Prod.: USA
Cin. and dir.: Martin Johnson
An expedition to Borneo.

Das Leben in den Abgründen des Meeres
Prod.: Ambrosio Film / Germany
Distr.: Siegel, Dresden

Mysteriums of Snow
Prod.: Goldwyn Bray / USA

Pearls and Savages
Prod.: Frank Hurley / Australia
Cin.: Frank Hurley
Distr.: Stoll Pictures Productions
The pearl fishers of New-Guinea. Parts of the film are tinted and include color photos.

Skovbækken
Prod.: Denmark
Dir. and Cin.: Richard Lund and H.F. Rimmen
A.k.a. *The Forest Brook*

Snowflake Land
Prod.: Svenska Biograf / Sweden
Jämtland, Sweden

The Spider
Prod.: Ensign / USA

Spiders and Their Victims
Prod.: Urban / Great Britain
Dir.: Percy Smith / Charles Head
Entry in the *Kineto Review Series.*

The Spider's Web
Prod.: Ensign / USA
Silk and spiders.

The Story of the Heron
Prod.: Hepworth Manufacturing Co. / Great Britain
Cin.: C.W.R. Knight
An entry in a series of films consisting of two parts — *Wildlife in the Tree Tops* and *The Story of the Kestrel*— that also offers continuity editing.

Under Polar-Kredsens Himmel
Prod.: Norway
Dir.: Reidar Lund
Novaja Semlja.

Vogelleben im Winter
Prod.: Bund für Vogelschutz, Stuttgart / Germany
A.k.a. *Life of Birds During Wintertime*
Nature preservation.

1922

Across the Great Sahara
Prod.: Great Britain
Cin.: T.A. Glover
Expedition Leader: Angus Buchanan

Aus dem Naturgeschichte des Kleinen Moritz (Der Maikäfer)
Butantan. Brasiliens Kampf Gegen die Giftschlange
Ein Heu-Schreckenleben
Im Bienenstaat

In Froschkönigs Reich — Intimes von der Grossen Weinbergschnecke
Intimitäten aus dem Leben Deutscher Schlangen
Mit der Kamera Durch Feld, Wald und Wiese
Tiere im Winterschlaf
Prod.: Decla (Decla-Bioscop-Ufa) / Germany
Distr.: Ufa (Universum-Film A.-G.)
Parts of the series of films *Natur im Film.*

The Battle of the Ants
The Buzzard
Cin: Oliver Pike
Children of Nature
The Common Butterfly
Fathoms Deep Beneath the Sea
Cin.: H.M. Lomas
Frocks and Frills
How animals use camouflage.
Hands Versus Feet
How animals and humans use hands and feet in different ways and for different purposes.
Infant Welfare in the Bird World
The Labyrinth Spider
The Lair of the Spider
The Marine Parade
The movement patterns of marine animals.
Nature's Gliders
Dir.: Oliver G. Pike
The Rook
Cin.: C.W.R. Knight
The Sea Shore
**Skilled Insect Artisans*
The Sparrow Hawk
The Story of Peter the Raven
Cin.: Charles Head
The Story of the Cuckoo
Cin.: Oliver Pike
Studies in Animal Motion
The White Owl
Cin.: Oliver Pike
Titles in the series of films *Secrets of Nature.*
Prod.: British Instructional Films / B. Woolfe / Great Britain
Distr.: Regent Film Company and New Era Film
Edit: W.P. PyCraft

Coorab on the Island of Ghost
Prod.: Australia
Dir.: Francis Birtles
A bicycle adventure.

The Cuckoo's Secret
Prod.: British Instructional Film / W.P. PyCraft
Cin.: H. Bruce Woolfe or Oliver Pike
This first film in the series *Secrets of Nature* was

filmed under the guidance of ornithologist Edgar Chance.

Fra Fjordens Sandbund
Prod.: Filmfabriken Danmark / Denmark
Dir.: Richard Lund
Cin.: H.F. Rimmen
A.k.a. *From the Sandy Bottom of the Fjord*
An inventive nature film.

Geschütze eine Vogelinsel
Prod.: Svensk Filminsustri / Sweden
Distr.: Decla
A.k.a. *Saving an Island for Birds*

The Harvest of the Sea
Prod.: Grangers Exclusives / Great Britain
This entry in the series *Marvels of the World* focuses on the Shetland Islands.

Headhunters of the South Seas
Prod.: USA
Cin.: Martin Johnson
Cannibals watching themselves on a big screen.

Hunting Big Game in Africa with Gun and Camera
Prod.: Universal Film Studios / USA
Cin: H.A. Snow and Sidney Snow
A.k.a. *Mit Auto und Kamara Zwischen Afrikanischem Grosswild*
Music: Gino Severi.

Livet På Havbunden
A.k.a. *Life at the Bottom of the Sea*
Fra Hæk og Gærde
A.k.a. *From the Hedge and Fence*
Gnavere
A.k.a. *Rodents*
I Skovens Udkant
A.k.a. *In the Outskirts of the Wood*
Holm og Klop (Maager)
A.k.a. *Seagulls*
Lidt om Livet ved Saltvands Stenbund
A.k.a. *A Few Facts About the Stone Sea-Floor in Salt Water*
Søelefanter
A.k.a. *Sea Elephants*
Væddeløbs-Mynder
A.k.a. *Racing Greyhounds*
Prod.: Filmfabriken Danmark / Denmark
Dir.: Richard Lund
Cin: H.F. Rimmen
Parts of a series of biological films.

The Long Road to Tibet
Our Adventures in Tibet

Dance Festival in Tibet
Laying Seige to the Great Mountain
The Assault on the Mountain
Prod. and Cin: J. B. L. Noel / Great Britain
Distr.: Royal Geographic Society
This entry in the series of films called *Climbing Mt. Everest* chronicles the second expedition to Everest.

Meandering in Africa
Prod.: American Museum of Natural History
Cin: Carl Ethan Akeley
Editor: Martha Miller Bliven
The Akeley African Expedition to Belgian Congo (Zaire).

Med Prins William på Afrikanske Jaktstigar
Prod.: Svensk Biograf Co. / Sweden
Cin.: Oscar Olsson
A.k.a. *The Cradle of the World*
An expedition to Northern Kenya, the Virunga Volcano and the Ituri Forest.

Mit dem Kurbelkasten durch die Vogelwelt
Prod.: Bernhardt-Film, Berlin / Germany
A.k.a. *With the Cine-Camera Through the World of the Birds*

Nanook of the North
Prod.: Revillon Fréres / Canada / France
Distr.: Pathè Exchange
Dir. and Cin.: Robert J. Flaherty
Focusing on Nanook the Inuk from Hudson Bay, this film revolutionized the way documentary films were made.

Eine Reise durch Zentralasien
Prod.: Germany
Dir.: Colin Ross
A journey from Bucharest to Samarkand.

Der Rhein in Vergangenheit und Gegenwart
Prod.: Ufa Kulturfilm / Germany
Dir.: Felix Lampe
A popular educational film.

Som Flyttfågel i Afrika
Prod.: Svenska Filmbyrå / Sweden
Cin.: Bengt Berg
A.k.a. *Like Flying Birds in Africa*

Song of the Sea
Prod.: Stoll / USA?
A more sophisticated film of waves.

Southward on the "Quest"
Prod.: Great Britain / Australia
Cin.: Frank Hurley and Claude McDonnel
Shackleton-Rowett's Antarctic expedition in 1921.

The film was later reedited and re-titled *Endurance*.

Den Store Grønlandsfilm
Prod.: Fotorama / Denmark
Dir.: Edvard Schnedler-Sørensen
Cin.: H.F. Rimmen
Manuscript: H.H. Seedorph Petersen
A.k.a. *The Great Greenland Film*
Knud Rasmussen's 5th Thule Expedition.

Von Deutschen Tieren und Deutchen Mooren
Prod.: Bund für Vogelschutz, Stuttgart / Germany
Distr.: Kösel & Pustet
A.k.a. *From German Animals to German Bogs*
Nature preservation.

Die Wisente in Bialowiecs
Prod.: Germany
A.k.a. *The Bison in Bialowiecs*

With Eustace in Africa
Prod.: Harry K. Eustace / Great Britain
Filmed between 1914 and 1918.

Wonders of the Sea
Prod.: Williamson, New York / USA
Cin. and Manuscript: J. Ernest Williamson
Six reels of life under the surface and on the floor of the sea.

1923

Aben ved Hundehovedet
Chimpansen og den Grønne Abe
Dyrenes Børneværelse
Dyrenes Vuggestue
Fra Fuglelivet
Insekternes Beskyttelseslighed
Papegøjer
Peberfrugten
Ræve
Prod.: Filmfabriken Danmark / Denmark
Dir.: Richard Lund
Cin.: H.F. Rimmen
Entries in a series of nature films.

Adventures in the Far North
Prod.: USA
Dir.: Captain Kleinschmidt
The Kleinschmidt couple is in Alaska, where they film different animal species.

Aus dem Mäusereich
A.k.a. *From the Mice Reich*
Im Schatten der Eiche
A.k.a. *In the Shadow of the Oak Tree*
Kröten
A.k.a. *Toads*

Merkwürdige Fischen
A.k.a. *Strange Fish*
Schutzkleider und Schauspiel-Künste der Natur
Protective clothing and behavior in nature.
Von Grillen und Zikaden
A.k.a. *Grasshoppers and Cicadas*
Von Salaman-Dern und Molchen
A.k.a. *Newts and Amphibians*
Prod.: Tyskland / Decla
Distr.: Ufa (Universum-Film A.-G.)
Entries in the film series *Natur im Film.*

Autumn
Betty's Day at the Zoo
Cabbage and Things
Crabs and Camouflage
*Fear!
Editor: F. Martin Thornton
A Fly Fisher's Festival
The Gannet
Cin.: Oliver Pike
Giant Snails
Dir.: P. Chalmers Mitchell
The Grouse
Cin.: Oliver Pike
The Hunting Spider
The May-Fly
The Pond
Sea Breezes
The Stickleback
*Strange Friendship
The Tiger Beetle
Editor: Maxwell Lefroy
The Tiger of the Stream
Editor: G. Southcote
The Wasp
*Winter
Prod.: British Instructional Films / Bruce Woolfe
Distr.: Regent Film Company and New Era Film
Parts of the series *Secrets of Nature.*

Beast of the Veldt
Prod.: William N. Selig / USA
Distr.: Export and Import Film

Bêtes ... comme les hommes
Prod.: Pathé Frérés / France
Dir.: Alfred Machin and Henry Wulschleger
Cin.: Mario Badouaille
Animals dressed up as humans.

The Bird Photographer at Work
Gulf Storks Analyzed
In Fiery Depths
The volcano Kilanea Iki.
Mistress Lark at Home

Original Owners of Furs
Prod.: Pathé / Great Britain
The series of films *Pathé Pictorial.*

Domestic Secrets of the Eider Duck
Skies in the South Seas
When Mr. and Mrs. Bluebird Took Up Housekeeping
Zoo Neckers
Prod.: Pathé Exchange / USA
The series of films *Pathé Review.*

Evolution
Prod.: Red Seal Pictures
The beginning of life on Earth.

Hunting Lions in Africa
Prod.: USA
Dir.: Lyman H. Howe

Mellum, das Vogelparadies in der Nordsee
Prod.: Schonger Naturfilm, Berlin / Germany
A.k.a. *Mellum, a Paradise for Birds in the North Sea*

Mit Kurbelkamera und Büchse Durch Sumpf und Urwald Afrikas
Prod.: Pathé, Paris / France
Distr.: German Distributor — Comenius, Bochum
A.k.a. *With a Film Camera and Rifle Through Wetland and Jungle in Africa*

Motoring in Cloudland
Prod.: Canadian Government Motion Picture Bureau
A journey along a 4200-mile circular run through Canada and the USA.

On the Equator
Prod.: Great Britain
Dir. and Cin.: Cherry Kearton

Running Animals
Prod.: USA
Cin.: J. B. Shackelford
Roy Chapman Andrews on an expedition to Africa in 1923, where running animals were successfully filmed from a moving car.

Sagan om de Sista Örnarna
Prod.: Bengt Berg / Sweden
Dir. and Cin.: Bengt Berg
A.k.a. *The Last Sea Eagles*
A very fine nature film with a conservation message.

Through Sheep's Eyes
Prod.: Hepworth / Great Britain
The first year of a sheep's life "seen" through its own eyes.

Trailing African Wild Animals
Prod.: USA
Dir. and Cin.: Martin Johnson
Martin and Osa on their search for Paradise Lake in Kenya.

The Wonderland of Big Game
Prod.: Dugmore-Harris productions / Great Britain
Cin.: A. Radclyffe Dugmore
The Dugmore-Harris expedition to East Africa.

1924

Australia's Lonely Lands
Prod.: Australia
Cin.: Francis Birtles?

Der Berg des Schicksals
Prod.: Germany / Switzerland
Dir.: Arnold Fanck
Cin.: Fanck and Sepp Allgeier
One of Fanck's fictional mountain films

Big Game in the Sub-Arctic of Canada
Prod.: Urban / Great Britain
Cin.: J.C.C. Bullock
British Columbia, Yellow Knife.

Birds of Scotland
Prod.: Great Britain
Dir.: H.A. Gilbert
Made around 1924–25.

Epic of Everest
Prod. and Cin.: J.B.L. Noel / USA
Distr.: Explorers' Films
The third Mt. Everest expedition in 1924, Mallory and Irvine's last attempt to reach the top.

Equatorial Africa: Roosevelt's Hunting Grounds
Prod.: USA
Cin.: A.J. Klein
Kenya and Uganda, Tanganyika, Lake Victoria, Mt. Ruwenzori.

Filmreise Nach dem Feuerland
Prod.: Germany
Dir.: Kaptajn C. Herbert
From Rio to Patagonia.

The Flight of a Dragon Fly
Dir.: Lucien Bull

The Formation of Volcanoes
Prod. and distr.: Visual Education

Gefiederte Räuber
Prod.: Linke, Dresden / Germany
A.k.a. *Thieves with Feathers*

Germination and Accelerated Growth of a Plant
Dir.: Dr. Jean Comandon

The Great White Silence
Prod.: Great Britain
Cin.: Herbert G. Ponting
A reediting of footage from the 1910–13 expedition to Antarctica conducted by Robert Falcon Scott.

Die Letzten Wisente (Bison Europaeus)
Prod.: Ufa / Germany

Mensch und Tier im Urwald
Prod.: Germany
Dir.: Hans Schomburgk
Cin.: Paul Lieberenz
A.k.a. *Man and Animals in the Jungle*
Schomburgk's expedition to Liberia and Monrovia in 1923–24.

Mit der Kamera Durch den Deutschen Wald
Prod.: Schonger Naturfilm, Berlin / Germany
A.k.a. *With a Camera Through the German Forest*

Räuber in der Natur — Fleischfressende Pflanzen
Prod.: Emelka-Kulturfilm, München / Germany
Distr.: Sternwarte, Berlin
A.k.a. *Thieves in Nature — Flesh-Eating Plants*

Salmon Fishing
Prod.: Germany
Uses fine continuity editing.

A Strange Courtship
Spiders.
Concerning Bills
The Dipper
The Swallows
The Swallow-Tail Butterfly
The Vapourer Moth
Prod.: British Instructional Films / Great Britain
Distr.: New Era Films
Edited by different people, including F. Martin Duncan and W.P. PyCraft.

The Vast Sudan
Prod.: Stoll Film Company / Great Britain
Cin.: A. Radclyffe Dugmore
There is some uncertainty surrounding this title.

1925

Abu Markub och de Hundrade Elefanter
Prod.: Sweden
Dir. and Cin.: Bengt Berg
A film about elephants and a shoebill bird.

Akeley's African Film
Prod.: Metro Pictures, New York
Cin.: Mr. and Mrs. Carl Akeley

Aus der Zoologie: Tiere, die Man Selten Sieht
Prod.: Cohinoor-Film, München / Germany
A.k.a. *From Zoology: Animals That Man Rarely Sees*

Bird Manor
Prod.: USA
Dir.: T. Walter Eeiseman

Colin Ross: Mit dem Kurbelkasten um die Erde
Prod.: Germany
Dir. and cin: Colin Ross
A.k.a. *Colin Ross: With the Cine-Camera Around the World*
The Philippines, India, Japan, Indonesia, China and the USA, among other places.

Domestic Secrets of the Eider Duck
Prod.: Pathé Exchange / Great Britain
Cin.: Howard H. Cleaves
The Labrador coastline.

Eine Mittelmeer und Orientreise mit dem Peer Gynt
Prod.: Germany
A.k.a. *A Mediterranean and Oriental Journey with Peer Gynt*
From Triest to Cairo

Eve Africaine
Prod.: Leon Poirier / France

The Flower Isle of the Pacific
Prod.: Pathé / Great Britain

Grass
Prod.: Famous Players–Lasky Corporation / USA
Dir.: Merian C. Cooper
Cin.: Ernest B. Shoedsack
Script: Marguerite Harrison
Editor: Terry Ramsaye and Richard P. Carver
A sophisticated travelogue including a surprisingly powerful story about the Baktyari nomads. In their search for grass they have to cross roaring rivers and the mountain pass Zardeh Kuh.

Insulinde
Prod.: Germany
Java.

Life in Sudan
Prod.: Great Britain
Distr.: Visual Education

Nature's Side Show
Prod.: American Nature Association / USA
Cin.: William L. Finley and Arthur N. Pack
Finley's expedition to Arizona in 1925.

Der Naturschutz der Bergwacht
Prod.: Bergwacht, München / Germany
A mountain ranger's preservation of nature.

Nionga
Prod. and distr.: Stoll Picture Productions / Great Britain
Distr.: Film Company
A drama documentary about Central Africa.

Osprey: The Great Fish Hawk
Prod.: Pathé Exchange / USA

The Ostrich and Feather Industry
Whaling
Prod.: African Film Productions / South Africa
Entries in the series of films *South African Industries*.

Palestine
Prod.: British Instructional Film / Great Britain
The Jordan River, the Dead Sea, Bethlehem and Hebron.

Queer Creatures of Cactus County
Prod.: American Nature Association / USA
Cin.: William L. Finley and Arthur N. Pack
From Finley's expedition to Arizona in 1925, a very fine nature film, including lots of humor.

Schützet die Tiere!
Prod.: Velox / Germany
A.k.a. *Save the Animals*
Nature preservation.

Secrets of the Eagle and a Merlin's Nest
Prod.: Great Britain
Cin.: H.A. Gilbert and Arthur Brook
Scotland.

The True North
Prod.: Great Britain
Dir.: Jack Robertson
Siberia.

Urwelt im Urwald
Prod.: Germany
Dir.: Adolf von Dungern
A.k.a. *Prehistoric Times in the Virgin Forest*

Vom Kilimandscharo zum Nil Durchs Verbotene Afrika
Prod.: Germany
Dir.: H.A. Aschenborn
A.k.a. *From Kilemanjaro to the Nile Through the Forbidden Parts of Africa*

Der Waldbrand
Prod.: Prizma, Jersey City / USA
Distr.: Germania
A.k.a. *The Forest Fire*
Nature preservation.

When Mr. and Mrs. Bluebird Took Up Housekeeping

Prod.: Pathé Exchange / USA
From the *Pathé Review* series.

Wild Men and Beast of Borneo
Prod.: USA?
Cin.: Lou Hutt
Hutt travels from Hong Kong to Malaysia.

Wings to the South
Prod. and Cin.: William L. Finley
Probably recorded between 1922 and 1925, this film covers birds along the Texas coastline.

Wisent in Not
Prod.: Schonger Naturfilm, Berlin / Germany
A.k.a. *Bisons at Risk*

Wonders of the Wild
Prod.: Burr Nickle Pictures / USA
Burr Nickle travels trough Mexico, Japan and Borneo.

Wunder der Wildnis
Prod.: Germany
Dir.: Hans Schomburgk
A.k.a. *The Wonders of the Wild*

Zum Schneegipfel Afrikas
Prod.: Ufa Kulturfilm / Germany
Dir.: Carl Heinz Boese
A.k.a. *To the Snowcapped Top of Africa*
The first time a film crew climbed Kilemanjaro.

1926

Alaskan Adventures
Prod.: C. C. Griffin / Great Britain–Canada(?)
Dir.: Jack Robertson (Anderson)
Distr.: Pathé Exchange
Editor: Paul D. Hogan.
Jack Anderson and Arthur Young travel through the wilds of Alaska and Siberia. They survive by shooting and eating wild animals.

Auf Tierfang in Abessinien
Prod.: Germany
Dir.: Ernst Garden
A.k.a. *Catching Wildlife in Abessinia*
An expedition film that shows how wildlife is being caught and placed in the Berlin Zoo.

The Battle of the Plants
Busy Bees
The Emperor Moth
The Gnat
The Golden Eagle
Cin.: H.A. Gilbert and Arthur Brook.
The Phantom
The Puss Moth

Seed Time
Prod.: British Instructional Films / Great Britain
Distr.: New Era Films
Entries in the series *Secrets of Nature*.

Die Biene Maja und Ihre Abendteure
Prod.: Kultur-Film AG / Germany
Dir.: Wolfram Junghans
A.k.a. *Maja the Bee and Her Adventures*

Big Game Parade
Prod.: American Nature Association / USA
Cin.: William L. Finley and Arthur N. Pack
From the Finley-Church expedition to Northland in 1926.

Cruising North (Bird Islands)
Prod.: American Nature Association / USA
Cin.: William L. Finley and Arthur N. Pack

Denver African Expedition
Prod.: University of Denver and Cape Town / USA
Dir.: E. Cradle and J. Grant

The Fiji Islands
Prod.: British Instructional Film / Great Britain
Distr.: Pro Patri Films
A part of the series of films called *The Empire*.

Getting Our Goat
Prod.: American Nature Association / USA
Cin.: William L. Finley and Arthur N. Pack
From the Finley-Church expedition to Northland in 1926.

Gorilla Hunt
Prod.: Great Britain(?)
Dir.: Ben Burgridge?
Burgridge leads an expedition, the purpose of which is to catch live gorillas.

The Great Bear of Alaska
Prod.: American Nature Association / USA
Cin.: William L. Finley and Arthur N. Pack
From the Finley-Church expedition to Northland in 1926.

Der Heilige Berg
Prod.: Germany
Dir.: Arnold Fanck
Cin.: Fanck and Sepp Allgeier?
A.k.a. *The Holy Mountain*
Fiction, starring Leni Riefenstahl.

The House-Fly
Prod.: British Instructional Film / Great Britain

Moana — A Romance of the Golden Age
Prod.: Paramount Pictures / Zukor and Lasky / USA

Dir. and Cin.: Robert J. Flaherty
Editor: Julian Johnson
On the Samoa island of Savie lives Moana. This film gave a name to the genre: documentary.

Der Naturur-Kunden aus dem Dickschen Wald
Prod.: Bergwacht, München / Germany
A.k.a. *A Nature Document from the Dense Forest*
Nature preservation.

Off to Glacier Bay
Prod.: American Nature Association / USA
Cin.: William L. Finley and Arthur N. Pack
From the Finley-Church expedition to Northland in 1926; Alaska and Kenai.

Partite di caccia grossa in Africa
Prod.: Italy / V. Z. Tedesco
Dir.: Vittorio Zammarano Tedesco
Cin.: Zammarano Tedesco and Aurelio Rossi

Primeval World of the Forest
Prod.: Ufa / Germany
Cin.: August Brückner

Primitive Love—An Epic of the Frozen North
Prod.: Edward L. Klien Corporation / USA
Distr.: Stoll Picture Productions
Dir.: Frank E. Kleinschmidt

Ramparts of the North
Prod.: American Nature Association / USA
Cin.: William L. Finley and Arthur N. Pack
From the Finley-Church expedition to Northland in 1926; Alaska and Kenai.

Segelfahrt ins Wunderland
Prod.: Germany
Dir.: Günther Plüschow
Argentina.

Varanus Komodensis
Prod.: USA
Dir.: William Douglas Burden
Burden traveled to Ostindia in 1926 to film the Komodo Dragon.

Voyage au Congo
Prod.: André Gide / France
Dir.: Marc Allégret
Distr.: Film Society
André Gide travels to the Congo.

Wild Animal Outpost
Prod.: American Nature Association / USA
Cin.: William L. Finley and Arthur N. Pack
From the Finley-Church expedition to Northland in 1926; Umiak.

With Cherry Kearton in the Jungle
Prod.: Cherry Kearton Films Ltd. / USA
Cin.: Cherry Kearton

A Zoo Tea Party
Prod.: British Instructional Film / Great Britain
Chimpanzees acting like humans by smoking, among other things.

Zulu Native Life
Prod.: South Africa
The Majozi tribe.

1927

The Ant-Lion
Denizens of the Garden
Insects.
Floral Cooperative Societies
Insects and flowers.
The Home Wrecker
Plant Magic
Flowers recorded by using macro and time-lapse photography.
The Plants of the Pantry
The Praying Mantis
Romance of the Flowers
The Story of a Glass of Water
The Story of a Leaf
The Story of the Grasses
Prod.: British Instructional Film / Great Britain
Distr.: Pro Patria Films
Entries in the film series *Secrets of Nature*.

Babes in the Woods
Prod.: American Nature Association / USA
Cin.: William L. Finley and Arthur N. Pack
From the Pack-Finley expedition to the Pacific Northwest region.

Bali
Prod.: Germany
Dir.: Lola Kreuzberg

Basutoland and Its People
Prod.: Great Britain

Big Game Animals of North America
Prod.: Canada

Chang—a Drama of the Wilderness
Prod.: Paramount / USA
Dir. and Cin.: Ernest B. Schoedsack and Merian C. Cooper
Intertitles: Achmed Abdullah
Fiction in which the animals play a very important part.

The Flea, Bug and Louse

Prod.: Great Britain
Distr.: Bermondsey Borough Council

The Forest
Prod.: American Nature Association / USA
Cin.: William L. Finley and Arthur N. Pack
This filming of the Pack-Finley expedition to the Pacific Northwest region includes footage of both industrial and natural usage of wood.

The Great Australian Bush, Its Wonders and Mystery
Prod.: Edward Percy Bailey / Australia?
Cin.: Edward Percy Bailey
Focuses on nature, plants, wildlife and the aborigines.

Med Hundeslæde Gennem Grønland
Prod.: Fotorama / Denmark
Cin.: Leo Hansen
A.k.a. *On Dog Sledge Through Greenland*
The 5th Thule Expedition by Knud Rasmussen, 1921–24.

Mountaineering in Lakeland
Prod.: Gaumont Company / Great Britain
Distr.: Travel Association of Great Britain
Mountain climbers climbing Great Gable.

L'Oeuf d'epinoche: De la fécondation à l'éclosion
Prod.: France
Dir.: Jean Painlevé
Cin.: André Raymond
A film about sticklebacks.

Riding the Rim Rock
Prod.: American Nature Association / USA
Cin.: William L. Finley and Arthur N. Pack
From the Pack-Finley expedition to the Pacific Northwest region; Oregon and Wyoming.

So This Is America
Prod.: Castle Films / USA
Distr.: Film Distributers
Natural tourist attractions in the USA: the Rocky Mountains; Oregon's Crater Lake; Mt. Shasta; the Sierra Nevadas; others.

Sunlight Is Life
Prod.: Dr. Ulrich Kaiser / Great Britain
Distr.: Bermondsey Borough Council
Health propaganda.

Thar She Blows
Prod.: American Nature Association / USA
Cin.: William L. Finley and Arthur N. Pack
From the Pack-Finley expedition to the Pacific Northwest region; a film about whales.

Through Darkest Africa, in Search of White Rhinoceros
Prod.: Great Britain
Dir. and Cin.: Harry K. Eustace
Hunting.

When Mountains Call
Prod.: American Nature Association / USA
Cin.: William L. Finley and Arthur N. Pack
From the Pack-Finley expedition to the Pacific Northwest region; the wildlife and climate in the mountains.

1928

Als Dreijähriger Durch Afrika
Prod.: Germany
Dir.: Colin Ross
A.k.a. *Traveling Through Africa at the Age of Three*
The title refers to director's son.

Baluchistan
A Persian Caravan
Through the Back Door Into India
Prod.: British Instructional Films / Great Britain
Distr.: Pro Patria Film
Entries in the film series *Heart of Asia*.

La Daphnie
Prod.: France
Dir.: Jean Painlevé
Cin.: André Raymonds
Water fleas.

Great Arctic Seal Hunt
Prod.: USA?
Dir.: Varick Frissel
A.k.a. *The Swilin' Racket*

The Great White North
Prod.: H.A. Snow / USA
Dir.: Manuscript and Cin.: Sidney Snow
Distr.: Fox
Hunting whales, walruses and polar bears.

Heia Safari!
Prod.: Ufa Kulturfilm / Germany
Dir.: Martin Rikli
Colonial Africa and the first woman to climb Kilemanjaro.

Mit Sven Hedin Durch Asien Wüsten
Prod.: Lufthansa / Lieberenz / Germany/Sweden
Dir.: Paul Lieberenz and Rudolf Biebrach
A.k.a. *With Sven Hedin Through the Asian Desert*
Sven Hedin's great expedition through Central Asia in 1927 and 1928.

OO-Tang
Prod.: Butchers Empire Picture / USA

An odd mixture of travelogues and dramatic fiction in which animals are turned into wild beasts.

L'Oursin
Prod.: France
Dir.: Jean Painlevé
Cin.: André Raymonds
Sea urchins.

På Skidor Till Syltopparne
Prod.: Svensk Filmindustris Skolfilm / Sweden
A.k.a. *Skiing to Syltopparne*
Skiers climb the mountains of Norrland in Sweden.

La Pieuvre
Prod.: France
Dir.: Jean Painlevé
Cin.: André Raymonds
Octopuses.

The Rhineland
Prod.: Germany
Tourist film.

Samba
Prod.: Germany
Dir.: August Brückner
Life of African tribes and animals of the jungle.

Secrets of the Water
Prod.: Unite / Great Britain

Simba, King of Beasts: A Saga of the African Veldt
Prod.: Martin and Osa Johnson, and different companies / USA
Cin.: M. Johnson, C. Akeley, A. J. Klein.
Editors: T. Ramsaye, M. Johnson and L. Seebach
Both sound and silent versions exist; *Die Ring Des*

Niebelungen by Wagner is used in the sound version. A classic among safari films, this formed the basis for the makings of 3 additional short films: *Adventuring Johnsons, Naked Man Versus Beast,* and *Safari.*

Västlandet
Prod.: Sweden
Distr.: Svensk Films Skolfilm-Avdeling
Sailing through Sognefjorden in Sweden.

The Victoria Falls of South Africa
Prod.: British Screen Productions / Great Britain

West Africa Calling
Prod.: British Instructional Films / Great Britain
This colonial propaganda film covers wild nature, industry and development.

192?

Fortune-Builders: Life Story of the Lowly Silk Moth, Which Weaves and Spins for Mankind
Prod.: Kineto Company / USA / Great Britain
Cin.: F. Percy Smith and Charles Head
This could be part of the British series *Secrets of Nature.*

Monstrosities of Pondland
Prod.: Great Britain
A tinted version.

Renting Houses for Songs
Prod. and Cin.: William L. Finley
How to take care of the birdlife in your garden.

Swat That Fly: The Life History of the Fly and How to Combat the Pest
Prod.: Kineto Company / USA / Great Britain
Cin.: F. Percy Smith

CHAPTER NOTES

Getting Around the Subject

1. Nørfelt 1992, p. 19.
2. Barsam 1973, p. 11.
3. The historical sections in Nørfelt 1992, are to be found on pp. 10–20 and have an additional summary on the history of nature films on pp. 93–95; the section on nature film in Norstad 1995, pp. 7–24.
4. Bousé 2000, pp. 37–52, 57–59.
5. Bousé 2000, pp. 20–25.
6. Griffith in Hampton 1931/1970, v.
7. Dench 1919, pp. 120, 127.
8. James and Imperato 1992, p. 209.
9. Allen and Gomery 1985, p. 30.
10. Allen and Gomery 1985, pp. 28–31.
11. Tybjerg in Jensen 1997, p. 134; Usai 2000, p. 10.
12. Surowiec (ed.) 1996, p. 88.
13. Larsen 1995.
14. Barber 1993, pp. 68–69.
15. Boudet 1967, pp. 280–292.
16. Larsen 1997, p. 79.
17. Bousé 2000, pp. 94–5.
18. Barber 1993; Larsen 1997; Peter Ravn 1978.
19. Hampton 1931/1970, p. 8.
20. Coe 1981, pp. 60–62; Hill and Herbert 1998, pp. 104–107; Sadoul 1964, p. 148; Bordwell and Thompson 1994, pp. 8–10; Hampton 1931/1970, p. 7.
21. Usai 2000, p. 4.
22. Barsam 1973, p. 136.
23. Salt 1983, p. 222; Coe, 1981, p. 89; Bordwell and Thompson 1994, pp. 177–8.
24. Neale 1985, pp. 91–93.
25. Talbot 1912, pp. 139–140.
26. Muybridge 1899/1918, pp. 9–14; Bordwell and Thompson 1994, p. 5; Hill and Herbert 1998, pp. 98–107; Coe 1981, p. 43.

1895–1902

1. Honri in Low (ed.) 1948a, pp. 243–244.
2. Salt 1983, pp. 48, 51, 56, 60.
3. Kevin Brownlow 1978, pp. 408, 455; Pike 1946, pp. 142–144; Coe 1981, p. 84; Salt 1983, pp. 41–42, 76, 191.
4. Allen 1980, pp. 23–28; Low and Manvell 1948, pp. 36–38; Hampton 1931/1970, p. 62; Tybjerg 1997, pp. 126–147.
5. Barnes 1976, pp. 64–65.
6. We cannot be 100 percent certain that these films were filmed on this exact date, and quite possibly some of the films were shot in late 1900 by T. Crahan and R.K. Bonnie. If they were filmed in 1897, they must have been made by J. White and Blechynden. Musser 1997, p. 319.

7. Low and Manvell 1948, pp. 51, 72.
8. Blom (ed.) 1999, pp. 263–266.
9. *Thjodolfur* (Icelandic newspaper) Sept. 20, 1901, p. 179.
10. Anrick 1919 p. 76.
11. Imperato 1992, p. 51.
12. Tarleau, 1920 pp. 46–47, 100; Brownlow 1978, pp. 420–421.
13. Fielding (ed.) 1967, pp. 60–64.
14. Caldwell (ed.) 1977.
15. Imperato 1992, p. 9; Johnson 1947 (original 1940), pp. 15, 30, 165.
16. Johnson 1947, pp. 22–27; Imperato 1992, pp. 26–28, 34.
17. Imperato 1992, p. 48; Brownlow 1978, pp. 466–467.
18. Johnson 1947, pp. 57–67.
19. Brownlow 1978, pp. 421–425.
20. Lowry in Fell 1983, pp. 131–141.
21. Musser 1997, p. 345.
22. Edmondson and Trustrum in Lansell and Beilby (eds.) 1982.

1903–1906

1. Usai in Abel (ed.) 1996, p. 23; Usai 2000, p. 21; Barnes 1976, pp. 114–115.
2. All four methods have been described in detail by Usai 1996, pp. 21–30.
3. Salt 1983, p. 87.
4. Engberg 1977 (1), p. 187; Engberg 1977 (2), p. 377; Hampton 1931/1970, pp. 29–31; Allen 1980, pp. 288, 297; Bordwell and Thompson 1994, p. 37; Low and Manvell 1948, p. 45.
5. Bordwell and Thompson 1994, pp. 22, 40–44; Salt 1983, pp. 51, 56, 111.
6. Griffiths 1999, p. 294; Depue in Fieldings 1967, p. 62.
7. Talbot 1912, pp. 84–86.
8. Herbert 2000, p. xv.
9. Talbot 1912, p. 130; Low and Manvell 1948, pp. 38–39.
10. About Canada. Browne 1979, p. 1. About England. Low and Manvell 1948, pp. 38–39. About France. Abel 1994, p. 24. About Denmark. Tybjerg 1997, pp. 126–147. About Italy. Bordwell and Thompson 1994, pp. 26–29.
11. Herbert 2000, p. xv.
12. Bloom 1999, pp. 263–264.
13. Herbert 2000, p. xv; Low and Manvell 1948, p. 25.
14. Niver 1971, p. 8; Low and Manvell 1948, p. 26.
15. Low and Manvell 1948, pp. 17–19.
16. Low and Manvell, 1948, p. 60.
17. Bordwell and Thompson 1994, pp. 22, 37, 43–44.
18. Bordwell and Thompson 1994, pp. 40–42.
19. Reprint of Urban Film Catalogue 1905. Herbert 2000, p. 100.
20. Sanderson 1961, pp. 110–112; Low and Manvell 1948, pp. 40, 51–70.
21. The numbers have been taken from Engberg 1977 (1), p. 187; Engberg 1977 (2), p. 378; Sanderson 1961, pp. 110, 112.
22. Allen 1980, pp. 212–220.
23. Abel 1994, p. 23; Allen 1980, p. 218; Musser 1990, pp. 276–277.
24. About landscape scenic films. Musser 1990, pp. 123, 132; Edmondson and Trustman 1982, p. 23.

1907–1910

1. Pike 1946, pp. 18–19; Honri 1948, p. 244.
2. Pike 1946, pp. 168, 183.
3. Salt 1983, p. 83. The information concerning the competition between the various showing venues comes from Allen, 1980, pp. 220–229.
4. Hampton 1931/1970, p. 46.
5. Horwitz, Harrison, and Wendy 1980, p. xiii; Abel 1994, pp. 25–31; Bordwell and Thompson 1994, pp. 26–29. Usai writes that the renting of films was introduced in 1909, but George Kleine began earlier (Usai 2000, p. 11).
6. Hampton 1931/1970, pp. 27, 59–60, 66–73.

7. Bush 1914c, pp. 16–52; Abel 1994, note 336 (the note refers to p. 486).
8. Abel 1994, p. 35.
9. Nørrested and Alsted 1987, pp. 58–59.
10. Long in Lansell and Beilby (eds.) 1982a, p. 24
11. Ramsaye 1926, pp. 519–522; Brownlow 1978, p. 405. I neglect to refer to Cherry Kearton as the film's cameraman. This is partly due to Hoffman 1910, p. 683 and Guggisberg 1977, pp. 70–71.
12. These special Selig "Thrills" are mentioned in Hampton 1931/1970, pp. 34–35.
13. Hosking and Lowers 1947, p. 22. See also. *Kinematograph and Lantern Weekly*, Sept. 5 (1907): 263, 267.
14. Kearton 1914, pp. 272–277.
15. Guggisberg 1977, pp. 70–75.
16. Steele 1913, p. 337.
17. Guggisberg 1977, p. 24.
18. Steele 1913, pp. 329–337; *The Moving Picture World* Sept. 10, 1910, pp. 567–568.
19. Brownlow 1978, p. 126.
20. Hosking 1947, p. 22.
21. Guggisberg 1977, p. 18.
22. Pike 1946, pp. 14–16.
23. Pike 1946, p. 17.
24. For more information concerning Pike's production for Pathé Frerès, see Pike 1946, pp. 18–19, 117.
25. Copy from the British Film Institute and Pike 1946, p. 178. It is worth noting that the shots are only half as long as he had originally intended.
26. Pike 1946, p. 188.
27. Dench 1919, p. 126.
28. Croy 1918, pp. 249–250; Field and Smith 1934, pp. 106–107.
29. Lefebvre in Hertogs (ed.) 1997, p. 96.
30. Talbot 1912, pp. 264–276. Electric Spark Company.
31. Croy 1918, pp. 238–239.
32. Talbot 1912, p. 272.
33. *The Independent* Dec. 13, 1915.
34. Field and Smith 1934, pp. 138–141.
35. Field and Smith 1934, p. 147.
36. Croy 1918, p. 242.
37. Field and Smith 1934, pp. 142, 144; Woolfe 1941, p. 8.
38. Smith 1931, p. 990.
39. Field and Smith 1934, p. x; Talbot 1912, pp. 191–192.
40. Smith 1931, p. 994.
41. Information concerning Percy Smith and his experiments. Talbot 1912, pp. 191–194.
42. David 1916.
43. Cosandey in Horteg (ed.) 1997, pp. 44–45; Thys om Kuyper (ed.) 1995; Guggisberg 1977, p. 71.
44. Thys 1995, pp. 6–14.
45. Legg and Hurley 1966, pp. 83–109.
46. Bertrand 1974, p. 33.

1911–1921

1. Gregory (ed.) 1920/1927, pp. 366–367; Honri 1948, p. 244.
2. Coe 1981, p. 87; Talbot 1912, p. 308.
3. Salt 1983, p. 151; Honri 1948, p. 244; Gregory 1920/1927, pp. 347–350.
4. Salt 1983, p. 87; Honri 1948, p. 244; Pike 1946, pp. 58, 156.
5. Salt 1983, p. 227.
6. Abel 1994, pp. 31, 54–55; Allen 1980, pp. 230–246; Tybjerg 1997, pp. 126–147.
7. Brownlow 1978, p. 406; Imperato 1992, pp. 84, 96–97.
8. Boeses 1926, pp. 59, 173.
9. Long, "1910s Australia," 1982, p. 25; Legg 1966, pp. 83–109; Surowiec 1996, pp. 82–83.
10. Legg 1966, pp. 112–113; Pike in Lansell and Beilby (eds.) 1982, p. 29.
11. Legg 1966, pp. 137–138.
12. Lynch 1989, p. 292.
13. Additional source. Legg 1966, p. 24.

14. Brownlow 1978, p. 426; *Scientific American* June 21, 1913, p. 568.

15. The information stems from Ponting 1921/1923, pp. 152, 168–171.

16. Surowiec 1996, p. 82.

17. Brownlow 1978, p. 433; Lynch 1989, p. 302.

18. *The Moving Picture World* Sept. 26 (1914): 1762.

19. *The Independent* July 12, 1915, p. 68.

20. Boesgaard Jan. 17, 1922.

21. Lund 1978.

22. *Kinobladet* 1921 (21), pp. 664–665.

23. Lund 1978.

24. *Kinobladet* Mar. 15, 1920; *Dansk Arbejde* April 1, 1921.

25. *Kinobladet* 1921 (21), p. 664.

26. Nielsen 2003, pp. 816–817.

27. *Social-Demokraten* 1957; Lund 1978; Unpublished article, April 8, 1958, found in the file on Richard Lund at the library of The Danish Film Institute.

28. Nielsen 2003, p. 823.

29. Furhammer 1982, p. 14; Birkvad and Diesen 1994, p. 21.

30. Film program for *Blandt Vilde og vilde Dyr* (*Amongst Wild People and Wild Animals*) Jan. 2, 1924.

31. Von Heland 1966, pp. 109–118.

32. Prince William 1923. In Sweden he is known as Prins Wilhelm.

33. As far as I know, Mathewson has written the only existing book on William Finley. Mathewson 1986, pp. 1–17.

34. Mathewson 1986, p. 14.

35. Ellis and Thornborough 1923, pp. 254–255.

36. *Literary Digest* 1913, pp. 576–577.

37. Ellis and Thornborough 1923, pp. 34–36.

38. I saw the film at Library of Congress (FLA 1551) I think this film version is incomplete, for the last focus ends very abruptly.

39. Ditmars 1934/1970, pp. 98–113.

40. I saw this film at the American Museum of Natural History in New York.

41. Bush 1913, p. 592.

42. Lola Kreutzberg 1929. The BFI copy of *Salmon Fishing* is incomplete. It only lasts some 1.07 minutes and the beginning of the film is missing.

43. Guggisberg 1977, p. 113.

44. Field and Smith 1934, pp. 70–72, describes a couple of the primary requirements.

45. I have the English titles from reviews in *The Moving Picture World*. Nov. 18, 1911, p. 552; Nov. 15, 1913, p. 724.

46. Bordwell and Thompson 1994, p. 42.

47. Field and Smith 1934, pp. 73–79.

48. Croy 1918, pp. 329–330; Williamson 1914, pp. 25–26

49. Dench 1919, pp. 150–153.

50. Dench 1919, p. 151. Other sources. Croy 1918, p. 330; *The Independent* Nov. 2, 1914, p. 171.

1922–1928

1. Gregory 1920/1927, pp. 353–356; Bodry-Sanders 1991/1998, pp. 142–144.

2. This time estimation is mentioned in *American Cinematographer* 1987, p. 96.

3. Bodry-Sanders 1991/1998, pp. 144–145.

4. Other sources. Coe 1981, pp. 82–83; Salt 1983, pp. 200–201; *American Cinematographer* 1987, p. 96.

5. Dugmore 1925, p. 145.

6. Coe 1981, p. 86; Salt 1983, pp. 202, 227 Johnson 1929, pp. 181–182.

7. Pike 1946, pp. 58, 156; Salt 1983, pp. 42, 191; Brownlow 1978, p. 456.

8. Coe 1981, p. 143.

9. Hampton 1931/1970, pp. 204–205; Bordwell and Thompson 1994, p. 184.

10. Barnouw 1983, p. 42; Jacobs 1971, p. 7; Brownlow 1978, pp. 471–485.

11. Furhammer 1982, pp. 15–16.

12. Furhammer 1994, pp. 13–15; *Aftonbladet*, Nov. 27, 1923; Birkvad and Diesen 1994, p. 23; Ellis and Thornborough 1923, pp. 254–255; Guggisberg 1977, pp. 85–86.

13. More information about this and the following about *The Story of the Last Eagles* can be found in Berg 1927b, pp. 60–106.

14. *Aftonbladet* Nov. 27, 1923. De Sista Örnarna.

15. Guggisberg 1977, p. 87; *Stockholms-Tidningen* Mar. 20, 1925; Furhammer 1982, pp. 15, 40.

16. Surowiec 1996, p. 86.

17. *Kristeligt Dagblad* Jan. 1, 1924.

18. Low 1979, p. 20; Woolfe 1941, p. 8; Field and Smith 1934, pp. x–86.

19. Brownlow 1978, p. 411; Imperato 1992, p. 93.

20. Guggisberg 1977, pp. 98–100.

21. Mitman 1999, p. 29; Akeley 1929, p. 209.

22. Bodry-Sanders 1991/1998, pp. 208–213.

23. *Nationaltidende* Feb. 10, 1924.

24. Guggisberg 1977, pp. 52–60.

25. Behlmer 1966, pp. 19–22; Brownlow 1978, pp. 523–529; *Dagens Nyheder* and *Ekstra Bladet,* Feb. 19, 1926.

26. *Scientific American* Aug. 1927, pp. 127–129.

27. Mitman 1999, pp. 39–40; Griffith 1971, pp. 22–24; Brownlow 1978, pp. 529–541.

28. Mitman 1999, p. 46.

29. Brownlow 1978, pp. 558–559; Mitman 1999, p. 47.

30. The section on Painlevé's life, upbringing, and film production can be found in Berg in Bellows, McDougall, and Berg (eds.) 2000, pp. 3–19; Hutchins 1937, pp. 101–102.

31. Johnson 1931, pp. 138–140; Imperato 1992, p. 73; Johnson 1947, p. 100.

32. Imperato 1992, p. 81.

33. Johnson 1947, p. 151.

34. Johnson 1947, p. 242; Johnson 1928, p. 178.

35. Danish press material for *Blandt Vilde dyr I Afrika*; Imperato 1992, p. 112.

36. Mitman 1999, p. 26.

37. Imperato 1992, p. 102; press material from Det Danske Filminstitut (The Danish Film Institute).

38. Johnson 1947, pp. 153, 163; Imperato 1992, pp. 99–102.

39. Johnson 1929, p. 143.

40. Johnson 1929, p. 123.

41. Johnson 1947, pp. 172–173, 182, 184.

42. Johnson 1947, pp. 135, 164, 170–171, 179, 181.

43. Johnson 1928, pp. 143, 147, 149; Imperato 1992, p. 105. Osa herself mentions that she learnt to speak a South Sea dialect which she calls *Bêche-de-mer* in Johnson 1947, p. 103.

44. This particular point of view is evident in her book about their life. Johnson 1947, pp. 69, 130, 149, 151, 163, 217, 238, 295.

45. Imperato 1992, pp. 121–122; Johnson 1929, p. 72; Johnson 1928, p. 8.

46. Johnson 1947, p. 225.

47. Johnson 1928, pp. 79–80, 89, 134; Johnson 1929, p. 47.

48. Bodry-Sanders 1991/1998, pp. 212–213; Johnson 1928, p. 6.

49. Hampton 1931/1970, pp. 421–422; Mitman 1999, pp. 30–33.

50. Johnson 1928, pp. 51, 127–129; Imperato 1992, p. 142; Bousé 2000, p. 207; Bodry-Sanders 1991/1998, p. 213.

BIBLIOGRAPHY

Abel, Richard. 1994. *The Ciné Goes to Town: French Cinema, 1896–1914.* Berkeley: University of California Press.

Aftonbladet. Nov. 27, 1923. De Sista Örnarna. Section Filmvärlden. Stockholm.

Agger, Jens Peder, and Ole Hansen. 1974. *Tegneserien — Fortælleteknik, funktion, udvikling.* Copenhagen: Borgen Forlag.

Akeley, Mary Jobe. 1929. *Carl Akeley's Africa.* New York: Dodd, Mead.

Allen, Robert Clyde. Spring 1978. "Contra the Chaser Theory." *Wide Angle,* vol. 3, no. 4, 4–11.

_____. 1980. *Vaudeville and Film 1895–1915: A Study in Media Interaction.* New York: Arno Press.

Allen, Robert Clyde, and Douglas Gomery. 1985. *Film History: Theory and Practice.* New York: Alfred A. Knopf.

Anrick, Carl Julius. 1919. "Känn Ditt Land." *Filmjournalen,* no. 3, 76.

Armanski, Gerhard. 1981. "Historie og Naturbevidsthed. Social og idehistoriske rids af forholdet mellem menneske og natur.*" hug!* Årgang 6, no. 31, 14.

Armour, Robert A. 1980. *Film: A Reference Guide.* Westport, CT: Greenwood.

Barber, Theodore. 1993. "The Roots of Travel Cinema: John L. Stoddard, E. Burton Holmes and the Nineteenth-Century Illustrated Travel Lecture." *Film History,* vol. 5, 68–84.

Barnes, John. 1976. *The Beginnings of the Cinema in England.* Newton Abbot [UK]: David & Charles.

Barnouw, Erik. 1983. *Documentary: A History of the Non-Fiction Film.* New York: Oxford University Press.

Barsam, Richard Meran. 1973. *Nonfiction Film: A Critical History.* New York: E.P. Dutton.

Behlmer, Rudy. 1966. "Merian C. Cooper Is the Kind of Creative Showman Todays Movies Badly Need." *Films in Review,* January, vol. XVII, no. 1.

Belfrage, Cedric. 1931. "Ugly Ducklings of Wardour Street." *Listener,* December 30, 6:1155.

Bellows, Andy Masaki, Marina Mcdougall, and Brigitte Berg, eds. 2000. *Science Is Fiction: The Films of Jean Painlevé.* Translated by Jeanini Herman. San Francisco: Brico Press.

Berg, Bengt. 1925. *Med Tranerne til Afrika.* Copenhagen: Povl Branner.

_____. 1926. *Abu Markúb. På Jagt efter Kæmpefugle og Elefanter.* Copenhagen: Povl Branner.

_____. 1927a. *Min Ven Fjeldpiberen.* Copenhagen: Povl Branner.

_____. 1927b. *De Sidste Ørne.* Copenhagen: Povl Branner.

Berg, Brigitte. 2000. "Contradictory Forces: Jean Painlevé, 1902–1989." In *Science Is Fiction: The Films of Jean Painlevé.* Edited by Andy Masaki Bellows, Marina Mcdougall, and Brigitte Berg. San Francisco: Brico Press.

Berg, Gustaf. 1919. "Svensk Bygd på Film." *Filmjournalen,* no. 1, 3.

Bertrand, Ina. 1974. "Francis Birtles — Cyclist, Explorer, Kodaker." *Cinema Papers,* January, 31–35.

Birkvad, Søren, and Jan Anders Diesen. 1994. *Autentiske Inntrykk. Møte med skandinaviske dokumentarfilmskaparar.* Oslo: Det Norske Samlaget.

Blaisdell, George. 1914. "Hemment Brings African Scenes." *The Moving Picture World,* May 2, 20:675.

Blandt Vilde og vilde Dyr (Amongst Wild People and Wild Animals) Film program, 1924.

Blom, Ivo, ed. 1999. "Chapters from the Life of a Camera-Operator: The Recollections of Anton Nögerath — Filming News and Non-Fiction, 1897–1908." *Film History,* vol. 11, no. 3, 262–281.

Bodry-Sanders, Penelope. 1991/1998. *Carl Akeley: African Collector, Africa's Savior.* New York: Paragon House.

Boeses, Karl Heinz. 1926. *Zum Schneegipfel Afrikas.* Berlin: Vossische Buchhandlung.

Boesgaard, Eric. 1922. "Hvor Filmen vinder nyt Land." Interview with Richard Lund. *BT,* January 17.

Bordwell, David. 1997. *On the History of Film Style*. Cambridge: Harvard University Press.
_____, and Kristin Thompson. 1994. *Film History: An Introduction*. New York: McGraw-Hill.
Boudet, Jacques. 1967. *Mennesket Dyrenes Herre*. Translated by Per Skar from *L'homme et l'animal*. Copenhagen: Forlaget Union.
Bousé, Derek. 2000. *Wildlife Films*. Philadelphia: University of Pennsylvania Press.
Braaten, Lars Thomas, Jan Erik Holst, and Jan Kortner. 1995. *Filmen i Norge*. Oslo: Notam Gyldendal.
British Film Institute, National Film Archive Catalogue Vol. 1, Non-Fiction Films. 1980. London: British Film Institute.
Browne, Colin. 1979. *Motion Picture Production in British Columbia: 1898–1940*. British Columbia Provincial Museum.
Brownlow, Kevin. 1978. *The War, the West and the Wilderness*. New York: Alfred A. Knopf.
Burch, Noël. 1990. *Life to These Shadows*. Berkeley: University of California Press.
Bush, W. Stephen. 1913. "How Wild Animals Live." *The Moving Picture World*, November 8, 592.
_____. 1914a. "Arctic Hunts." *The Moving Picture World*, February 21, 19:956.
_____. 1914b. "A New Star." *The Moving Picture World*, February 28, 19:1095–6.
_____. 1914c. "Theories vs. Facts." *The Moving Picture World*, March 28, 19:1652.
Caldwell, Genoa, ed. 1977. *The Man Who Photographed the World: Burton Holmes: Travelogues, 1886–1938*. New York: Harry N. Abrams.
Chalmers, J.P. 1909. "Another Lost Opportunity." *The Moving Picture World*, October 16, 4:326.
Chang. En roman fra siams jungle. 1928. Copenhagen: Fr. Palm Greisens Forlag.
Coe, Brian. 1981. *The History of Movie Photography*. London: Ash & Grant.
Cooper, "Caribou Bill." 1919. "The Non-Fiction of the Movies." *Motion Picture Magazine*, February, 17:40–1, 102.
Cosandey, Roland. 1997. "Some Thoughts on 'Early Documentary.'" In *Uncharted Territory: Essays on Early Nonfiction Film*. Edited by Daan Hertogs. Amsterdam: Stichting Nederlands Filmmuseum.
Croy, Homer. 1918. *How Motion Pictures Are Made*. New York: Harper.
"Dansk Dyreliv i levende Billeder." Apr. 1, 1921. *Dansk Arbejde*.
David, Adam. 1916. *Jagden und Abenteuer in der Gebieten des obern Nil*. Basel: Friedrich Reinhardt.
Dench, Ernest Alfred. 1919. *Making the Movies*. New York: Macmillan.
Ditmars, Raymond Lee. 1934/1970. *Confessions of a Scientist*. New York: Books for Libraries Press.
Dugmore, Arthur Radclyffe. 1910. *Camera Adventures in the African Wilds: Being an Account of a Four Months Expedition in British East Africa*. New York: Doubleday.
_____. 1925. *The Wonderland of Big Game: Being an Account of Two Trips Through Tanganyika and Kenya*. London: Arrowsmith.
Edmondson, Ray, and Jenny Trustrum. 1982. "1900's World Wide and Australia." In *The Documentary Film in Australia*. Edited by Ross Lansell and Peter Beilby. Melbourne: Cinema Papers.
Ellis, Don Carlos, and Laura Thornborough. 1923. *Motion Pictures in Education: A Practical Handbook for Users of Visual Aids*. New York: Thomas Y. Crowell.
Ellis, Jack C. 1989. *The Documentary Idea: A Critical History of English-Language Documentary Film and Video*. Englewood Cliffs, NJ: Prentice Hall.
Elsaesser, Thomas, and Adam Barker. 1990. *Early Cinema—Space, Frame, Narrative*. London: BFI.
Engberg, Marguerite. 1977. *Dansk Stumfilm. Vol. 1–2*. Copenhagen: Rhodos.
_____. 1977. *Registrant over Danske Film, 1896–1914. Vol. 1–3*. Copenhagen: Institute for Film & Media.
The Era. October 31, 1896. "A Sea Cave Near Lisbon." 19.
Field, Mary, and Percy Smith. 1934. *Secrets of Nature*. London: Faber & Faber.
Fielding, Raymond, ed. 1967. *A Technological History of Motion Pictures and Television: An Anthology from the Pages of* The Journal of the Society of Motion Pictures and Television Engineers. Berkeley: University of California.
Fildew, William E. 1917. "Trials of the Cameraman." *The Moving Picture World*, July 21, 33:391–2.
Finley, William L. 1923. "Hunting Birds with a Camera." *The National Geographic Magazine*, vol. XLIV, no. 2, August, 160–201.
Fledelius, Karsten, and Finn Løkkegaard. 1985. *Film, TV og Historie. En Metodisk og Didaktisk Introduktion*. Copenhagen: Institute for Film & Media.
Furhammar, Leif. 1982. "Svensk Dokumentär—Filmhistoria Från PW till TV." *Filmhæftet* 9, no. 38–40, December, 6–42.
_____. 1994. *Med TV i Verkligheten. Bind 1*. Borås: Centraltrykkeriet.
Gad, Urban. 1919. *Filmen. Dens midler og mål*. Copenhagen: Nordisk Forlag.
Gifford, Dennis. 1986. *The British Film Catalogue 1895–1985: A Reference Guide*. London: David & Charles.
Gregory, Carl Louis, ed. 1920/1927. *Motion Picture Photography*. New York: Falk.

Griffith, Richard. 1931/1970. Introduction to *History of the American Film Industry from Its Beginnings to 1931,* by Benjamin B. Hampton. New York: Dover.

Griffiths, Alison. 1999. "'To the Worlds the World We Show': Early Travelogues as Filmed Ethnography." *Film History,* vol. 11, no. 3, 282–307.

Guggisberg, Charles A. W. 1977. *Early Wildlife Photographers.* New York: Taplinger.

Guynn, William. 1990. *A Cinema of Nonfiction.* Rutherford, NJ: Fairleigh Dickinson University Press.

Hampton, Benjamin B. 1931/1970. *History of the American Film Industry from Its Beginnings to 1931.* New York: Dover.

Hardy, Forsythe, Michael Balcon, Ernest Lindgren, and Roger Manvell. 1947. *Twenty Years of British Film: 1925–1945.* London: The Falcon Press Limited.

Hazéra, Hélène, and Dominique Leglu. 2000. "Jean Painlevé Reveals the Invisible." In *Science Is Fiction: The Films of Jean Painlevé.* Edited by Andy Masaki Bellows, Marina Mcdougall, and Brigitte Berg. San Francisco: Brico Press.

Heland, Erik von. 1966. *Mina Afrikaår.* Stockholm: LT's Förlag.

Herbert, Stephen. 2000. *A History of Early Films. Volume 1.* London: Routledge.

Hertogs, Daan, ed. 1997. *Uncharted Territory: Essays on Early Nonfiction Film.* Amsterdam: Stichting Nederlands Filmmuseum.

_____, and Nico de Klerk, eds. 1994. *Nonfiction from the Teens.* London: British Film Institute.

Hill, Paul, and Stephen Herbert. 1998. "Eadweard Muybridge and the Kingston Museum Bequest." *Film History,* vol. 10, 98–107.

Hoffman, H.F. Apr. 30, 1910. "The Roosevelt Pictures." *The Moving Picture World,* 683.

Honri, Baynham. 1948. "British Film Studios 1900–1920: A Technical Survey." In *The History of the British Film, 1906–1914.* Edited by Rachael Low. London: George Allen & Unwin.

Horwitz, Rita, H. Harrison, and W. Wendy. 1980. *The George Kleine Collection of Early Motion Pictures in the Library og Congress.* Washington, D.C.: Library of Congress.

Hosking, Eric, and Harold Lowers. 1947. *Masterpieces of Bird Photography.* London: Collins.

Hutchins, Patricia. 1937. "Painlevé, Scientist and Filmmaker: A Survey of His Contribution to Educational Cinema." *Sight and Sound,* Summer, 101–2.

Imperato, Pascal James, and Eleanor Imperato. 1992. *They Married Adventure: The Wandering Lives of Martin & Osa Johnson.* New Brunswick, NJ: Rutgers University Press.

The Independent. Apr. 6, 1914. "Snakes and Spider and The Hunting Spiders."

The Independent. Aug. 31, 1914. "Paul Rainey's African Hunt."

The Independent. Oct. 5, 1914. "Captain F.E. Kleinschmidt's Arctic Hunt."

The Independent. Nov. 2, 1914. "Thirty Leagues Under the Sea."

The Independent. May 17, 1915. "Bird Life in Scotland."

The Independent. June 14, 1915. "Native Gamefish and Birds."

The Independent. July 12, 1915. "Lady McKenzie in Afrika."

The Independent. Dec. 13, 1915. "The Birth of a Flower and the Otter."

Jacobs, Lewis. 1968. *The Rise of the American Film.* New York: Teachers College Press.

_____. 1971. *The Documentary Tradition: From Nanook to Woodstock.* New York: Hopkinson and Blake.

Johnson, Martin. 1928. *Safari.* Translated from *Safari. A Saga of the African Blue* by Poul Boisen. Copenhagen: Nordisk Forlag.

_____. 1929. *Lion: African Adventure with the King of Beasts.* London: Knickerbocker Press.

_____. 1931. *Gongorilla. Adventures with Pygmies and Gorillas in Africa.* New York: Blue Ribbon Book.

Johnson, Osa. 1947. *Gift med Eventyret.* Translated from *I Married Adventure* by Peter Boisen. Odense: Skandinavisk Bogforlag.

Kearton, Cherry. 1914. *Wild Life Across the World.* London: Hodder and Stoughton.

_____, and Richard Kearton. 1898. *British Birds' Nests.* London: Cassell.

Kinematograph and Lantern Weekly. Aug. 29, 1907. "Lion Hunt."

Kinematograph and Lantern Weekly. Sept. 5, 1907. "Oliver Pike and Kearton Brothers Bird Film."

Kinobladet. Mar. 1920. "Den Danske Film."

Kinobladet. Mar. 1921. "Nye Veje for dansk Film."

Kreutzberg, Lola. 1929. *Tiere, Tänzerinnen und Dämonen. Mit der Filmkamera durch Bali und Indien.* Dresden: Carl Reissner.

Lansell, Ross, and Peter Beilby, eds. *The Documentary Film in Australia.* Melbourne: Cinema Papers.

Larsen, Peter Harms. 1990. *Faktion som Udtryksmiddel.* Copenhagen: Amanda.

Larsen, Svend Erik. 1995. "Natur." In *Natursyn—?* Edited by Hans-Henrik Sass. Glumsø.

_____. 1997. "Naturen Begynder i Byen." *Samvirke,* no. 10, 78–82.

Lefebvre, Thierry. 1997. "Popularization and Anthropomorphism: On Some Prewar 'Animal Films.'" In

Uncharted Territory: Essays on Early Nonfiction Film. Edited by Daan Hertogs. Amsterdam: Stichting Nederlands Filmmuseum.

Legg, Frank, and Toni Hurley. 1966. *Once More on My Adventure.* Sydney: Ure Smith.

Leonard, Harold, ed. 1941. *The Film Index, Vol. 1—The Film as Art.* New York: The Museum of Modern Art and H.W. Wilson.

Literary Digest 47, "Edison's Revolutionary Education." Oct. 14, 1913. Literary Digest, 47, 576–577.

Littell, Robert. 1923. "Big Game in the Movies." *The New Republic,* January 31, 251–52.

Long, Chris. 1982a. "1910's Australia." In *The Documentary Film in Australia.* Edited by Ross Lansell and Peter Beilby. Melbourne: Cinema Papers.

_____. 1982b. "1930's Australia." In *The Documentary Film in Australia.* Edited by Ross Lansell and Peter Beilby. Melbourne: Cinema Papers.

Low, Rachael. 1948a. *The History of the British Film, 1906–1914.* London: George Allen & Unwin.

_____. 1948b. *The History of the British Film, 1914–1918.* London: George Allen & Unwin.

_____. 1979. *The History of the British Film, 1929–1939. Documentary and Educational films of the 1930's.* London: George Allen.

_____, and Roger Manvell. 1948. *The History of the British Film, 1896–1906.* London: George Allen.

Lowry, Edward. 1983. "Edwin J. Hadley: Travelling Film Exhibitor." In *Film Before Griffith.* Edited by John L. Fell. Berkeley: University of California Press.

Lund, Jørgen-Richard. 1978. "Lærte os at opleve naturen." *Embedsmanden,* no. 4.

Lynch, Dennis. 1989. "The Worst Location in the World: Herbert G. Ponting in the Antarctic, 1910–1912." *Film History,* vol. 3, 291–306.

MacCann, Richard Dyer, and Edward S. Perry. 1975. *The New Film Index: A Bibliography of Magazine Article in English, 1930–1970.* New York: E.P. Dutton.

Macdonald, Kevin, and Mark Cousins. 1996. *Imagining Reality.* London: Faber and Faber.

Manvell, Roger. 1944. *Film.* Middlesex: Penguin.

Mathewson, Worth. 1986. *William L. Finley. Pioneer Wildlife Photographer.* Corvallis: Oregon State University.

Maurice, Georges. 1913. *Film Revue,* no. 4, January 17, 13.

Mitman, Gregg. 1999. *Reel Nature. America's Romance with Wildlife on Film.* Cambridge: Harvard University Press.

Morris, Peter. 1978. *Embattled Shadows: A History of Canadian Cinema, 1895–1939.* Montreal: McGill-Queens University Press.

_____. 1983. "Images of Canada." In *Film Before Griffith.* Edited by John L. Fell. Berkeley: University of California Press.

The Moving Picture World. May 11, 1907. "Vesuvius and the Eruption of 1906."

The Moving Picture World. Sep. 21, 1907. "Carl Hagenback's Wild Animal Park."

The Moving Picture World. Sep. 5, 1908. "The Cult of the Motion Picture."

The Moving Picture World. Feb. 19, 1910. "On the Screen. Travelogue."

The Moving Picture World. May 21, 1910. "The Egret Hunter."

The Moving Picture World. Sep. 10, 1910. "Cherry Kearton and His Work."

The Moving Picture World. Feb. 25, 1911. "Lassoing Wild Animals in Africa."

The Moving Picture World. Nov. 18, 1911. "Life at the Bottom at the Sea."

The Moving Picture World. Dec. 30, 1911. "Sea and Landscapes."

The Moving Picture World. Apr. 20, 1912. "The Paul Rainey African Pictures."

The Moving Picture World. Oct. 5, 1912. "Photoscenes of Travel."

The Moving Picture World. Mar. 1, 1913. "Col. Roosevelt Speaks for Kearton."

The Moving Picture World. Nov. 15, 1913. "The Bee og Among the Fishes. The Stickleback."

The Moving Picture World. Sep. 26, 1914. "Hemment Brings African Scenes."

Musser, Charles. 1990. "The Travel Genre in 1903–1904. Moving Towards Fictional Narrative." In *Early Cinema—Space, Frame, Narrative.* Edited by Thomas Elsaesser and Adam Barker. London: BFI.

_____. 1997. *Edison Motion Pictures, 1890–1900. An Annotated Filmography.* Washington, D.C.: Smithsonian Institution Press.

Muybridge, Eadweard. 1899/1918. *Animals in Motion. An Electro-photographic Investigation of Consecutive Phases of Muscular Actions.* London: Chapman and Hall.

Narwekar, Sanjit. 1992. *Films Division and the Indian Documentary.* New Delhi: Publications Division, Ministry of Information and Broadcasting, Gov't of India.

Neale, Steve. 1985. *Cinema and Technology. Image, Sound, Colour.* London: Macmillan.

Neergaard, Ebbe. 1948. *Documentary in Denmark.* Copenhagen: Den Danske kortfilmproduktion. Jean Painlevé's Film. 1930. Section 8: Drama & Music, *New York Times,* June 29.

Nichols, Bill. 1991. *Representing Reality: Issues and Concepts in Documentary.* New York: Library of Congress.

Nielsen, Jan. 2003. *A/S Filmfabrikken Danmark — SRH/Filmfabrikken Danmarks Historie og Produktion.* Copenhagen: Multivers.

Niver, Kemp R. 1967. *Motion Pictures from the Library of Congress Paper Print Collection 1894–1912.* Berkeley: University of California Press.

_____. 1971. *Biograph Bulletins, 1896–1908.* Los Angeles: Artisan Press.

Nørfelt, Tomas Fibiger. 1992. "*Naturbilleder.* Analyse af naturfilmgenren med særligt henblik på bestemmelse af naturprogramsubgenren." Thesis, Copenhagen University.

Norstad, Kari. 1995. "*Natur i Naturprogrammer.*" Thesis, Oslo University.

Nørrested, Carl, and Christian Alsted. 1987. *Kortfilmen og Staten.* Copenhagen: Eventus.

Olsen, Lau. "Den Etnografiske Dokumentarfilm." Thesis, Copenhagen University.

Ottley, D. Charles. 1935. *The Cinema in Education. A Handbook for Teachers.* London: Routhledge & Sons.

Painlevé, Jean. 1955, 2000. "Scientific Film, La Technique Cinématographique." In *Science Is Fiction. The Films of Jean Painlevé.* Edited by Andy Masaki Bellows, Marina Mcdougall, and Brigitte Berg. San Francisco: Brico Press.

Peterson, Jennifer. 1997. "'Truth Is Stranger Than Fiction': Travelogues from the 1910s in the Nederlands Filmmuseum." In *Uncharted Territory: Essays on Early Nonfiction Film.* Editor Daan Hertogs. Amsterdam: Stichting Nederlands Filmmuseum.

Petterson, Palle. 1996. "Naturopfattelser og Stumfilm." Thesis, Copenhagen University.

Pike, Andrew. 1982a. "Documentary Traditions Before Grierson. The Case of Frank Hurley." In *The Documentary Film in Australia.* Edited by Ross Lansell and Peter Beilby. Melbourne: Cinema Papers.

_____. 1982b. "1920's World Wide and Australia." In *The Documentary Film in Australia.* Edited by Ross Lansell and Peter Beilby. Melbourne: Cinema Papers.

Pike, Oliver G. 1946. *Nature and My Cine Camera.* London: The Focal Press.

Polimanti, O. Dec. 26, 1911. "Der Kinematograph in der Biologischen und Medicinischen Wissenschaft." *Naturwissenschaftliche Wochenschrift,* no. 49, 769–774.

Ponting, Herbert George. 1908. "Photographing Alligators." *Scientific American, Supplement* 65, 353–54.

_____. Sept. 1914. "Cinematographing the Antarctic." *Pearson's Magazine,* 235–249.

_____. 1921/1923. *The Great White South — or with Scott in the Antarctic.* London: Duckworth Co.

Ramsaye, Terry. 1926. *A Million and One Nights: A History of the Motion Picture.* London: Frank Cass.

Ravn, Peter. 1978. *Turisme.* Copenhagen: Gyldendal.

Reeves, Louis. 1912. *The Moving Picture World,* October 5, 21.

Renov, Michael. 1993. *Theorizing Documentary.* New York: Routhledge.

Root, Nina J., ed. 1987. *Catalog of the American Museum of Natural History Film Archives.* New York: Garland.

Rotha, Paul. 1936. *Documentary Film.* New York: Hastings.

Sadoul, Georges. 1964. *Louis Lumière.* Paris: Edition Seghers.

Salt, Barry. 1983. *Film Style and Technology. History and Analysis.* London: Starword.

Sanderson, Richard. 1961. "A Historical Study of the Development of American Motion Picture Content and Techniques Prior to 1904." Ph.D. diss., The University of Southern California.

Schepelern, Peter. 1981. *Film og Genre. Filmens genrebegreb i kommerciel praksis og kritisk teori.* Gylling: Gyldendal.

Schillings, C. G. 1905. *With Flashlight and Rifle.* London: Hutchinson.

"To the South Pole with the Cinematograph. Film Records of Scott's Ill-fated Expedition." 1913. *Scientific American. The Weekly Journal of Practical Information,* vol. CVIII, no. 1, 560–568.

Smith, F. Percy. 1931. "Making the 'Secrets of Nature' Series." *International Review of Educational Cinematography,* no. 3, 990–1006.

_____, F. Durden, and Mary Field. 1941. *Cine-Biology.* Middlesex: Penguin.

Steele, Wilbur Daniel. 1913. "The Moving Picture Machine in the Jungle." *McClure's Magazine,* vol. XI, no. 3, January.

Surowiec, Catherine A., ed. 1996. *The Lumiere Project: The European Film Archives at the Crossroads.* Lissabon: Projecto Lumiere.

Talbot, Frederick A. 1912. *Moving Pictures: How They Are Made and Worked.* London: William Heinemann.

Tarleau, Allen D. 1920. "A Temple in the Sky." *Motion Picture Magazine,* July, 19: 46–7.

Thys, Marianne. 1995. "The Adventure of Alfred and Mimir." In *Alfred Machin Cinéaste / Film-maker.* Edited by Eric de Kuyper. Bruxelles: Royal Belgian Film Archive.

Tjek. 1957. "Han har gjort det hele med." *Social-Demokraten.* July 7.

Tsivian, Yuri, and Paulo Cherchi Usai, eds. 1989. *Silent Witnesses: Russian Cinema, 1908–1919*. London: Pordenone Biblioteca dell'Imagine.

Tybjerg, Casper. 1997. "Billeder i Bevægelse." In *Dansk Mediehistorie, Bind 2*. Edited by Klaus Bruhn Jensen. Copenhagen: Samleren.

Urban, Charles. 1907. "The Cinematograph in Science and Education." *The Moving Picture World*, no. 21, July 27, 324.

Usai, Paolo Cherchi. 1996. "The Color of Nitrate: Some Factual Observations on Tinting and Toning Manuals for Silent Films." In *Silent Film*. Edited by Richard Abel. New Brunswick, NJ: Rutgers University Press.

_____. 2000. *Silent Cinema. An Introduction*. London: BFI.

Waldron, Gloria. 1949. *The Information Film. A Report of the Public Library Inquiry*. New York: Columbia University Press.

Weaver, J. T. 1971. *Twenty Years of Silents, 1908–1928*. New York: Scarecrow.

William, Prince. 1923. *Among Pygmies and Gorillas. With the Swedish Zoological Expedition to Central Africa 1921*. Copenhagen: Gyldendal.

Williamson, John Ernest. 1914. "J.E. Williamson Taking Moving Pictures at the Bottom of the Ocean." *Scientific American*, no. 111, July 11, 25–26.

Winston, Brian. 1988. "Before Flaherty, Before Grierson: The Documentary Film in 1914." *Sight & Sound*, vol. 57, no. 4, Autumn.

Wood, Ben E., and F. Freeman. 1929. *Motion Pictures in the Classroom*. Boston: Houghton Mifflin.

Woolfe, Bruce. 1941. "I Remember..." *Sight and Sound*, vol. 10, no. 37, Spring, 8–9.

INDEX

Numbers in *bold* italics indicate pages with photographs.